QUICK
ESCAPES
from
Detroit

Quick Escapes Series

QUICK ESCAPES

from
Detroit

22 Weekend Trips
from the Motor City

by
Khristi Sigurdson Zimmeth

A Voyager Book

The Globe Pequot Press

Old Saybrook, Connecticut

Cover photograph: Copyright (c) New England Stock Photo

Photo Credits: Pp. 1, 86: Courtesy of Michigan Travel Bureau; pp. 3, 41, 80: © Bob Brodbeck; p. 12: by Robert De Jonge, courtesy Michigan Travel Bureau; p. 22: courtesy Traverse City Convention and Visitors Bureau; p. 31: courtesy Maxwell Advertising; p. 48: courtesy Finley Films Holiday Color Slides; p. 55: courtesy Ann Arbor Hands-On Museum; p. 63: courtesy Marshall Area Chamber of Commerce; p. 71: courtesy Fairchild House Bed & Breakfast; pp. 95, 97: Peter J. Schulz, courtesy of the City of Chicago; p. 107: © Elder Photo; p. 109: courtesy Maumee Bay State Park; p. 121: by Dan Feicht, courtesy of Cedar Point; p. 127: by Joan Tuefei, courtesy of the Convention and Visitors Bureau of Greater Cleveland; p. 137: courtesy of the Ohio Department of Development; p. 147: courtesy of the Greater Cincinnati Convention and Visitors Bureau; p. 157, 167: courtesy of Metropolitan Toronto Convention and Visitors Association; p. 179: © Michael Vough Photography; p. 181: © Banayote Photography; p. 188: courtesy of La Porte County Convention and Visitors Bureau

Library of Congress Cataloging-in-Publication Data

Zimmeth, Khristi Sigurdson.
    Quick escapes from Detroit: 22 weekend trips from the Motor City / by Khristi Sigurdson Zimmeth.—1st ed.
    p. cm.
"A voyager book."
Includes index.
ISBN 0-7627-0040-8
1. Detroit Region (Mich.)—Guidebooks. 2. Ann Arbor Region (Mich.)—Guidebooks. 3. Middle West—Guidebooks. I. Title. 96-49231 F574.D43Z56 1997
917.74'340443—dc21

                                       CIP

Manufactured in the United States of America
First Edition/First Printing

To Maria Shaw, who got me into the business, and to Ron Garbinski, who kept me in it, and to Susan Alpert, whose love of travel inspires me still.

Acknowledgments

Thanks are due to a number of people who helped me during the process of putting this book together: Gina Newell, who helped with research; my sister, Kerry Sigurdson, who babysat; and my husband, John, and my children, Nate and Claire, who were supportive in more ways than I can count.

Contents

Introduction

Some say that Henry Ford indirectly invented the weekend getaway when his first "horseless carriage" rolled off the assembly line. Before that, huge ships and slow-moving railways took well-off vacationers and countless overstuffed steamer trunks on holidays that lasted at least a month, sometimes two or three. There was no such thing as "traveling light."

With the invention of the automobile, however, shorter trips became possible and soon became popular. Travel became less expensive and more accessible to a wider range of people. Months at the shore or on the continent became weekends by the beach, at the cottage, or soaking up the sights in a nearby city. By the mid-1950s, almost everyone could enjoy that delicious otherworldly feeling of "being somewhere else" that pleasure travel provides.

Whether we were the first to enjoy them or not, metro Detroiters have certainly perfected the art of the weekend getaway. While half the state's population lives in the Detroit metropolitan area, an excellent network of freeways and secondary roads allows us to zip easily out of the city into the surrounding countryside. And zip we have. As our area belched out the fast-moving cars we became known for and built more and more factories, we've increasingly escaped to the bucolic lands in the western and northern parts of the state.

"If you seek a pleasant peninsula, look around you," the state motto asserts. And pleasant it is—from charming small-town Marshall, with its treasure trove of nineteenth-century architecture and antiques shops, to increasingly cosmopolitan Traverse City and the lovely links that make Gaylord one of the golf capitals of the Midwest. Great weekends exist throughout the state, each with its own attractions and flavor. For that reason, the majority of the getaways described in this book are right here in our own backyard.

While Michigan offers an incredible variety of adventures, Detroit and Ann Arbor also have the enviable position of being in the heart of the Midwest. Within a 300-mile radius (the limit for this book and, I think, for a comfortable weekend drive) are some of the region's most fascinating cities, including Chicago, Illinois; Cincinnati, Ohio; and Toronto, Ontario. All make easily accessible quick escapes for metro Detroiters.

This book contains some of my favorite short trips, ones I've enjoyed as an editor at *Michigan Living Magazine* and during more than thirty years of residing in the Wolverine State. Some I've enjoyed as a footloose single traveler; others have seen me accompanied by a husband and laden with two kids, one black Lab, and a Jeep Cherokee full of swim toys. There are benefits to both, of course, so I've tried to give you an assortment of escapes, some family friendly, others for adults only.

A word or two about prices: for restaurants, a meal is considered inexpensive if entrees are less than $10; moderate ($10–$15); or expensive ($15 and up). I've attempted to be as accurate as possible with other fees, but prices change often and many vary with the season.

A few caveats: Unless you're an avid skier, you'll agree that Michigan and most of the Midwest are at their best in the milder seasons. Therefore, a number of these trips are geared toward fair weather, although they are certainly available to travelers year-round. I have also tried to seek out getaways that can be enjoyed during other seasons and note that whenever possible. There are also many more great destinations than space to accommodate them in these pages, however. If this book doesn't include your favorite, let me know and I'll do my best to include it next time. Finally, be aware that the information contained herein was current as of September 1996. As with any business, change occurs rapidly, and the hotel or restaurant that was once extraordinary may now be just average—or may not be there at all. It's always a good idea to call ahead to avoid disappointment.

Let me know if I've missed any of your favorites or if you have comments or corrections. In the meantime, there's enough here to keep you busy for at least the next few years—or at least until the second edition hits the bookstores.

Happy Traveling!

Khristi Sigurdson Zimmeth

Michigan Escapes

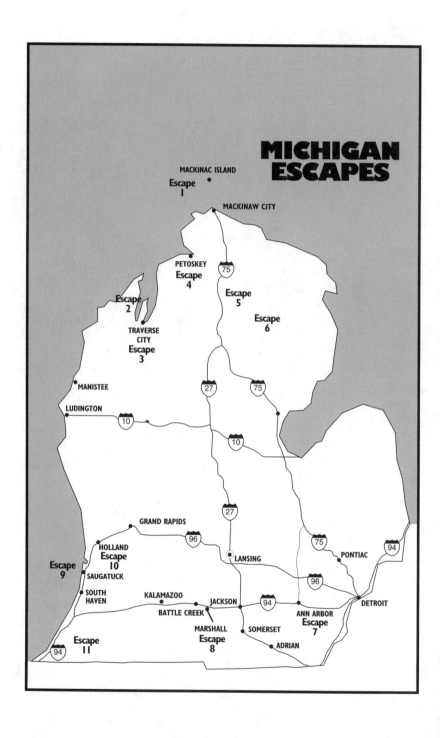

MICHIGAN ESCAPES

MACKINAC ISLAND
Escape 1

MACKINAW CITY

PETOSKEY
Escape 4

Escape 2

Escape 5

75

Escape 6

TRAVERSE CITY
Escape 3

27

75

MANISTEE

LUDINGTON

10

10

27

GRAND RAPIDS

96

75

PONTIAC

94

HOLLAND
Escape 10

LANSING

Escape 9

SAUGATUCK

96

SOUTH HAVEN

KALAMAZOO

JACKSON

94

DETROIT

BATTLE CREEK

MARSHALL
Escape 8

SOMERSET

ANN ARBOR
Escape 7

Escape 11

94

ADRIAN

Mackinac Island

Horse-drawn carriages are one of the most popular ways to get around Mackinac Island.

An Island Idyll

4 NIGHTS

Bicycling • Beaches •History •Sight-seeing

A nineteenth-century Fort Mackinac physician was known to prescribe stays on Mackinac Island for those "suffering from overworked brain or muscle." A century later, the island is still a favorite tonic for anyone looking to escape the hassles of modern living. Once on the island, visitors discover that the nonmotorized pace is just what the doctor ordered and the perfect antidote to workweek stress and other twentieth-century trials and tribulations.

In the summer, the population of this 3-mile-long island swells from just five hundred year-round residents to thousands of day-trippers, also known as "fudgies" (due to their fascination with the island's fudge shops) who try to cram the many attractions into a frantic daylong stay.

Savvy travelers prefer to stay at least a weekend (some stay the whole summer), which allows them to slow down enough to enjoy the island's pace and peace. If you're looking to really escape the crowds, consider a visit in the fall, when the air cools, the leaves turn (colors peak from mid-September to mid-October), and rates fall dramatically in the island's often-expensive hotels. An added plus: You can catch the end-of-the-season sales in the island's shops. (For other useful tips, consider picking up a copy of the *Mackinac Connection: An Insider's Guide* by local author Amy McVeigh, available in the Island Bookstore or by special order).

Day 1

Afternoon

From Detroit, Mackinac Island is a fairly lengthy drive of approximately 280 miles. To get there, take Interstate 75 north to exit 337, 338, or 339. Plan on spending at least three full days on the island to build in time for relaxing and to make the drive worthwhile.

Lodging: A good idea is to spend the first night in Mackinaw City. The **Hampton Inn** (800–301–1765) was built in 1995 and was quickly awarded three diamonds by AAA. It features 300 feet of sandy beach, private balconies, and free continental breakfast. It's also closest to the ferryboats and offers handy discount coupons for island attractions. Skip the city's nightlife, however, since you'll be catching the first ferry the next morning. Rates: $78–$108 per night, including continental breakfast.

Day 2

Morning

Breakfast: Hampton Inn, Mackinaw City (it's included in your room rate). After, it's time to strap on your sea legs. Mackinac Island is accessible only by ferry or seaplane, and three companies offer frequent ferries from Mackinaw City in the Lower Peninsula and St. Ignace in the Upper Peninsula. The oldest and largest is the **Arnold Line,** which has been serving the island since 1878. **Shepler's** is the second largest and is known for its personal service (they'll even fill up and wash your car and do minor repairs while you're on the island). **Star Line** is the newcomer. All take approximately fifteen minutes to make the trip and offer incredible vistas along the way.

Once on board, be sure to take an outside seat for the best views. Along the way, you'll pass the **Mackinac Bridge,** which joined the state's Upper and

Lower peninsulas in November 1957. Known as "Mighty Mac," it's the world's longest suspension bridge and took years of planning and $96 million to complete. Today it features 4 miles of uninterrupted steel superstructure and is considered one of the world's marvels of human engineering.

Afternoon

Once on the island, reserve the remainder of the first day for relaxing and checking out your hotel. Linger over dinner in the **Point Dining Room** or take in a movie in the resort's 575-seat theater. There's plenty of time to see the sights tomorrow.

Lunch: A rustic yet comfortable place for lunch on the island is the **French Outpost** (Cadotte Avenue, across from the Little Stone Church; 906–847–3772). The menu is mostly soups, salads, pizza, or sandwiches; but there's also an excellent raw bar. You can choose from three dining areas—the main restaurant, the deck overlooking the straits, or the screened-in porch. Moderate.

Lodging: With its signature red roof and white clapboard sides, **Mission Point Resort** (1 Lakeshore Boulevard; 906–847–3312 or 800–833–7711) blends well with the island's Victorian architecture. Surprisingly, it was built in the 1950s and 1960s as home to the Moral Rearmament, a Christian activist group. Perfect for travelers with or without children, this sprawling resort is spread out over eighteen acres and located near enough to Main Street to be convenient but far enough away to be relaxing. And unlike the more famous Grand Hotel, its prices are palatable.

Included in the room rates ($109–$289 per night) are use of the 3,000-square-foot health club (with sauna, steam rooms, and massages as well as bike rentals and in-line skates), cassette tours of the island, and tennis and volleyball courts. The 236 guest rooms are decorated in sunny tans, yellows, and peaches, with an English-country feel. The hotel's signature space, however, is the breathtaking Great Hall, built to resemble a sixteen-sided, 36-foot-tall teepee. If you've brought the kids, Mission Point has an innovative Kid's Klub program, with an extensive menu of activities including an Indian Pow Wow, scavenger hunts, freighter watching, and a new 3,000-square-foot activities center. An added bonus: Kids eat free in the hotel's three restaurants.

If you have kids in tow, tonight's the night to take advantage of the hotel's Kid's Eat Free deal. But if you're adults looking for something a little more atmospheric, stroll through downtown (you'll be amazed how much quieter it is in the evening) to the **Carriage House** (906–847–3321). Tucked behind the Hotel Iroquois, many consider it the island's best restaurant. This relaxed but elegant waterfront restaurant offers fine food in an intimate setting. There's a great view of the straits as well as fresh and imaginative fare that includes broiled whitefish and fettuccine Alfredo with morels, a chef's specialty. Reservations are always a good idea. Moderate to expensive.

After dinner you can opt to take in a play back at the resort. Mission Point operates the only live theater on the island. Performances are offered six nights a week in season and range from comedies to dramas.

Day 3

Morning

Breakfast: Your room rate at Mission Point include the generous breakfast buffet. Served in the dining room, it includes both hot (eggs, bacon, hash browns) and cold (yogurts, fruits, juice) items. If you sleep in and miss the buffet, the resort's **Freighters Deli** has croissants and cappuccino and is decorated with old photos of Great Lakes ships. It's also an ice-cream parlor and serves the only Pizza Hut pizza on the island, something you may want to remember if you're prone to late-night cravings.

A good way to get your bearings and an orientation to the island is to take a carriage tour. More than thirty local families pooled their resources forty years ago to start this cooperative business; today they operate about seventy-five carriages, with three hundred horses that take visitors on tours that last either forty-five minutes or an hour and a half. Both tours include all the top island attractions, including **Fort Mackinac** and **Arch Rock** (with stops to let you get out and enjoy the view) as well as an optional drop-off at the Grand Hotel at the end of the tour. Call (906) 847–3573 for information.

Lunch: Many of the island's eateries can be expensive and sometimes the food is average at best. Consider a picnic instead. Pick up your pleasure at **Doud's Mercantile** (906–847–3551) at Main and Fort streets. Enjoy it overlooking the water and the marina's many beautiful boats. Inexpensive.

Afternoon

After lunch is the time to explore on your own. To do so, make your first stop the handy island Visitor's Center across from Marquette Park. It's a good place to pick up information, learn more about the island, and chat with the friendly staff (its well-maintained restrooms are also a good place for a pit stop).

From the Visitor's Center, turn left on Main Street to take you downtown. Many of the shops are closed on Sundays, so if you plan on exercising your credit cards, do it on Saturday. Main Street has the usual souvenir and gift shops as well as a number of small, independent clothing boutiques that feature all things pricey and preppy. A few more unusual highlights include **Maeve's Art & Antiques** (906–847–3755), with great jewelry and original island scenes. It's owned by Maeve Croghan, whose Irish ancestors lived and worked on the island. Across the street, the **Island Scrimshander** (906–847–3792) is run by three brothers who make their living at this ancient mariner's art. If you're lucky, you'll catch one of them at work.

If exploring the island has piqued your curiosity, learn more at **Island Books** (906–847–6202) in the lobby of the Lilac Tree Hotel (Main Street). Here you'll find good regional titles, current best-sellers, and lots of steamy beach reading. Also in this complex is **La Belle Provence** (906–847–3358), which imports French country antiques as well as new merchandise that ranges from soap to sideboards.

If you're allergic to T-shirt and gift shops as well as to the ubiquitous fudge shops (the most in the world!), you'll prefer Market Street, which runs parallel to Main and reflects the island's quieter side. A street of fishing crews and fur traders, it's a refreshing contrast to the teeming throngs that often crowd Main Street. Some fourteen historical buildings are furnished in 1880s style; many offer tours and a glimpse of a bygone way of life.

Dinner: Reserve one night for an all-out splurge at the **Grand Hotel** (906–847–3331), indisputably the most famous spot on the island. One of the classic pleasures of a weekend on Mackinac is getting all dressed up and walking or biking to the Grand, as travelers have been doing for more than a century. The classic white Greek Revival structure (the world's largest summer-only hotel) was built in 1887 by steamship and railroad barons. It sits high on a bluff overlooking 50 acres of Victorian gardens and the town below. Its veranda is one of the most photographed sites in the state. It's 660 feet long and contains more than a dozen white rockers. (Be forewarned, however: There's a $5.00 fee per person just to stroll the porch and explore the hotel if you're not staying or eating there. A swim in the famous serpentine pool costs $8.00 per person.) Rooms, of course, are decorated in antiques and command prices of up to $350 per night. Even the least expensive room is $225 in the off-season.

The Grand is also the only place in Northern Michigan where you're still expected to dress for dinner (men must wear a coat and tie). The main dining room has an unmatched setting, along with drill teams of uniformed Jamaican waiters at your beck and call. The food is surprisingly good despite the fact that the large dining room serves so many at a time, with a popular five-course feast that includes seafood cocktail with mustard sauce, smoked salmon, fresh whitefish, and aged prime rib. Dinner is included for hotel guests; nonguests pay a fixed per-person price of $65. It's worth it for this once-in-a-lifetime experience.

After dinner, watch the sun set from the hotel's rooftop piano bar, with its breathtaking view of the straits. If you're on a budget or you've brought the kids and you'd still like to experience the Grand, consider having breakfast or lunch in one of the hotel's other eateries, including Carlton Teas, which serves breakfast and light lunches, the Geranium Bar, or the Jockey Club Grand Stand.

Day 4

Morning

Breakfast: Mission Point. Time to work off some of last night's Grand Hotel meal with a little exercise, island style. As two days on Mackinac have revealed, bikes are more at home here than cars. Take advantage of the fresh air and burn a little energy with a trip around the island on a bike. Check out the ones built for two, or if you're really ambitious (and in good physical condition), consider renting in-line skates from the hotel.

Bike rentals can be found at Mission Point or at a number of places along Main Street (try Rybas, 906–847–3829), with three locations, or Island Bike Rental (906–847–6288), Livery near Shepler Dock). Or you can bring your own wheels and pay an extra $3.00 to ferry them across.

A good route for beginners and families is the **South Bicycle Trail,** which takes in most of the island's natural highlights, including dramatic limestone Arch Rock, which rises to 146 feet and is the site of awe-inspiring vistas. From there, take Rifle Range Road inland and turn right on Garrison Road to Skull Cave. Legend has it that a British trader spent the night here during an Indian attack only to find it full of bones. Continue on Garrison past the cemeteries, then turn right on Fort Holmes Road to Fort Holmes. The incredible view from the stockade alone is worth the trip. From there, the road leads to British Landing, about 2 miles, or left into town.

British Landing, roughly halfway around the island on the western shore, has a half-mile nature trail, a bluff with a good bridge view, and a friendly and informative on-duty naturalist. Nearby is the Croghan Water Wetland Area, home to a variety of native flora and fauna. British Landing is also where, in winter, an ice bridge forms across to St. Ignace to allow year-round residents to snowmobile off the island.

Another popular cycling choice is the 8-mile shoreline route around the island. Insiders, however, agree, that to really experience Mackinac's magic, you have to explore its interior. You'll bike along wooded trails, explore ancient geological formations, and spot bald eagles along island bluffs. A free map at the Visitor's Center details this and other worthwhile routes.

The majority of the natural and historical attractions and some 80 percent of the island itself are set aside as the **Mackinac Island State Park** (906–847–3328). Congress made the island the country's second national park in 1875; in 1894 much of it became Michigan's first state park, thereby protecting it from extensive development. More recently, *National Geographic Traveler* named it one of the top ten parks in the nation. Its highest point is Fort Holmes, which offers great views.

Another fort worth checking out is **Fort Mackinac** (906–847–3328), located high on a bluff overlooking the harbor. This restored eighteenth- and nineteenth-century British and American outpost is now preserved as a museum. All of the 1780 buildings are original and include period furnishings, audiovisual presentations, and costumed guides. Kids love the Children's Discovery Room, where they can roll hoops and play other nineteenth-century games and pose for silly photos in authentic military costume. The whole family will love the stirring military music, battle reenactments, and cannon and rifle demonstrations. Admission is $6.50 for adults, $4.00 for children ages six through twelve; $20.00 for a family.

Lunch: The fort is also the site of a charming tearoom, with a terrace that offers great views of the straits. The food is made by the Grand Hotel and includes soups, salads, personal-size pizzas, and hearty sandwiches. Afterward, indulge in the popular pecan fudge ice-cream ball, which is big enough for two. Inexpensive.

Afternoon

Charming St. Anne's church, the island's largest parish, has a pretty public garden and a basement full of artifacts that relate to the island's history. From there, you can cut through the garden path and head for McGulpin Street, where the **Mackinac Island Butterfly House** (906–847–3972) is a favorite spot of visitors of all ages. Hundreds of species in free flight fill the house.

If architecture is your thing, don't miss a walk pass the island's "summer homes" located on Front Street. The row of Victorians includes the governor's warm-weather digs, built in 1909 in the shingle style. The state bought the governor's home for just $15,000 in 1945; it's worth at least a million dollars today. It's open for tours on Wednesday mornings only.

Dinner: The **Island House** (906–847–3347) across from the marina is known for its fine Governor's Room restaurant. Entrees include specialties such as Barbarie duckling in Beaujolais wine sauce and slow-roasted prime rib. There's also a popular breakfast buffet (All-U-Can-Eat for just $13) and the casual Garden Grill, a handy place for a burger, ribs, or chicken. Moderate to expensive.

Besides late dinners and watching the breathtaking sunsets, the island isn't known for its scintillating nightlife. One notable exception, however, is the **Pink Pony Bar & Grill** (adjacent to the lobby, in the Chippewa Hotel on Main Street; 906–847–3341), long a favorite of yachtsmen and women competing in the Port Huron-to-Mackinac and Chicago-to-Mackinac races. Recently doubled in size, it still has the trademark pink steed outside the front window and still serves up outstanding views of the marina and the straits. The one-hundred-year-old serpentine bar and live entertainment attract crowds after dinner; in summer, diners spill outside onto a new, two-tiered deck. Popular dinner choices include Chicago-style baby back ribs, herb-crusted whitefish, and spicy Caribbean-inspired shrimp. Moderate.

If the kiddies are in tow, skip the bar and head back to Mission Point in time for the nightly hayride. You'll enjoy a memorable—if a bit bumpy—ride as well as a different perspective of this timeless island.

Day 5

Breakfast: Enjoy the view and a leisurely meal before hitting the ferry and heading home. Don't forget to pick up some of that famous fudge!

There's More

Freighter Watching. A free and fun pastime for the entire family is watching the many freighters from around the world that pass through the straits. Many freighter fans, much like bird-watchers, keep an ongoing log.

Gaming. Mission Point arranges nightly junkets to nearby Kewadin Casinos in St. Ignace and Sault Ste. Marie. You can take the 11:30 P.M. ferry back to the resort or plan on stopping on your own once you leave the island.

Golf. The Mackinac Straits area has six championship courses, including one at the Grand Hotel. For more information, contact the Mackinac Island Chamber of Commerce at (906) 847-6418.

Horseback Riding. The back of a steed is another way to explore the island. Try Cindy's Riding Stable (906-847-3572) or Jack's Livery Stable (906-847-3391).

Sailing and Fishing. Sailing cruises with departures from Mackinac Island marina yield bountiful catches of king salmon, whitefish, perch, and chinook. Ask your hotel concierge about charters and other offerings.

Special Events

June. Lilac Festival, Mackinac Island
      Mackinac Island Chamber Music Fest
July. Fireworks, Mackinac Island
      Chicago-to-Mackinac and Port Huron-to-Mackinac Yacht Races
August. Bike Races, Mackinac Island
September. Labor Day Bridge Walk, St. Ignace

Other Recommended Restaurants and Lodgings

Restaurants

Village Inn (Hoban Street; 906-847-3542) is a favorite wateringhole for island natives and an excellent spot for cozy family dining. It's known for its steakburger, planked whitefish, and outdoor patio. Moderate.

Lodgings

The **Chippewa Hotel** (Main Street; 906-847-3341) has been an island landmark since 1902. It recently received a $2.5 million renovation, updating its guest rooms and doubling the size of its popular Pink Pony Bar & Grill. Accommodations are in thirty-five standard rooms and twenty-six waterfront suites, all with oak trim, marble, wicker, and brass. Rates: $120-$160 per night.

The **Island House** (800–626–6304 or 906–847–3347) has ninety-four rooms in a renovated four-story 1852 hotel across from the marina. The island's oldest hotel, it offers Victorian guest rooms and three two-bedroom suites with private veranda. There's also a new indoor pool as well as the respected Governor's Dining Room. Rates: $130–$160 per night.

Lilac Tree Hotel (906–847–6575) is a newer, all-suite hotel in the heart of downtown. Twelve rooms have Jacuzzis; all feature antiques and reproductions. The Lilac Tree is one of the few hotels to have winter packages. Rates: $150–$225 per night.

For More Information

Mackinac Island Chamber of Commerce, Mackinac Island, MI (906) 847–6418.

Leelanau County

The Sleeping Bear Dunes are a challenge for even the most physically fit.

Michigan's Little Finger

_____ 3 NIGHTS _____

Beaches • Restaurants • Shopping • Wineries

Whole books have been written about the Leelanau Peninsula, the area known as Michigan's Little Finger, located on the Lower Peninsula northwest of Traverse City. For many, Leelanau is "Up North" at its best, with 100 miles of Lake Michigan shoreline overlooked by sandy bluffs and challenging dunes, picturesque back roads full of fruit farms, beaches, and historic lighthouses as well as charming country towns, most of which still cater more to residents than tourists (the county didn't even get its first traffic light until 1991, a result of encroaching sprawl from Traverse City).

Summers can be a bit crowded, with tourists who are heading for the beaches or the casino clogging the main roads. Slip off onto a back road, however, and you're virtually assured of solitude and scenery that's sure to take your breath away. Or consider a trip in the off-season, when the towns and the area's signature cherry orchards are blanketed in a shroud of snow. Whenever you come, you're sure to agree with the original Native American inhabitants, who named this peninsula *Leelanau*—"Land of Delight."

If you're looking for a longer stay, consider combining Leelanau County with Traverse City (Michigan Escape Three). Although geographically close to one another (it's just 30 miles from Traverse City to Suttons Bay in Leelanau County), each offers more than enough to fill a weekend—or longer.

Day 1

The peninsula is about 275 miles northwest of Detroit. Get an early start on Friday morning to beat the weekend gridlock on Interstate 75 and plan on arriving in time for a late lunch. To get to the peninsula, take I–75 north to State Highway M–72, then north on M–22 to Glen Arbor.

Afternoon

Lunch: The **Western Avenue Grill** (6140 Western Avenue, Glen Arbor; 616–334–3362) is the quintessential Northern Michigan eatery, with a rustic lodge atmosphere and great food. The menu is surprisingly varied, from New Zealand mussels and fresh Great Lakes whitefish, an area staple, to the famous "Glen Arbor Greek" salad, homemade pizza, and signature sixteen-ounce top sirloin served blackened or chargrilled with fries. Moderate.

Lodging: One of the many pleasures of the peninsula is its lack of anonymous chain hotels. The majority of rooms are in charming bed and breakfasts, upscale condominiums, or full-service resorts. One of the best places to stay in the area is the **Homestead** (Wood Ridge Road, Glen Arbor; 616–334–5000), with 271 spacious condolike units and 1 mile of breathtaking Lake Michigan waterfront. Surrounded by the Sleeping Bear Dunes, the resort includes outdoor pools, water slide, clay tennis courts, a noted golf academy as well as biking, hiking, and children's programs. Its central location makes exploring the rest of the peninsula easy. Rates start at $125 for a one-bedroom condo.

After checking in, you may choose to explore nearby Glen Arbor, just a few miles south on State Highway 22, or hang out on the Homestead's beautiful beach. Glen Arbor has just one main street, but it's full of intriguing shops such as **Leelanau Interiors** (616–334–4754), with interesting things for the home; the **Cottage Book Shop** (5970 South Lake Street; 616–334–4223), full of good reads, and the **Glen Lakes Artists Gallery** (behind the book shop; 616–334–4230), with quirky and colorful paintings by this local artist. It also has one of three outpost galleries of area jewelry designer **Becky Thatcher** (5975 South Lake Street; 616–334–3826); the others are in Leland, Michigan, and Key West, Florida.

Dinner: The Homestead's romantic restaurant, known simply as **"The Inn,"** is one of the best in the area. Overlooking Lake Michigan, it serves "Modern American" cuisine, such as Pacific salmon smothered in maple-glazed whole-grain mustard and other innovative entrees. The wine list is well known and includes a number of local wines. Note: A coat and tie are necessary in the main room. Moderate to expensive.

Day 2

Morning

Breakfast: Fuel up with a hearty breakfast in your condo at the Homestead or at the **Good Harbor Grill** in Glen Arbor (6584 Western Avenue; 616–334–3555). Good Harbor specializes in fresh and natural homemade fare made with local produce and whole grains. You won't go wrong with the one of the three egg omelettes, the vegetarian eggs Benedict, or the "Big Bear" breakfast—three eggs, bacon, sausage, and hash browns cooked in a skillet and topped with melted cheese. If you're looking for something a little lighter, try the multigrain pancakes or the maple-almond-crunch granola. Inexpensive to moderate.

You'll need that early-morning energy for your next stop: the **Sleeping Bear Dunes National Lakeshore.** The 70,000-acre park is located just south of your hotel off State Highway 109. If you have kids, this will be the thing they'll tell their friends about when they get home. A masterpiece of ice, wind, and water, the dunes are named after a Chippewa Indian legend about a mother bear and her two bear cubs who attempted to cross Lake Michigan to escape a forest fire. The two cubs drowned and are today represented by the Manitou Islands. The massive Sleeping Bear dune represents where the mother waited for her offspring.

For a good overview of the park, stop at the handy Visitors Center operated by the National Park Service. A slide program, books, and free maps offer information about the dunes and their history. There's also a snack bar where you can get something to drink after you climb. Depending on how ambitious you are (and what kind of shape you're in), you may choose to climb the dunes or take the car on the 7.1-mile route known as the **Pierce Stocking Scenic Drive.** If you choose to use your oxygen power, you'll be rewarded with a great cardiovascular workout as well as breathtaking view of Glen Lake and the Manitou Islands. Choices for hikers range from the 130-foot **Dune Climb** (maybe they should have called it the "Dune Crawl") to the Dunes Trail, a 3.5-mile round-trip, or the 2.8-mile walk to Sleeping Bear Point. Be forewarned: There is no water or shelter provided, and it's easy for kids to get lost in the expanse of sand at the top. It's best to wear sturdy shoes and take a map and a canteen of water. Call (616) 326–5734 for more information.

If you prefer to drive, the scenic Pierce Stocking offers panoramic views of the dunes, Glen Lake, and Lake Michigan. It's open from mid-April through mid-November, weather permitting, and can get a little crowded on peak summer weekends. The route is also a breathtaking—if challenging—bike trail.

Afterward, stop at the **Coast Guard Maritime Museum** located on Sleeping Bear Point in Glen Haven. The museum recounts the region's maritime history and contains a replica of a Great Lakes steamer pilothouse, shipwreck artifacts, and other relics of the area's shipping past, including remains of boats that fell prey to Lake Michigan's legendary fury. Other things to do at the Dunes: hike Pyramid Point off Port Oneida Road for a great vista of wind and water; seek out the views of Inspiration Point off the southwest side of Glen Lake; laze on the sand and take a dip in the clear but cold Lake Michigan at one of the beaches within the park, including **D. H. Day Park** in Glen Haven, North Bear Lake, and Good Harbor Bay; hike the Empire Bluffs off Wilco Road south of Empire and canoe along the Platte and Crystal rivers, both within park boundaries. Crystal is a short, shallow river that's ideal for beginners or families with young children; the Platte is also gentle, while the Upper Platte is fast and for experienced canoers only. In winter, the park has 50 miles of marked cross-country trails.

Afternoon

Lunch: If you're starving, stop at **Boone Docks** (5858 South Manitou Boulevard; 616–334–6444) in Glen Arbor, where you can enjoy a rustic setting and homemade soups, sandwiches, and seafood. Try the patio if the weather permits. Moderate. Otherwise, hold off until you get to Leland, about 25 miles up Highway 109.

The most famous eatery in Leland is the **Blue Bird** (102 River Road; 616–256–9081). This casual Northern Michigan institution is known for its huge cinnamon rolls as well as its homemade soups and Great Lakes whitefish. Moderate.

Leland is one of the peninsula's main tourist towns, with shops that range from tacky to trendy. If you're looking for some good beach reading, don't miss **Leelanau Books** (109 North Main Street; 616–256–7111), which was recently enlarged and stocks a wide selection of titles for both children and adults. Other shops along Main Street worth a look include **Tampico** (112 North Main Street; 616–256–7747), importers of Central American goods, **Ragamuffin** (113 North Main Street; 616–256–9675), with adorable and affordable clothes for kids; and **Becky Thatcher Designs** (110 North Lake Street; 616–256–2229), with high-quality Native American–inspired jewelry crafted of local materials such as the popular Petoskey stone. Farther down the Main Street you'll find **Stone House Breads** (407 South Main; 616–256–2577), owned and operated by Bob Pisor, whom Detroit-area TV watchers will remember from the Channel 4 news.

Leland is also home to **Fishtown,** set along Lake Michigan. Fishtown is a tad touristy for some tastes, but is worth a stop if only for its breathtaking location. Here old fishing shanties-turned-shops have been renovated to sell leatherworks, candy, baked goods, pottery, and a bevy of other merchandise.

Dinner: To escape the crowds in downtown Leland, head for the serenity of the **Leland Lodge** (565 Pearl Street; 616–256–8812). The Leland Room is a quiet New England–style spot that offers elegant dining with a great view overlooking the adjacent golf course and Leelanau valley. Moderate to expensive.

Day 3

Morning

Breakfast: Grab a bite at your hotel before setting off to explore. Today's itinerary includes tours of North Leelanau and the peninsula's other towns as well as a stop at the Indian-run casino near Suttons Bay.

From the Homestead you'll want to head north on Highway 22. You'll pass through Leland and can stop if you missed anything the day before. Otherwise, continue to Northport, a charming town at the tip of the peninsula. Resist the urge to stop and shop, however, until after you've visited a few sites at the peninsula's tip. The drive alone is worth the trip, winding through beautiful countryside beside blue water.

Ready for a snack? Stop at **Kilcherman's Christmas Cove Farm** (Christmas Cove Road/DeLong Road, off Route 201; 616–386–5637), just north of Northport, home to two hundred varieties of apples. Many are historic brands that date back as far as 1600. It's one of the few antique apple farms in the country.

Head another 3 miles north and you'll find another not-to-be-missed attraction, the **Grand Traverse Lighthouse,** registered as a National and State Historic Site. The lighthouse is located 5 miles north of the village of Northport in the 1,300-acre **Leelanau State Park** (616–386–7553). Visitors are free to roam the grounds and explore the buildings as well as climb to the top of the historic structure. From it you can see Charlevoix, a popular resort town that's some 77 miles by car but just 17 miles by sea. Other favorite stops include Peterson Park, site of some of the peninsula's best sunsets, and the rocky yet scenic Northport Point.

Afternoon

Lunch: **Stubb's** (115 Waukazoo, Northport; 616–386–7611) is a casually elegant eatery that specializes in regional cuisine such as freshly prepared fish and local wines. Once an area bar and grill, it was recently purchased by two Culinary Institute of America graduates, who have transformed it into Northport's best restaurant. Moderate.

After lunch is the time to explore Northport. The tiny village nestles into the tip of the peninsula and remains much as it has for centuries, save for a few new shops and restaurants. Streets are lined with tidy homes and bed and breakfast inns, restaurants are casual and friendly. A few highlights include **Barb's Bakery** (112 North Mill Street; 616–386–5851), where you can grab a freshly baked pastry (try the doughy cinnamon twists) and some fresh coffee while chatting with the owner; **North Country Gardens** (Waukazoo Street at Nagonaba Street; 616–386–5031), a large gift shop with unusual merchandise by local artists located in a restored building (the building also is home to the local chamber of commerce, where you can pick up brochures and other information); and **Bird N' Hand Antiques** (123 East Nagonaba Street; 616–386–7104), which features vintage clothing and vintage-inspired millinery by owner-designer Barbara Pare (Northport also has seven other antiques stores). And if art's your thing, Northport is home to two worthwhile spaces: **Zoon Gallery** (122 West Nagonaba; 616–386–5937), featuring art and crafts by Cranbrook graduate Char Bickel that revolve around whimsical animal themes; and **Joppich's Bay Street Gallery** (109 North Rose; 616–386–7428), a seasonal spot that features local Michigan artists. A few steps away is the local marina, where you can ogle the sailboats from as far away as Florida and relax with an ice-cream cone from the nearby **Ship's Galley** at the public beach and park.

From Northport, head south on Highway 22 to Suttons Bay. Another popular resort town, Suttons Bay is the largest town on the peninsula's eastern shore. Originally called Suttonburg and Pleasant City, it was named after Harry C. Sutton, who came to the area in 1854 to clear the woods and supply fuel for wood-burning steamboats. By 1876 the town had grown, with three hotels that did a flourishing summer business and a number of shops (one, Bahle's Department Store, remains today and is run by the original family).

Suttons Bay is a pretty port town with good shopping and restaurants from family-style to fancy (the town's trademark red phone booths were imported from England to add a dash of color). It also has some of the peninsula's best shopping, with intricate stained-glass windows at **Leelanau Architectural Antiques** (301 St. Joseph Street; 616–271–6821); wearable art by local artists at the **Painted Bird** (216 St. Joseph Street; 616–271–3050); funky fashions at the **Lima Bean** (222 St. Joseph Street; 616–271–5462); and everything for the palate at **Bacchus and Brie,** with a wide selection of wine as well as pastas, cheeses, and coffees. Others also worth a stop include **Hats and Haberdashery** (30 St. Joseph Street; 616–271–5226), and the historic **Bahle's Department Store** (210 St. Joseph Street; 616–271–3841). If the kids need to let off some steam or you've a mind to take a dip, the city park and marina has an attractive sand beach and a playscape for kids. Want to take in a movie? Suttons Bay has one of the few cinemas on the peninsula, housed in a historic storefront (216 St. Joseph Street; 616–271–3772).

Dinner: Suttons Bay also has some of the most diverse dining on the peninsula. If you're feeling like splurging, there's no better place than **Hattie's** (111 St. Joseph Street; 616–271–6222), which serves up fine dining in a simple and elegant atmosphere of tiny, twinkling lights. Specialties include the unusual morel ravioli as well as grilled range hen with barbecue sauce, Thai-style scallops, and the signature dessert, Chocolate Paradise with Raspberries. Expensive.

If the kids are along, you might feel more at home at the casual **Boone's Prime Time Pub** across the street (102 St. Joseph Street; 616–271–6688), an outpost of the popular Boone's Long Lake Inn in Traverse City. It's known for its family dining, specializing in steaks, shrimp, and tasty sandwiches. Get here early or there will be a wait. Moderate.

Feeling lucky? After dinner you may want to head for the nearby **Leelanau Sands Casino** (2521 North West Bay Shore Drive [Highway 22], Suttons Bay; 616–271–4104). Owned and operated by the Grand Traverse Bay band of Chippewa Indians, the casino offers blackjack, craps, Caribbean stud poker, live keno, and 450 slot machines from 25 cents to $5.00. The casino is open seven days a week and is open until 3:00 A.M. nightly. You must be at least eighteen years old to enter and twenty-one to play craps, blackjack, and Caribbean stud poker.

Day 4

Morning

Breakfast: The **Leelanau Country Inn** (149 East Harbor Highway; 616–228–5060) is located halfway between Glen Arbor and Leland off Highway 22. The 104-year-old inn has been cited as the area's best restaurant as well as the best Sunday brunch, with more than fifty homemade items as well as the region's largest selection of locally produced wines. Reservations are always a good idea. Moderate.

Oenophiles who have had a chance to taste the fruits of the area may want to use their final day to explore the wineries themselves. The Leelanau Peninsula and nearby Traverse City area are perfectly situated on the 45th parallel, halfway between the equator and the North Pole, and have rich soil as well as four distinct seasons. That makes it the perfect climate for growing and harvesting premium wine grapes. The region boasts seven renowned wineries, four of which are on the Leelanau Peninsula.

Boskydel Vineyards (7501 East Otto Road; 616–256–7272) is owned by Bernie Rink, who began testing hybrid grape vines in 1965 and installed Leelanau County's first bonded wine cellar. Today it produces French-American hybrid grapes that combine the French wine quality with disease-resistant American roots. The winery is best known for its Vignoles, Seyval Blanch and De Chaunac, Boskydel red, white and rosé blends and for its atmosphere, which is reminiscent of Germany's Rhine region and New York's Finger Lakes. It's off South Lake Leelanau Drive between State Highway 204 and County Road 633 and is open from 1:00 to 6:00 P.M. year-round for tours and tastings.

Good Harbor Vineyards (34 North Manitou Trail West; 616–256–7165) is known for its white grape varieties grown on the premises and aged in French Oak barrels and stainless steel vats. Favorites include Trillium, named after the ubiquitous area wildflower, Fishtown, and Northern Lights. Self-guided tours and tastings are available, as are the vineyard's acclaimed products, such as the 1991 Good Harbor Riesling. Located 3 miles south of Leland behind the Manitou Farm Market; open from 11:00 A.M. to 6:00 P.M. during the week and noon to 6:00 P.M. weekends from May through October; call for November–April hours.

On the other side of the peninsula are the remaining two area wineries. **Leelanau Wine Cellars** (12693 East Tatch Road, Omena; 616–386–5201) is a 65,000-gallon winery that produces a full line of vinifera, hybrid, and fruit wines. Try the Vis-a-Vis or the 1995 Chardonnay. Tasting facilities are open daily year-round (call for hours) at the winery itself on County Road 626 and Kalchik Road as well as in Empire, Leland, and downtown Traverse City.

L. Mawby Vineyards (4519 Elm Valley Road, Suttons Bay; 616–271–3522) the smallest of the area wineries, produces fewer than three thousand cases of estate-grown table and methode champenoise sparkling wines from their vineyards on the hills overlooking Suttons Bay. Wines are filtered only when necessary, creating a unique method for wines that mature and develop in the bottle. Worth noting are the 1994 Vignoles and the Cremant Brut NV. Tastings and sales are available from May through October, Thursdays through Saturdays from 1:00 to 6:00 P.M. or by appointment.

Whichever vineyard you visit and wine you choose, all make sweet reminders of your weekend in the Leelanau Peninsula to savor long after you've returned home.

There's More

Canoes. The Crystal River Canoe Livery (6052 Western, Glen Arbor; 616–334–3090) takes adults and children on two and one-half-hour excursions along the easy yet scenic Crystal River.

Golf. Northern Michigan abounds with excellent courses, including Crystal Mountain Resort (12500 Crystal Mountain Drive, Thompsonville; 800–968–7686), with twenty-seven holes, and Sugar Loaf Resort (616–228–5461 or 800–968–0574), where a new Arnold Palmer course has opened. There are also a number of good public courses nearby.

Herbs. Busha's Brae Herb Farm (2540 North Setterbo Road, Suttons Bay; 616–271–6284) is a working herb farm that features a garden of biblical herbs, a Shakespearean garden, a cottage garden, and a production garden, all open to visitors. Teas and herbal luncheons plus an herbal newsletter and catalog are all available on request. Open May through December.

Sailing. Interested in learning more about the science of sailing? The Inland Seas Educational Association (ISEA) offers half-day, full-day, and overnight programs for all ages on board the *Inland Seas*. The association specializes in ecology, aquatic biology, family schoolship, and navigation programs and is based in Suttons Bay. For more information, contact ISEA, P.O. Box 218, Suttons Bay, MI 49682; (616) 271–3077.

If you're looking for something a little more relaxing, consider a three- or six-day Windjammer cruise (13390 Southwest Bay Shore Drive, Box 8, Traverse City, MI 49684; 800–968–8800) on the tall ship *Manitou*. Docked in Northport, it sails to Beaver Island, Harbor Springs, legendary Mackinac Island, and secluded islands and bays to view area wildlife. It's the perfect add-on to a weekend getaway if you're looking to extend your trip.

Special Events

July. Fireworks Celebration, Northport
Harbor Days, Northport

August. Annual Arts Festival, Suttons Bay
Leelanau Peninsula Wine Festival, Northport

Other Recommended Restaurants and Lodgings

Restaurants

Cafe Bliss (420 St. Joseph Street, Suttons Bay; 616–271–5000) serves up vegetarian and ethnic-inspired cuisine in a gray, turn-of-the-century home on the outskirts of town. Moderate.

The **Cove** (111 River, Leland; 616–256–9834) is a local landmark that overlooks historic Fishtown. It's known for its signature Fishtown stew as well as for its freshwater fish, burgers, and sandwiches. Open May through October. Moderate.

Fischer's Happy Hour Tavern (State Highway 22 between Leland and Northport; 616–386–9923) is an area institution that specializes in good food, great service, and a family-friendly atmosphere. It's also one of the few places that's open seven days a week, year-round. Inexpensive to moderate.

Hose House Deli (303 St. Joseph Street, Suttons Bay; 616–271–6303) is housed in the city's former firehouse and features deep-dish pizza, deli sandwiches, and salads. Inexpensive.

Woody's Settling Inn (116 Waukazoo, Northport; 616–386–9933) is a casual, family-style bar and restaurant that's open year-round and known for its cherry-smoked chicken, nachos, and fresh fish. Lunch and appetizers can be eaten on the patio that overlooks downtown Northport. Moderate.

Lodgings

Leelanau Country Inn (149 East Harbor Highway, Maple City; 616–228–5060) has six rooms in a historic 104-year-old inn between Glen Arbor and Leland. Summer rates start at $55 per night.

Omena Shores B&B (13140 Isthmus Road, P.O. Box 154, Omena, MI 49674; 616–386–7313) is a lovingly restored 1850s barn full of antiques, wicker, and handmade quilts. Rates: $65–$85 per night.

Open Windows B&B (613 St. Mary's Avenue, Suttons Bay; 800–520–3722) is a century-old home with three guest rooms near downtown Suttons Bay. Room rates ($70–$95) include homemade breakfast served on the porch or in the kitchen.

Sugar Loaf Resort (4500 Sugar Loaf Mountain Road, Cedar; 616–228–5461 or 800–968–0574) is the largest resort on the peninsula, with more than five hundred hotel rooms, townhouses, and luxury condos. It also features free golf packages, an all-grass miniature golf course, scenic chairlift rides (it's also a popular winter destination), and a new Arnold Palmer–designed golf course.

For more accommodations, see Traverse City (Michigan Escape Three).

For More Information

Traverse City Convention and Visitors Bureau, 101 West Grandview Parkway, Traverse City, MI 49684; (800) 872–8377.

Traverse City

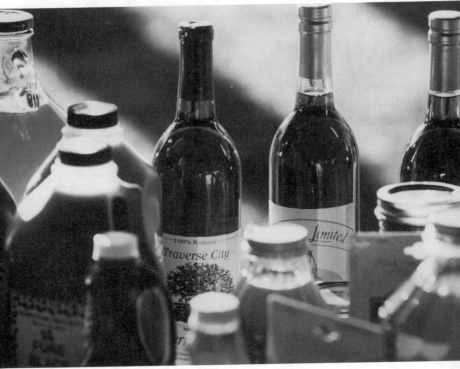

Cherry trees blanket the Traverse City area, and their fruits make popular souvenirs.

Life Is Just a Bowl of Cherries

_____ 3 NIGHTS _____

Shopping • Sun and Sand • Restaurants • Skiing • Sailing
_____

If Northern Michigan had a capital, it would be Traverse City. The city is the largest in the northern part of the state, and among the most popular with visitors. Besides Florida, this is where downstaters dream of retiring or opening an antiques shop or bed and breakfast. Purists claim the city's original charm has been lost to excessive development, but most visitors find Traverse City to be a delightful mix of small-town friendliness and big-city amenities.

The area earned its name from the early French fur trappers. Traveling by canoe across the stretch of open water between the tip of the Leelanau Peninsula and Charlevoix, they would call their venture *le grande traverse,* or "the great crossing." Thus the area became known as Grand Traverse Bay. Lumbermen followed the fur traders, tapping the area's rich resources. Lumbering thrived into the early 1990s, when two other industries—cherry farming and tourism—began to flourish. Both continue to impact the local economy today.

Strategically located at the head of Grand Traverse Bay, Traverse City is also known as the Cherry Capital of the World, with a huge eight-day festival celebrating the harvest each July. Many of those cherries are grown on the Old Mission Peninsula, where a number of the area's vineyards are also located.

Day 1

Afternoon

Hit the road in the morning and plan on being in town in time for a late lunch. Traverse City is about a four-hour drive northwest of Detroit. To get there, take Interstate 75 north and exit near Grayling onto State Highway 72, which heads west directly into Traverse City.

Lunch: One of the best places for lunch in Traverse City is **Cousin's Jenny's Cornish Pasties** (129 South Union Street; 616–941–7821), a cozy downtown eatery that serves seven varieties of pasties as well as homemade soups, salads, and scones. Inexpensive.

Lodging: **Bayshore Resort** (833 East Front Street; 616–935–4400 or 800–634–4401) manages to be both elegant and convenient to nearby downtown. The 120 rooms are classically decorated in taupe stripes with rose and teal accents and antique reproduction furniture. Some have a whirlpool and/or fireplace. There are also a sugar sand beach, a large indoor pool, and a fitness area. A tip: Kids love the rooms on the ground floor that lead directly onto the beach. Rates: $120–$275 per night.

Day 2

Morning

Breakfast: One of the nicest things about a stay at Bayshore is its continental breakfast, served in a spacious room near the lobby from 6:00 to 10:00 A.M. More than just coffee and a doughnut, it includes self-serve yogurt, fresh fruit, juices, cereals, and your choice of breads and pastries.

After breakfast it's time to wander downtown and start exploring. The compact central city is just a few blocks from your hotel and is lined with well-maintained nineteenth- and early twentieth-century storefronts where you'll find more than one hundred shops, from fashionable to funky. Be sure to stop at **Horizon Books** (243 Front Street; 616–946–7290), housed in a former J.C. Penney store, which is considered by bibliophiles to be among the best bookstores in the state. It was also one of the first to have it's own in-house coffee bar. Not far away is the **Opera House** on Front Street, a Victorian landmark built in 1891 and one of just eighteen opera houses left in the state. It's still used for occasional concerts and is open for tours by appointment. Call (616) 922–2070.

Other stores worth exploring include **Cali's Cottons** (242 East Front Street; 616–947–0633), where owner Alison Knowles stocks comfy 100 percent cotton clothing; **Dandelion** (130 East Front Street; 616–933–4340), known for its adorable and unusual selection of duds for kids; and the **Firehouse Fair** (118 Cass Street; 616–935–4442), which is housed in a former firehouse and stocks a wide assortment of interesting gifts and goodies. Not far away is **Wilson's Antiques** (616–946–4177), near Cousin Jenny's on Union Street, where more than fifty dealers set up shop in booths that are filled with just about every kind of collectible imaginable. If you're looking for some souvenirs for the folks back home, don't miss **American Spoon Foods** (616–935–4480), also on Front Street, a local Northern Michigan institution that serves up gourmet jams, jellies, and foodstuffs, including a few more unusual selections such as cherry salsa and cherry hot pepper jelly. Chocoholics may also want to take a few of the edibles from **Kilwin's Candies** (129 East Front Street; 616–935–2403) home as a sweet reminder of a Traverse City stay.

Afternoon

Lunch: **Poppycock's** (128 East Front Street; 616–941–7632) is a delightful restaurant in the heart of downtown. Lunch selections include an excellent Front Street Salad (greens, grilled chicken breast, sun-dried cherries, fresh goat cheese, sprouts, and pecans) as well as sandwiches (try the herb-crusted whitefish or the Portabella mushroom stack) and pastas (Poppycock's marinara is made with sun-dried tomatoes, pine nuts, feta cheese, and marinara sauce over whole-wheat fettuccine). Moderate.

After lunch it's time to take in some of the other area attractions. One you won't want to miss is the **Dennos Museum Center** (1701 East Front Street; 616–922–1055), not far from your hotel. Part of Northwestern Michigan University, it's devoted to the hands-on exploration of science, art, and technology. Three changing galleries house temporary and traveling exhibitions. The museum is best known, however, for its spectacular collection of contemporary Eskimo art, one of the best in the country. Here you'll find more than 550 pieces of sculpted soapstone and prints depicting the culture of these fascinating Arctic people in a permanent space known as Inuit Art Gallery. In summer, the museum is also home to the Michigan Ensemble Theater, which performs in the auditorium.

Another local favorite away from downtown is the **Music House** (7377 U.S. Highway 31 North, Acme; 616–938–9300), a "performing museum" of beautifully restored and rare antique musical instruments in an authentic turn-of-the-century decor. The unusual museum features everything from tiny music boxes to a seventy-year-old hand-carved Belgian dance organ. While there, you can trace the history of sound reproduction in the phonograph and radio galleries, listed to a huge Regina Corona Music Box, even sip a soda to the tunes of the Nickelodeons at the in-house Hurry Back Saloon. Open May through October.

Dinner: Head back downtown to catch one of the area's newest attractions, the **Traverse City Dinner Train** (642 Railroad Place; 616–933–3768 for reservations). It winds its way along a 33-mile track, giving diners an incredible view of the bay and the surrounding landscape. Downstate chef Ron Stewart cooks up one of the most romantic meals imaginable on four 1950s vintage dining cars that once ran between New Orleans and Los Angeles. The five-course meal costs $55 per person but is worth the price for appetizers such as smoked salmon pâté, changing soups such as cream of wild morels, and your choice of four entrees, including garlic-roasted prime rib, farm-raised rainbow trout with Chateau Grand Traverse pan sauce and herb-scented orzo, breast of chicken stuffed with smoked duck and apples, or tri-color pasta with roast vegetable stuffing. Expensive.

If you still haven't had enough of the bay and you'd sooner go by schooner, consider a sail on the **Tall Ship *Malabar*** (13390 West Bay Shore Drive; 616–941–2000 or 800–678–0383). It's an authentic replica of an eighteenth-century topsail gaff-rigged sailing vessel, with more than 105 feet of pure sailing pleasure. It sails three times daily between late May and early October: a noon sail with a picnic meal, an afternoon sail, and a breathtaking sunset sail with a picnic meal. Reservations are needed.

Day 3

Morning

Breakfast: If you're looking for something heartier with which to start the day, **Mabel's** (472 Rumson Street; 616–947–0252) has raked in the *Traverse Magazine* awards, from "best breakfasts" and "Northern Michigan's Top Ten Restaurants" to "Best Place to Bring Kids." The huge morning meals (served all day) include overstuffed omelettes, thick slabs of home-baked French toast, and more. Pick up a few of the famous sticky buns on the way out. Inexpensive. Mabel's is about a half mile from your hotel.

Traverse City is known for its vineyards and its cherries, both of which dominate the scenic Old Mission Peninsula. No visit would be complete without exploring this thin 18-mile-long spit of land that bisects Grand Traverse Bay. Its hilly topography and rich soil are some of the finest in the country for

growing cherries and grapes, with the bay moderating temperatures and pre-
venting the early spring warming that endangers fruit buds.

Today the western shore is a fashionable address for Traverse City residents. The east shore is less crowded and more scenic. For spectacular vistas
and panoramic views, follow State Highway 37 as well as East Shore Road,
Bluff Road, and Smokey Hollow Road.

Lunch: The **Boathouse** (14039 Peninsula Drive; 616–223–4030) is a clean-
lined, nautical-flavored eatery with a spectacular Bowers Harbor marina setting on Old Mission Peninsula. The food is equally good—with a wide range
of fare from burgers and salads to innovative daily specials including fish and
pastas. The restaurant's signature popovers come with all meals. Open just
two years, the restaurant has been recently discovered and can get crowded
on weekends. Reservations are always a good idea. Moderate.

Afternoon

Chateau Grand Traverse (12239 Center Road; 616–223–7355) is the first
winery you'll encounter on the Old Mission Peninsula. Owned by the O'Keefe
family since 1974, it's approximately 8 miles from downtown Traverse City
along Center Road (Highway 37). With panoramic views of both East and
West Grand Traverse Bays, it sits on more than 140 acres planted with grapes.
An inviting and newly expanded tasting room allows visitors to sample the
fruits of the vineyard in a French wine bar atmosphere. Standouts include a
1994 and 1995 Johannesburg Riesling and an impressive 1992 Ice Wine (don't
forget to ask how it's made).

Another family-owned winery is **Bowers Harbor** (616–223–7615), located
some 9 miles outside Traverse City. The first thing you'll notice as you approach is the spectacular view of the small hamlet of Bowers Harbor. Owners
Jack and Linda Stegenga got into wine making after abandoning a career rais-
ing Hereford cows. Today, their small winery is known for its sparkling Riesling Bruit, a light and lively fruity wine, as well as for the 1992 and 1993
Chardonnay and the 1992 Shiraz.

The newest kid on the block is **Old Mission Cellars** (616–223–4310),
founded in 1994. Located in the village of Old Mission, it has just 4 acres of
grapes planted among 180 acres of cherry trees. Winemaker Lee Lutes honed
his skills at a Long Island winery and a vineyard in Northern Italy. A Michigan
native, he returned a few years ago to help owners Dave and Joan Kroupa get
the winery on its feet. Old Mission Cellars is considered a "boutique" winery,
with just five wines: two white, one red, and two fruit wines. Try the 1995
Chardonnay or the 1995 Riesling or the cherry and apple wines, considered
the best in the area.

The most romantic of the vineyards, hands down, is **Chateau Chantal**
(15900 Rue du Vin; 616–223–4110). Located about 12 miles north of Traverse

City on 65 acres overlooking both the east and west bays, this winery began developing its vineyards in 1983 and opened its elegant tasting room and facility ten years later. Named after the owners' daughter, Chantal, it produces wonderful chardonnays, Rieslings, pinot noir, and merlot wines. It's open for tastings daily and is the site of a popular Jazz at Sunset series on Friday nights. The chateau is also a bed and breakfast, with three wonderful rooms overlooking the vineyards and the surrounding countryside. Not surprisingly, guests are encouraged to sip wine and watch the sun set from the chateau's charming patio.

If you're more interested in vintage lighthouses than vineyards, **Old Mission Point and Light** dates to 1870. The original frame keeper's dwelling is still here, as is a pretty beach with good swimming. Across the way you can see Omena on the Leelanau Peninsula and Eastport on Torch Lake. Also worth a visit is the **Old Mission Church,** off Old Mission Road in the hamlet of Old Mission, a replica of a house of worship built in 1839 by a Presbyterian missionary to the Chippewa Indians. The information-packed historical displays are a product of the Old Mission Women's Club, a group of enthusiastic volunteers.

Dinner: After a tour of the vineyards, you'll want to stay on the peninsula and dine at the **Bowers Harbor Inn** (13512 Peninsula Drive; 616–223–4222). Many area foodies consider this the most romantic eatery in the area, as much for its spectacular view and vintage summer house setting as for the fine food. The drive along the West Bay to the restaurant alone is worth the trip even if the food weren't good. But it is. Specialties include "fish-in-a-bag." If you're looking to go casual, the adjacent Bowery serves ribs, rotisserie chicken, and great burgers. Moderate to expensive.

Day 4

Morning

Brunch: **Park Place Hotel** (300 East State Street; 616–946–5000) is known to serve the area's best brunch. It includes both breakfast and lunch items—from cold boiled shrimp to savory pasta salads and freshly baked breakfast items—for under $15. Moderate.

If you've brought the kids, Sunday is a great day to take in the **Clinch Park Zoo** (616–922–4904). Its location along the waterfront makes it one of the prettiest zoos in the country. The tiny zoo specializes in animals that would be found in the woods around Traverse City, including a black bear mom and two adorable cubs, a repetitive crow, playful beavers, otters, and turtles as well as the more ominous coyote, wolf, and bison. Don't miss the chance to take the mini-locomotive for a roundabout view of the bay and beyond. Afterward, if weather permits, laze awhile on the adjacent Clinch Park Beach, one of the city's most popular. The zoo is open daily from April through November. Admission is $2.00 for adults; $1.50 for children ages five through thirteen; free for children under five.

Afterward, you may want to head back downtown to explore anything you missed or spend the rest of the day lazing around the beach before hitting the freeway and heading home. Another option is to head to **Interlochen Academy,** where music hath charms to soothe the savage beast. The renowned music school has more than two hundred performances each year by students, faculty, and big-name entertainers. From outdoor concerts in the open-air pavilion overlooking Green Lake to campus concerts by summer student campers, Interlochen offers a taste of the arts. For ticket information, call (616) 276–6230.

There's More

Apples. Amon Orchards (7404 U.S. Highway 31 North; 800–937–1644) is a family-owned and run fruit farm that's a favorite of family visitors. Trolley tours of the orchards, a farm market, and a petting zoo are among the many attractions.

Balloon Rides. You won't need eighty days to get a great view of Traverse City and the Old Mission Peninsula. Spectacular sights are daily fare at Grand Traverse Balloons (225 Cross Country Trail; 616–947–7433), which offers airborne tours in multicolored seven-story-tall hot air balloons. Flights are offered at sunrise and sunset, last one hour, and are followed by champagne celebrations.

Cooking Classes. The Traverse Cooking Academy (616–933–6042) offers weekends twice a year that feature the Midwest's finest chefs cooking up their signature regional fare.

Golf. The Traverse City area has more than twenty excellent courses on which to tee off. Highlights include A-Ga-Ming in Kewadin (800–678–0122), the Bear and Spruce Run at Grand Traverse Resort in Acme (800–748–0303); High Point Gold Club in Williamsburg (800–753–7888), Mistwood Golf Course in Lake Ann (616–275–5500), and the Legend at Shanty Creek in Bellaire (800–678–4111). For more information, contact the course directly or the Traverse City Convention and Visitors Bureau at (800) 872–8377.

History. The Con Foster Museum (Grandview Parkway; 616–922–4905) serves as the local history museum and is the place to discover the area's cultural heritage. Free.

Parasailing. Feeling ambitious? A number of area companies take visitors high in the sky on parasailing adventures. Grand Traverse Parasail (616–947–3938) is docked at Bay Winds Restaurant and sails from 11 A.M. to sunset in season.

Shopping Outlets. Caught the outlet fever? Horizon Outlets (616–941–9211) of Traverse City includes more than forty shops featuring deals and discounted goods. Among the best is the Eddie Bauer outlet, which has great "Up North" resort and casual clothing that you'll wear long after you return home.

Alden. *National Geographic* once called Torch Lake one of the most beautiful lakes in the world. This clear but cold lake is home to great fishing and water sports, as well as to the tiny town of Alden, which is among the state's most charming. **Spencer Creek Landing** (9166 Helena Street; 616–331–6147) is a gourmet restaurant on the town's main street, with spectacular sunsets over the lake and fine regional cuisine. Alden is also home to a couple of excellent antiques shops and **Talponia Books,** one of the most unusual used-book stores in the state, where you'll find vintage beach reading side by side with collectible first editions.

Special Events

May. Blossom Days, Old Mission Peninsula
June. Bay Day, Traverse City
July. Fireworks, Traverse City
     National Cherry Festival, Traverse City
     Outdoor Art Fair, Traverse City

Other Recommended Restaurants and Lodgings

Restaurants

Don's Drive Inn (2030 U.S. Highway 31 North; 616–256–9656) is the place for classic–style burgers, fries, and shakes. Inexpensive.

Kelly's Roadhouse Cafe (14091 Center Road; 616–223–7200) is considered one of the Old Mission Peninsula's favorite gathering places. Specialties include cherry–smoked ribs, fresh fish, fondues, and homemade soups. This is a casual place where you can take the kids without feeling self-conscious. Moderate.

Old Mission Tavern (17015 Center Road, Old Mission Peninsula; 616–223–7280) serves classic cuisine from Greece, Italy, France, and Poland. Diners flock here for the pierogies served on Thursdays and the leg of lamb served on Sunday. Moderate.

Omelet Shop. Another great choice for breakfast, it's a frequent winner of the "Best Breakfast" category in the *Traverse Magazine*'s reader polls. Two locations: 1209 East Front Street (616–946–0590), in a strip mall near the Bay Shore Hotel, or 124 Cass (616–946–0912) downtown. Inexpensive.

Schelde's (714 Munson Avenue; 616–922–2114) is known for its family–friendly menu and service. The all-you-can-eat salad bar is a favorite here and at other Schelde's restaurants across the state. Inexpensive to moderate.

Scott's Harbor Grill (12719 South West Bay Shore Drive; 616–922–2114) has one of the best views and patio dining that fills up quickly. The restaurant offers a wide range of salads, sandwiches, and entrees as well as daily specials. Moderate.

Sleder's Family Tavern (717 Randolph; 616–947–9213) is the state's oldest tavern (est. 1882) and well known for its buffalo burgers and Mexican entrees. Moderate.

Windows (7677 West Bay Shore Drive; 616–941–0100) is considered by many to be the city's best restaurant. With gourmet French-American cuisine and daily specialties, it's a must-visit when you're in Northern Michigan. Expensive.

Lodgings

The **Grand Traverse Resort** (100 Grand Traverse Village Boulevard, Acme, (800–678–1308) has 750 rooms, suites, and condos as well as ten restaurants, lounges, and a shopping gallery. Rates: $145–$365 per night.

Holiday Inn (615 East Front Street; 616–947–3700 or 800–888–8020) is a favorite family spot where kids eat free. Two blocks from downtown, it has 179 rooms on West Bay. Rates: $82–$160 per night.

Park Place Hotel (616–946–5000 or 800–748–0133) is the city's only multi-storied hotel located right in the heart of downtown. Rates: $115–$145 per night.

Pointes North Inn (2211 U.S. Highway 31 North; 616–938–9191 or 800–968–3422) has fifty-two luxury suites on 300 feet of sandy beach on East Bay. All rooms have water views, with private balcony, Jacuzzi, microwave, refrigerator, and VCR. This is a great spot for families. Rates: $125–$145 per night.

For More Information

Traverse City Convention and Visitors Bureau, 101 West Grandview Parkway, Traverse City, MI 49684; 616–947–1120 or (800) 872–8377.

Petoskey/Harbor Springs

Lake Michigan is popular with both anglers and sailors.

Papa's Place

———————————— 2 NIGHTS ————————————

Shopping • Golf • Arts • History • Nature

Don't wait too long to discover the vintage charms of Petoskey; the National Trust for Historic Preservation just named the city to its list of the United State's top ten endangered places. Faced with an approaching Wal-Mart and the kind of suburban sprawl that has transformed Traverse City, many fear the loss of one of the state's most charming areas.

Long a favorite of travelers, Petoskey and neighboring Harbor Springs became famous in the latter half of the nineteenth century, when they were established as summer resorts (settled originally by the Ottawa and Chippewa Indians, Petoskey was named after Ottawa chief Pe-to-se-ga). Petoskey became the choice of families who found its clean air and relaxed pace a welcome change from the harried city. Harbor Springs, on the north side of Little Traverse Bay, became famous for its excellent harbor and a regular stopping place for large passenger ships (passage to Petoskey from Chicago once went for $15 round-trip). The area's natural beauty also attracted wealthy Midwestern families, including the Fords, Upjohns, Gambles (of Proctor & Gamble), and Offields (Wrigley's gum), who built grand homes around the bay in neighboring Wequetonsing and Harbor Point.

Emmet County's two largest towns face each other across Little Traverse Bay and are just 9 miles apart via State Highway 119. Today, both towns have survived and continue to flourish as summer resorts. The population swells in warm weather, but the area attracts visitors year-round, with scenic back roads that blaze with color in autumn and nearby Boyne Mountain and Boyne Highlands, two of the state's best downhill ski resorts, which attract thousands of winter sports enthusiasts.

Day 1

Petoskey is approximately 260 miles north of Detroit. To ensure enough time to enjoy the weekend, take Friday off and plan on an early start to beat the midafternoon traffic along north Interstate 75. Take I–75 to State Highway 72 west to U.S. 131 North. U.S. 131 goes right into Petoskey. Plan on being in town early enough for a late lunch and a round of afternoon shopping. With more than 70 historic shops in a six-block area, downtown Petoskey offers a great escape from the mall maul.

Afternoon

Lunch: **Roast and Toast** (309 East Lake Street; 616–347–7767) is a great spot in the middle of downtown that specializes in simply prepared healthy food. *Traverse Magazine* named it one of the top ten places in Northern Michigan for lunch and one of the top three places for great coffee (they roast their own daily). It lives up to its many accolades, with two or three savory soups (try the great tomato-herb minestrone), a full-fledged deli menu, and fresh salads such as the grilled chicken Caesar or the tasty romaine with pecans, blue cheese, and vinaigrette. All baked goods are made fresh daily. Inexpensive.

Petoskey's downtown shopping area is known as the **Gaslight District** and is nationally known for its unusual and distinctive boutiques. With decorative nineteenth-century storefronts and vintage gas lamps, they're grouped along a few main streets and are an easy and enjoyable stroll. Some of the exclusive clothing, gift, and jewelry shops are open year-round; others are summer only and move south to West Palm Beach or Naples, Florida, during the long Michigan winter.

If you're interested in the area's fascinating history, head for **McLean & Eakin Books** (307 East Lake Street; 616–347–1180), the city's (and some say the state's) best bookstore. In an era of supermarket–style chains, it's fiercely independent and devoted to remaining so. An armchair in the window is often occupied by the shop's amiable cat or by captivated readers, who head here for the best in children's literature, local and regional publications (there's a great selection of Hemingway's Michigan works and books by native son Bruce Catton), and more.

A few steps away is **Arktos** (315 East Lake Street), a fine-arts studio and gallery that features charming and colorful art with an animal theme. More art by Michiganians is featured at **Made in Michigan** (311 East Lake), which has more than one hundred items by local craftspeople, including note cards by Gwen Frostic, porcupine quill boxes, Petoskey stone jewelry, and more.

Undoubtedly one of the downtown's best stores is **Northern Possessions** (317 East Lake Street), with three locations in Northern Michigan and a sophisticated yet fun mix of clothing, jewelry, and contemporary crafts from all over the world.

Not a shopper? Downtown also holds charms for history buffs and Hemingway devotees, who will want to stop by one of the local stores and pick up a copy of the city's "Walking Tour" brochure, which includes background on the vintage storefronts as well as a history of former inhabitants and owners, both famous and otherwise. Shoppers, foodies, and just about everyone else appreciates **Symon's General Store** (401 East Lake Street), built in 1879. It ranks as one of the city's oldest buildings and today stocks fresh coffees and other gourmet goodies. The front steps are also a good resting place when you need a break.

More history (and more Hemingway) can be found at the city's charming **Little Traverse Historical Society and Museum** (100 Depot Court; 616–347–4211), housed in an 1892 railroad depot just steps from downtown. Within the museum's glass showcases are reminders of Ernest Hemingway's time in Northern Michigan (his family had a cottage at nearby Walloon Lake), including Christmas cards, rare first editions, family photos, and even the kerosene lamp he wrote by on dark country nights. Don't miss the informative forty-five-minute video that traces the Hemingway sites in the area. It's beautifully photographed and well worth watching as a primer and basic area history lesson. Many of the sites still remain—including the Staffords Perry Hotel, your base for the weekend. The museum's an interesting and worthwhile stop even if you're not a "Papa" fan.

Also worth a trip is the city's **Virginia McCune Arts Center** (461 East Mitchell Street; 616–347–4337), which has two exhibition galleries, works by area artists, and a tempting gift shop. The excellent Crooked Tree Arts Council has its offices and its annual juried show here. If you're looking for a break, the city's **Waterfront Park** has a pond, a 35-foot waterfall, and a public wheelway that links all the waterfront along Little Traverse Bay and is a favorite of hikers, bikers, and Rollerbladers.

If you prefer to use a little horsepower instead of your own energy, consider a ride in one of the city's horse-drawn carriages. Tours are offered weekends from mid-June through Labor Day and take in the city's Gaslight District. Call (616) 347–7301 for a schedule and prices.

Dinner: **Andante** (321 Bay Street; 616–348–3321) is considered by many to be the city's best restaurant as well as one of the top eateries in all of Northern Michigan. Classical music and Impressionist paintings fill the elegant dining room, located in an unpretentious house at the edge of downtown. The fare is equally impressive, including dishes such as butternut squash bisque, whitefish baked in a potato crust and served with Gewurtztraminer butter, and chargrilled venison on spaetzles with Portobello mushroom sauce. It also has a great wine list. Moderate to expensive.

Lodging: Hemingway once stayed at the **Perry Hotel** (Bay at Lewis; 800–456–1917) for 75 cents per night. Advertised as the only fireproof hotel at the turn of the century, it's the only original resort hotel still operating in town. Today the yellow brick structure (now called Stafford's Perry) is a little more expensive but still retains the charm that Hemingway enjoyed in the 1920s. The city's first brick hotel, it's been a landmark since 1899 and is known for its attentive service as well as its convenient downtown location. The eighty rooms and three suites are spacious and well-decorated with painted furniture (some original to the hotel), deep colors, and vintage wallpaper. Rates range from $65 to $175.

Day 2

Morning

Breakfast: The **Flap Jack Shack** (314 West Mitchell Street; 616–347–1260) is a no-frills eatery (one of two in Northern Michigan) known for its amazing variety of pancakes—including buttermilk, silver dollar, blueberry, Alaskan sourdough, and buckwheat—as well as for other specialties such as multi-grain cinnamon cakes, pigs in a blanket, or a flapjack sandwich. Try the sampler plate (two pancakes of each variety), the blintzes, or the French rolled pecan cakes. Inexpensive.

After breakfast, jump on U.S. Highway 31 North to State Highway 119 into Harbor Springs. Along the way, stop at **Petoskey State Park** (800–543–2937) to hunt for Petoskey stones, the state stone. First-time visitors to the area are often surprised to see people strolling the beach with heads bowed, hoping to find these prized pieces of fossilized coral. The stones are thought to be at least 350 million years old. (If you're out of luck, they're also sold as souvenirs and jewelry in town.) The park is blessedly peaceful, even in the heat of summer, and is a great place to wander the beach, enjoy an early picnic lunch, or take a dip in the bracing waters of Lake Michigan.

Afternoon

Lunch: **Juilleret's** (130 State Street, Harbor Springs; 616-526-2821) has been in the Juilleret family for five generations and is the oldest family-run restaurant in the state. Originally an ice-cream parlor, it served briefly as a dance hall during Prohibition. Since 1960 it's been better known for its homemade ice cream than its hooch. Besides the ice cream, Juilleret's also offers three meals daily. Specialties include the planked whitefish, homemade soups, and the famous "Velvet"—a silky concoction of ice cream, marshmallow, and bittersweet chocolate. Open in season only. Inexpensive.

Although close to Petoskey geographically, Harbor Springs seems like another world. Founded by the Jesuits and once called *L'Arbre Croche* (Crooked Tree), it thrived as a lumber town from 1880 to 1920. More history can be found at the city's **Andrew Blackbird Museum** (368 East Main Street; 616-526-7731), where local tribal members provide tours of the museum that once served as the home of the town's first postmaster, Andrew Blackbird, an Odawa Indian. Also open to the curious is the **Ephraim Shay House** (396 East Main Street; 616-526-8966), the former home of the inventor of the Shay locomotive. The 1891 home is sheathed entirely in embossed metal and is open only in the summer.

Today's Harbor Springs caters to a decidedly affluent crowd, with its main draw being a Main Street full of antiques shops, art galleries, and exclusive boutiques filled with designer resort wear and home accessories. Redoing your decor? Pick up a few ideas along with some rustic-inspired furnishings at **Cedar Creek Interiors** (290 East Third Street; 616-526-9026) or an artful birdhouse at **Birds on the Bay** (137 East Bay Street; 616-256-5039). If you're looking for a more personal transformation, pick up something fun and funky at the many interesting clothing and accessories stores along Main Street.

If antiques are your thing, you'll be in heaven in Harbor Springs. **Elliot & Elliott** (616-526-2040) is known for its jewelry, early boat models, and Native American art. **Joie de Vie** (154 East Main Street; 616-347-1400) specializes in French country. Or head for the strange-sounding **Pooter Ooloms** (294 East Third Street; 616-526-6101), which imports antiques from Scandinavia, Austria, and France, including creamy pine pieces, painted furniture, and antique quilts.

After shopping, you may need to relax awhile. The **Zoll Street Beach** west of the piers is a nice spot to soak your feet or let the kids loose for a while, with a small arc of sand and a few welcome picnic tables. From here you can see the grand "cottages" of the summer community known as Wequetonsing.

Wequetonsing is one of the few exclusive old colonies where you can catch a glimpse of how the other half lives—at least in the summer. Although nearby Harbor Point is private, you can stroll or drive along the bay and enjoy Weque's (pronounced "wee-kwee") lavish summer homes. The resort was established by Presbyterians from Allegan, Michigan, and Elkhart, Indiana, so that "worn-out and sweltering humanity could repair to recover health and enjoy rational recreations."

The most impressive houses face Little Traverse Bay, while smaller cottages line back streets and pedestrian walkways. They range in size from small and simple to grand and glorious, complete with gingerbread, cupolas, and, of course, long, wide porches.

Finally, if the city's trendiness starts to be too much or if the kids are getting antsy, plan a stop at the charming **Deer Park** on the outskirts of town at Zoll and Main streets. Watch for it closely—there are few signs and you could easily miss it. Here you can watch the does cavort inside a pen area or buy a handful of feed for the wide-eyed babies, many of whom are orphans adopted from the surrounding woods.

Dinner: Head back to the Staffords Ferry Hotel for a dinner in the **Rose Room** (616–347–4000). It's famous for its elegantly rich atmospheere as well as for its excellent cuisine. Start with the Perry salad (bibb lettuce, walnuts, mushrooms, and dried cherries with creamy cherry vinaigrette), followed by the morel pasta roll or foie gras with Grand Marnier. For an entree, try the Chicken Perigourdine (chicken breast on linguine with truffle cream sauce) or the Maine lobster tails. There's piano music on Friday and Saturday evenings. It's expensive—but worth it.

Day 3

Morning

Breakfast: Many consider the brunch at Petoskey's **Stafford's Bay View** (616–347–2771) the best in Northern Michigan (yes, it's owned by the same people who own Stafford's Perry). With a charming Victorian atmosphere and a friendly and knowledgeable waitstaff, it's hard to deny the claim. The brunch spread includes a gluttonous array of breakfast and lunch-style foodstuffs, including made-to-order omelettes and waffles, ham, turkey, eggs Benedict, great sweet rolls, a gourmet table of smoked fish and pâtés, and more. It's a bargain at just $16.95 per person; children ages seven to eleven are $7.95; ages four to six are $4.95; under three are free. Brunches are offered once a month in winter, weekly other seasons.

Don't leave the area without a drive or walk through **Bay View,** the picturesque summer community founded in 1875 by the Methodist Church as a summer retreat for its members. The community has 430 homes on the National Historic Register and is the largest collection of historic homes in the country. Most are the product of Charles Caskey, a nineteenth-century architect who designed most of the gingerbread-trimmed confections, many of which are still occupied in summer by descendants of the original owners.

One-time guests include speakers such as William Jennings Bryant, Helen Keller, and Booker T. Washington. Attend a concert, lecture, or play, take a class, or just wander through the beautifully preserved enclave. Activities today are much as they were in the nineteenth century and include lectures, concerts, recitals, and Sunday evening services. A fascinating archives and museum in the Encampment tell the Bay View story (616–348–2599).

There's More

Camping. Petoskey State Park (800–543–2937) has both a prime location and a sandy shore, both of which make it one of the state's most popular campgrounds.

Canoeing. Bear River Canoe Livery (2517 McDougall Road, Petoskey; 616–347–9038) rents canoes for excursions of all skill levels on area rivers.

Fall Foliage. Some say autumn is the best time to visit, when the surrounding countryside is transformed into a tapestry of scarlet and gold. If you're planning an autumn adventure, pick up a copy of the *Fall in Northwest* "Michigan" guide, which details five area color tours, including the breathtaking and justly famous 20-mile road from Harbor Springs to Cross Village, known as the Tunnel of Trees. Call (800) 845–2828.

Fishing and Boating. Walloon and Crooked lakes, Lake Charlevoix, and Little Traverse Bay all offer superb fishing for trout, bass, panfish, and walleye as well as salmon and steelhead. Public fishing sites provide easy access. Stream fishers should try the Maple, Bear, Jordan, or Boyne rivers for trout. The Bear River in downtown Petoskey is stocked yearly with brook trout and steelhead. Burt Lake and Indian River are excellent spots for walleye, bass, and pike. Crooked Lake is where you'll find walleye, smallmouth bass, pike, and perch. If you like the big water, steelhead, lake trout, and coho and chinook salmon can be found in Lake Michigan's cold waters. Boaters will also find unlimited access on the aforementioned lakes and bays as well as on the 38-mile inland waterway that winds from Crooked Lake to Lake Huron.

Hemingway Haunts. Except for a year in Italy during World War I, the famous author spent his summers on Walloon Lake and Horton Bay from the age of seven weeks until he was twenty-two. He married his first wife, Hadley Richardson, in Horton Bay in 1921 and immortalized many haunts and friends in "Up in Michigan," "The End of Something," "Torrents of Spring," and the Nick Adams series. Today, Petoskey is considered a pilgrimage for "Papa" fans from all over the world. For more on area Hemingway sites or the annual Hemingway weekend, contact the Little Traverse Historical Society (616–347–2620) or write P.O. Box 162, Petoskey, MI 49770.

Herbs. Wintergreen Herbs & Potpourri (10970 Burnett Road, between Petoskey and Charlevoix; 616–347–7399) is located on a scenic hillside in the midst of an old apple orchard and is known for its culinary and ornamental herbs as well as for its everlasting flowers. Pick up something sweet-smelling to take home or tour the more than thirty theme gardens.

Hiking and Biking. The Tunnel of Trees supplies bluff views of Lake Michigan and is especially scenic for hikers and bikers in the fall. The Bear River Trail is a 1.5-mile hiking route that follows the river through downtown Petoskey. There are good access points at Sheridan Street or Lake Street in front of City Hall.

Golf. Many people come to this area just to golf. The area sports a variety of courses, including the new Bay Harbor, 15 miles south of Petoskey, as well as Chestnut Valley, Crooked Tree, Little Traverse Bay Golf Club, Pine Hill, and Wilderness Golf Course. Boyne Mountain and Boyne Highlands alone offer six eighteen-hole championship courses; *Golf Digest* recently named Boyne's Heather course and the Donald Ross Memorial among "America's 75 Best Resort Courses." For more information on which one suits your skills, contact the Boyne County Convention and Visitors Bureau at (800) 845–2828.

Kids. If you've brought the family, pick up a copy of *What Kids Like to Do in Harbor Springs and Petoskey* by two young area authors, Nathaniel Breighner and Todd Matelski. It's available at Between the Covers in Harbor Springs (152 East Main Street; 616–526–6658) and McLean and Eakin Books (307 Lake Street; 616–347–1180) in Petoskey.

Nature Preserve. Thorne Swift Nature Preserve (State Highway 119, north of Harbor Springs; 616–347–0991) is one of the many areas owned and operated by the Little Traverse Conservancy. Here you'll find trails for cross-country skiing, and great places for hiking as well as long stretches of wild and mostly deserted beach.

Skiing. While summer is the peak season in the Petoskey area, winter is close behind. Boyne Mountain and Boyne Highlands (800–GO–BOYNE), as well as other area resorts such as Nub's Nob (4021 Nub's Nob Road; 800–SKI–NUBS), attract thousands of downhill skiers each year and are probably the best-known runs in the state.

Special Events

January. Winter Sports Festival, Petoskey
June. Concerts in the Park, Petoskey
     Home Tour, Petoskey
July. Little Traverse Historical Festival, Petoskey
     Art in the Park, Petoskey
August. PowWow, Harbor Springs
     Emmet County Fair, Petoskey
October. Annual Hemingway Weekend, Petoskey

November. Christmas Tree Lighting, Harbor Springs
December. Christmas Walk, Petoskey and Harbor Springs

Other Recommended Restaurants and Lodgings

Restaurants

Harbor Springs Gourmet Take–Out (127 State Street, Harbor Springs; 616–526–9607) is a great resource for sandwiches, soups, and complete lunches that you can enjoy in the city's waterfront park. They also carry many Michigan–made products and gift baskets. Moderate.

Jesperson's (312 Howard Street, Petoskey; 616–347–6071) has been family owned since 1903 and is well known as the home of the "cherry berry pie" as well as homemade soups, sandwiches, and classic desserts. Inexpensive.

The **New York Restaurant** (101 State Street, Harbor Springs; 616–526–1904) was established in 1904 and retains much of its turn-of-the-century charm. Bistro-style cuisine includes "Up North" classics such as broiled whitefish as well as more creative offerings such as Pasta Pollo (bow–tie pasta tossed with chicken breast, artichoke hearts, wild mushrooms, and fresh chive cream sauce) or a pâté plate with country–style pâté, cornichons, and whole-grain mustard served with vegetable slaw and fresh French bread. Moderate.

Walloon Lake Inn (4178 West Street, Walloon Lake; 616–535–2999) is a one-hundred-year-old inn on the shores of Walloon Lake, with five guest rooms and an intimate dining room. Entrees range from regional specialties such as rainbow trout to French–inspired cuisine, all prepared with locally produced ingredients. Moderate.

Lodgings

Bay Winds Inn (909 Spring Street, Petoskey; 616–347–4193) offers attractive, Victorian-inspired rooms at an equally attractive price. Located on the strip of hotels off U.S. Highway 131, just minutes from downtown, it's a family favorite, with a cozy lobby with fireplace, a long front porch, and the area's largest indoor pool. Rates: $89–$125 per night.

Kimberly Country Estate (2287 Bester Road, Harbor Springs; 616–526–9502) is the place to stay when you're splurging. The 8,000-square-foot home has just six guest rooms, each decorated in an elegant English country theme, with fresh flowers, oil paintings, and lots of chintz. Rates: $135–225 per night; two-night minimum stay on weekends.

Staffords Bay View Inn (U.S. Highway 31, Petoskey; 800–456–1917) on the State Register of Historic Places, has twenty-five rooms, an unpretentious appeal, and a great view of Little Traverse Bay. The inn was founded in 1886 and is known for its Victorian parlor, sunroom, wide front porch, and period antiques. Lawn games and bikes are available for guests; Saturday night stays include the famous Sunday brunch. Rates: $88–175 per night.

For More Information

Boyne County Convention & Visitors Bureau, 401 East Mitchell Street, Petoskey, MI 49770; (800) 845–2828.

Gaylord

Gaylord has become one of the Midwest's premier golf destinations.

Golf Getaway

2 NIGHTS

Golf • Spa Weekend • Family Fun • Lumber Lore

Think Florida is the only place with lovely links? Guess again. The area around Gaylord has emerged as one of the premier golf destinations in the United States. Gaylord's rolling terrain—sculpted by glaciers millions of years ago and dominated today by majestic forests and sparkling lakes—has attracted some of the sport's most prestigious designers. Robert Trent Jones, Sr., Tom Fazio, Jerry Matthews, and Tom Doak have all designed signature courses in the area known as the "Gaylord Golf Mecca." At one point, Gaylord had the thickest concentration of designer courses in the country.

Whatever your skill level, the city's courses represent a level of quality, diversity, and distinction unmatched in the Midwest, with an awesomely beautiful Northwoods setting and lots of other things to do when—and if— you tire of teeing off. Prices can be expensive, however. If you're looking to save, consider a post–Labor Day weekend, when prices drop dramatically and you can have the links almost to yourself. The getaway is geared toward adult golfers.

Day 1

Afternoon

Gaylord is 225 miles from Detroit. It's a straight shot north on Interstate 75 to the city's three exits (270, 279, and 282).

Lodging: There are as many places to stay here as there are places to golf. Two top choices are Treetops Sylvan Resort and Marsh Ridge. Both resorts offer golf packages, which include lodging, golf, some meals, and more. Be sure to ask about them.

Treetops Sylvan Resort (3962 Wilkinson Road; 616–732–6711) is a deluxe full-service resort with 232 spacious guest rooms, sixty-three holes of spectacular golf, nineteen downhill ski runs, two outdoor and two indoor pools, and a state-licensed child development center as well as volleyball, hiking, tennis, ice-skating, tubing, sleigh rides, snowboarding, NASTAR ski races, and more. In 1994 the resort was awarded a silver medal from *Golf Magazine* as one of the United States's finest resorts. Rates: $99–$144 per night.

Marsh Ridge (4185 Old 27 South; 517–732–6794) on the other hand, is a smaller and more intimate resort 3 miles south of Gaylord. It's a great place for couples to stay if one golfs and the other doesn't. It's also the site of the pampering spa-style "Me Week" (weekends too), a program that's especially popular with women while their husbands golf. Rates: $125–$160 per night.

If you need to rest after the road trip, check out **Treetops Horizon Room,** which features piano music from 7:00 to 11:00 p.m., or head for the **Top of the Hill Sports Bar,** where you'll find pool tables, a putting game to get you in the mood for tomorrow, a dart board, and some five hundred brands of imported and domestic beer.

Day 2

Morning

Breakfast: Skip the shotgun start and fuel up for the fairways with a big breakfast at the **Flapjack Shack** (1251 West Main Street; 517–732–7886). It's known for its fabulous flapjacks that come in a variety of flavors, including buttermilk, silver dollar, blueberry, Alaskan sourdough, and buckwheat. Inexpensive.

Golf is the main reason people head for the Gaylord area. With twenty-one courses, it's a duffer's dream. There are courses to match every style and skill level. What follows is a rundown of some of the most popular. You may want to play one each day or hit the others on successive visits. For more on the individual courses, contact the Gaylord Convention & Visitors Bureau (800–345–8621) and ask for the Golf Travel Planner.

Black Bear (1500 West Alexander, Vanderbilt; 517–983–4505) is the newest course in the area as well as its first and only nineteen-hole layout. It opened in the fall of 1996 and was built mainly to satisfy the growing women's market.

The **Natural** (500 West Otsego Lake Drive, Gaylord; 517–732–1785) is also a new course. It was designed by Michigan architect Jerry Mathews to appeal to golfers of all abilities. The course includes some of the state's most scenic wetlands; keep an eye out for wildlife. The clubhouse overlooks the wetlands and seven of the eighteen holes.

Elk Ridge (9400 Rouse Road, Atlanta; 517–785–2275). Atlanta, about 10 miles from Gaylord, is home to one of the state's most challenging courses, honored as the second best new public course in the country and one of the top fifteen courses in the state. Sculpted from Northern Michigan woodlands, it's also home to one of the state's largest elk herds.

Garland (Box 364–M, Lewiston; 517–786–2211) is home to four respected courses: Fountains, Monarch, Reflections, and Swampfire. Fountains boasts the longest single-span log bridge in the world and a blend of six par fives, fours, and threes. Monarch is 7,188 yards from the back tees, with water in play on fourteen of the eighteen scenic holes. Reflections is a shorter course, with a unique combination of six par fives, fours, and threes that blend into the surrounding pine forests, lakes, and streams. Swampfire is a championship course, with 5,854 yards from the tips.

The **Loon** (4400 Championship Drive, Gaylord; 517–732–4454) is one of the area's newer courses, an exciting eighteen-hole championship layout designed and developed by Michael Husby. Gently rolling and expertly bunkered, it appeals to golfers at all levels of play.

Treetops Sylvan Resort (3962 Wilkinson Road, Gaylord; 517–732–6711). Tom Fazio's Premier is a user-friendly course that was recently voted by *Golf Digest* as the third-best new course in United States. The resort's classic course, the Robert Trent Jones, Sr. "Masterpiece," opened in 1987 with the highest slope rating in the state. *Golf Digest* named it twenty-seventh on a list of the top seventy-five U.S. resort courses. The par three sixth is the signature hole; from here Jones named the course Treetops. Treetops North is home to Rick Smith's signature course, a 6,653-yard par seventy design with a challenging combination of holes and distant views of the surrounding North country.

Wilderness Valley Black Forest (7519 Mancelona Road, Gaylord; 616–585–7090) is consistently rated among the nation's best by *Golf Digest*, *Golf*, and *Golf Week* magazines. Playable from four sets of tees, it offers North-woods seclusion and a challenging experience.

Afternoon

Lunch: Grab a bite at the clubhouse. If you're en route, good takeout can be had in Gaylord at **Albie's** (1403 West Main Street; 517–732–8000), known for its famous Cornish pasties. Inexpensive.

Dinner: The **Big Buck Brewery & Steakhouse** (550 South Wisconsin Avenue, Gaylord; 517–732–5781) is the new area hot spot and one of North-ern Michigan's first microbreweries. After a tough day on the course you can relax with one of the tasty specialty beers—all processed using that clean, and clear Northern Michigan water—and watch as your entrees are prepared over a natural wood charcoal fire in the dining room. Specialties here in-clude the steaks, seafood, and pastas, as well as the friendly Northwoods at-mosphere. Moderate.

Day 3

Morning

Breakfast: Downtown's **Sugar Bowl** (216 West Main Street; 517–732–5524) is a Northern Michigan institution, with vintage photographs of Gaylord and a menu that dates back to 1919. Moderate.

You may choose to check out one of the other golf courses today or in-stead to explore Gaylord's other attractions. Like most of Northern Michigan, this area was once covered with hemlock, pine, tamarack, and birch. By the 1800s the lumberers had moved on, leaving little behind (one remaining ves-tige of Michigan's tall-timber past is seen in **Hartwick Pines State Park,** just east of Interstate 75 between Gaylord and Grayling. (For more information, see "There's More.")

The area was officially organized in 1875 as *Otsego*, an American Indian word that means "beautiful lake." The town grew, but the town's topography is what lured vacationers, who eventually brought golf.

Because the town sits on the highest point in lower Michigan, Gaylord is today nicknamed "the Alpine Village." The downtown is decorated with bal-conies, window boxes, even a glockenspiel on Glen's supermarket on West Main Street. It plays every fifteen minutes. And while there are more Polish and German residents today than Swiss, the natives happily don dirndls and lederhosen each July during the annual Alpenfest.

Gaylord's picturesque downtown is the site of more than one hundred in-teresting shops. Most are set along Main Street and house everything from crafts to clothing. Check out the **Alphorn Sport Shop** (137 West Main; 517–732–5616) for duds for backpacking, biking, or fly-fishing, or browse among the heartwarming selection at **Glenda's** (128 West Main; 517–732–9111). Downtown is also home to three museums. The **Otsego County Historical Society Museum** (320 West Main Street; 517–732–4568) traces the area back to its Native American inhabitants and its later logging days. The **All-American Race Car Museum** (980 South Wisconsin Avenue; 517–732–4351) revs up race fans with assorted memorabilia, real racing machines, and a video wall. The **Call of the Wild Museum** (850 South Wisconsin Avenue; 517–732–4336) has been a family favorite for years. It displays taxidermied Northern Michigan wildlife in its natural habitat. The adjacent gift shop is a popular place to spend allowances.

Afternoon

Lunch: **Busia's** (2782 Old 27 South; 517–732–2790) is a rarity—an authentic Polish kitchen in Northern Michigan. The homey eatery is famous for its kielbasa and homemade breaded chicken as well as for its pierogi, *nalesniki,* (blintzes), and friendly atmosphere. Inexpensive.

Gaylord is also the gateway to Northern Michigan's natural world and a haven for environmental enthusiasts who come for activities from camping to canoeing. If you're a mountain biker, neighboring Otsego County offers great views and great workouts on a number of two-lane county roads that traverse bucolic farmland and tree-lined groves. The more adventurous find curious deer and turkey along dirt roads and two-track pathways in the **Pigeon River Country State Forest.** Both trails offers twists and turns as well as sharp climbs and descents with breathtaking views of rivers, lakes, and forests. These trails are also perfect for hikers. Pick up maps at forest headquarters or the downtown Gaylord Chamber of Commerce (South Otsego Avenue and First Street).

Pigeon River is a 95,000-acre forest in the corner of Otsego County (to get there, drive east out of Vanderbilt on East Sturgeon Valley Road). Stop at the forest headquarters for a handy visitors guide that details the park's offerings. Chief among them is the only elk herd east of the Mississippi. The gentle giants number more than one thousand and are best seen daily at dawn and dusk crossing the road or in an open grazing area. Best sighting spots include Whitehouse Trail, Whitmarsh, Tin Shanty, Hardwood Creek, Chandler Dam, Blue Lakes, and Sparr roads. If you're really lucky, you'll be treated to the animal's mystical bugle call. Other wildlife spotting includes coyote, bear, bobcat, fox, wild turkey, red-tailed hawk, even bald eagle.

There's More

Camping. Leave civilization behind at one of six campgrounds. Some, such as Pigeon River County State Forest, are rustic, while others, such as Otsego Lake County Park (517–732–6521), have electrical hookups and access to nearby stores. Ostego Lake State Park (517–732–5485), 6 miles south of Gaylord, has 203 campsites and modern restrooms.

Family Fun. If you brought the kids along, check out the Jimmy Jukebox Family Center (610 South Wisconsin Avenue, Gaylord; 517–732–5099). It has an arcade, video games, and a pool table as well as pizza and other fastfood favorites. Another family-friendly spot is Bavarian Falls Golf/Go Cart Track (850 South Wisconsin Avenue, Gaylord; 517–732–4087), an eighteenhole adventure golf course and a quarter-mile go-kart track open April through October.

Horseback Riding. If you're looking for a change of pace, El Rancho Stevens (Box 495, Gaylord; 517–732–5090) is a family-style ranch on Dixon Lake some 5 miles south of Gaylord. You'll find twenty-two rooms, a heated pool, boating, horses, and a well-run children's program. Open May through September only.

Lumber Lore. The Hartwick Pines Lumbering Museum (State Highway 93 south of Frederic; 517–348–7068) is housed in a state park that contains one of the largest remaining stands of virgin white pine. Get a taste of the lumbering life through its nineteenth-century logging camp and interpretive center, guided tours, camping, and fishing. While there, don't miss the charming Chapel in the Woods.

The Real Thing. The funky Bottlecap Museum (5 miles east of Gaylord on County Road 44; 517–732–1931) is one fan's passionate collection of Coca-Cola memorabilia, dolls, and miniatures.

Winter Sports. Fans of figure eights and doggie paddlin' have a home away from home at the new $4.5-million Sportsplex (1250 Gornick Avenue, Gaylord; 517–731–3546), with a huge rink walk-around track and an Olympic-size pool. It even has a junior hockey team, the Gaylord Grizzlies (for tickets, call 517–732–4447).

Special Events

June. Otsego Lake Fly-In
        Gus Macker Basketball Tournament
July. Alpenfest
August. Otsego County Fair
        Michaywe Arts & Crafts Fair
        Alpine Cup Snowmobile Drag Races

Other Recommended Lodgings

Hidden Valley Resort & Golf Club (State Highway 32 East, Gaylord; 517–732–5181) has 132 rooms, including condos and chalets, in a wide price range. Open May through October only. Rates: $60–$99 per night.

Holiday Inn of Gaylord (833 West Main Street, Gaylord; 517–732–2431) is a good budget–minded choice or a good spot if you've brought kids along. It has 140 newly renovated rooms and a Holidome with a heated indoor pool, whirlpool, and sauna. Rates: $74–$91 per night.

Michaywe Resort (1535 Opal Lake Road, Gaylord; 517–939–8919) is just 5 miles south of the city, with more than fifty condos, chalets, and lodges on or near the golf course. There are also tennis courts, a driving range, two private beaches, a lakeside clubhouse, and miles of cross-country and snowmobile trails to use in the winter. Rates: $110 and up per night.

For More Information

Gaylord Area Convention and Tourism Bureau, 101 West Main Street, P.O. Box 3069, Gaylord, MI 49735; (517) 732–6333 or (800) 345–8621.

Frankenmuth/Birch Run

After one of Frankenmuth's famous chicken dinners, you may want to exercise it off with a spin on a paddleboat.

Shop 'Til You Drop

_____ 1 NIGHT _____

Shopping • Christmas Wonderland • History • Sight-seeing

On their own, both Frankenmuth and Birch Run are popular and perennially appealing day trips for metro Detroiters. Together, however, they represent a great one-night getaway that offers excellent eating and super shopping close to home.

While this is a good escape year-round, it's especially appropriate in November and December, when you can do all your Christmas shopping in one weekend as well as stock up on goodies for your holiday tree at nearby Bronner's Christmas Wonderland. Frankenmuth gets into the holiday mood further with an elaborate downtown display of sparkling lights, towering trees, and a full plate of holiday happenings. Throw in a relaxing night at one of Michigan's most elegant inns, and it all adds up to the quintessential "quick escape."

Day 1

Morning

Plan on getting an early start so you can enjoy two full days. From Detroit, the **Outlets at Birch Run** (517–624–9348) are a straight, 125-mile shot northwest up Interstate 75. You can't miss the signs. If this is your first trip to an outlet mall, be prepared to be overwhelmed. Outlet fever has swept the country. Before 1986 Birch Run was an obscure village at the Frankenmuth exit off Interstate 75. Today it has grown to one of the largest centers in the Midwest, with more than one hundred stores as well as a surrounding community of fast-food restaurants.

You may want to check out a directory of stores ahead of time to plot your shopping strategy. As you'll soon discover, there's no way you can hit all the stores unless you devote an entire weekend to it (now that's not such a bad idea...). If you only have one full day, you'll have to be selective—come armed with a list and be prepared to check it twice.

Birch Run is divided into four main sections. The area closest to the freeway is the original and today includes stores such as **Carter's Childrenswear** (check out the Oops! racks for great deals on irregulars and clothes with slight, mostly unnoticeable, flaws), **Pfaltzgraff Pottery,** charming party dresses by **Polly Flinders, Totes** umbrellas and rain gear, the **Kitchen Collection,** and more. Behind that is a small section with **Black & Decker** (tools), **Publisher's Outlet** (books), and **Bugle Boy** (clothes), among others.

Many dedicated die-hard shoppers, however, skip those sections altogether and concentrate on the newest addition to the mall: the designer and upscale area located near the back. You can't miss it—you'll pass right by it as you enter the complex. Like anything else, outlet shopping can be a hit-or-miss proposition. But bargains are the rule rather than the exception at stores such as **Laura Ashley** (I've found wallpaper here for $2.00 a double roll), **Eddie Bauer, Ann Taylor,** and **Polo/Ralph Lauren**. Other favorites include the fun and funky fashions by **Esprit** for both kids and adults; leftovers from the popular mail-order catalog at the **Spiegel** store, sports wares at **Nike,** and the warm and woolly outerwear at **London Fog,** all necessities for long, midwestern winters.

Afternoon

Lunch: If you're not a fast-food fan, check out the **Pizzeria Uno,** a national chain that recently opened here, is located across from Polo/Ralph Lauren. Known for its deep-dish Chicago-style pizzas, its prices are inexpensive to moderate. Also a good choice is the new **Schlotzky's Deli,** near the entrance, which serves up fresh fare including salads, wood-smoked pizza, and sandwiches on their signature muffaleta-style bread. Inexpensive. Spend the afternoon hitting the stores you missed in the morning.

Dinner: Exhausted? If you're not in the mind for anything fancy and you just want to refuel, you won't go wrong at **Tony's** (517–624–5860) across from the mall. Descended from a famous Saginaw eatery, Tony's is known for its huge portions of everything, from subs and salads to lasagna. It's also a great place for breakfast, with equally large portions. Inexpensive.

Lodging: If you've a mind to splurge on one night at someplace really special (you saved all that money on your shopping, after all), there's no better place in the area than the **Montague Inn** (517–752–3939) in nearby Saginaw, just 16 miles north. It's housed in the former 12,000-square-foot mansion of civic leader Robert Montague, who made his fortune on an invention that used sugar beets to make hand creams and soaps, a process he later sold to the Jergens Company. The Inn is located in Saginaw's historic Grove District. Considered one of the best in the state, it sits on 8 acres overlooking Lake Linton and is furnished with antiques and reproductions. The sixteen tastefully decorated guest rooms have four-poster beds and wing chairs. A favorite is the Montague Suite, which features a fireplace, green Pewabic tile, and great views of the landscaped grounds. Rates: $85–$145 per night, including continental breakfast.

Day 2

Morning

Breakfast: Montague Inn. The room rate includes a continental breakfast of oatmeal, cereals, juice, and baked goods that you can enjoy in either of two dining rooms, one of which has a welcoming fire on cold mornings.

Set today aside for wandering the town of Frankenmuth, now the state's top tourist draw. It was settled in 1854, when pastors in Bavaria, concerned over the religious life of Lutheran immigrants and their American Indian neighbors, sent a colony of fifteen Franconians to the New World (*Frankenmuth* means "courage of the Franconians"). While the Indians soon moved elsewhere, the Bavarians remained, reinforced by later arrivals. The town became known as "Little Bavaria," with German remaining the principal language long after the turn of the century.

Today, that Bavarian heritage along the city's 2-mile strip is created and cultivated for increasingly large groups of tourists who travel here, attracted mostly by the notorious chicken dinners at Zehnder's and Bavarian Village. Much of the architecture, however, is still original, as is the town's genuine friendliness, known in German as *gemutlichkeit*.

On the way into town you'll pass **Bronner's Christmas Wonderland** (517–652–9931 or 800–255–9327). Check your skepticism at the door. Even the most die-hard Scrooges are enchanted by the more than fifty thousand ornaments, tree toppers, lights, and decorations in this cavernous, 200,000-square-foot store (unbelievably, it's the size of four football fields). Nativity scenes range from minute hand-carved figures to life-size scenes. There are also more than 260 artistically decorated trees, a multi-image slide presentation, and a spectacular outdoor light display each night. Everything isn't commercial however; Bronner's also includes a Silent Night memorial chapel, which is open daily, as well as Bibles in more than thirty languages. It also has a breathtaking collection of imported ornaments that are works of art in themselves. Bronner's also sells Precious Moments, Hummels, and other collectibles. Open 361 days a year. (It's closed New Year's Day, Easter, Thanksgiving, and Christmas).

In the center of downtown's business district is **School Haus Square.** Originally the St. Lorenz Lutheran School, it's now a collection of twenty-five specialty shops, including the colorful Kite Kraft. Check out the wall murals along the corridors, which depict the state's educational system in the late 1800s.

Afternoon

Lunch: Depending on your schedule, you may want to eat your main meal midafternoon and catch a quick bite for dinner later on the way home. No visit to Frankenmuth is complete without a visit to the city's main claim to fame, **Zehnder's** (730 South Main Street; 517–652–9925) and **Bavarian Village** (713 South Main Street; 517–652–9941). Located across the street from each other, the two restaurants are operated by the Zehnder family. While the meals are similar (both serve the trademark, all-you-can-eat chicken), the atmosphere is different. Zehnder's is reminiscent of a southern plantation on the exterior, with white pillars and a huge sweeping porch. Bavarian Village, on the other hand, is—not surprisingly—decorated in the Alpine style, complete with a thirty-five-bell automatic glockenspiel that plays three melodies followed by a presentation of carved wooden figures that depict the legend of the Pied Piper.

Whichever you choose, you're in for a family-style feast. For $13.50 per person you'll be served a multicourse meal that includes chicken, mashed potatoes and gravy, relishes, home-baked breads, even ice cream for dessert. If you're not a chicken lover, you can also enjoy German specialties such as Wiener schnitzel, spicy sausages, sauerbraten, and *kasseler rippchen* (smoked pork loin). While the lines can be long (they're generally shorter at lunch, another reason for visiting then), they move quickly. Dining rooms are surprisingly intimate considering the number of people they serve each day. Moderate.

After lunch, walk off those calories with a tour of the rest of the village. **Frankenmuth Historical Museum** (613 South Main Street; 517–652–9701) recounts the area's history, starting with the Indian mission days. More history can be found at **St. Lorenz Church** and the **Log Cabin Church** (Tuscola at Mayer; 517–652–6141), which is the largest congregation east of the Mississippi River of the conservative Missouri Synod of the Lutheran Church. Here contemporary stained glass reveals the area's Lutheran history, from St. Paul to Frankenmuth's missionary ministers. The adjacent log church is a re-creation of the original log church and pulpit.

A must-see attraction downtown is the enchanting **Zeesenagel Italian Alpine Village** (780 Mill Street; 517–652–2591) at the bottom of the hill south of Zehnder's. Interior designers David Zeese and Don Nagel were so inspired by an eighteenth-century nativity scene they saw in a Roman church that they decided to build one of their own. Today the scene comes alive with five hundred realistic figures, including haughty dignitaries, fishmongers, lace makers, and fruit vendors. The eclectic gift shop next door is also worth a stop and sells an unusual mix of merchandise including Lladro Spanish porcelains and Greek icons.

If you're a beer fan, you'll enjoy tours of the **Frankenmuth Brewery** (425 South Main Street; 517–652–6183), the largest of only two remaining in the state. Officially considered a microbrewery (it produces fewer than 15,000 barrels annually), it has a distinctive, old German style that's achieved using state-of-the-art German equipment. Two brews—Frankenmuth Dark and Frankenmuth Bock—have won awards, but the brewery also makes an American-style pilsner, a light beer, and an ale. Free half-hour tours include a video and a tour of the tanks and bottling line along with a taste of two beers of your choice (you must be twenty-one or older to taste).

Wine more your style? The **St. Julian Winery** (127 South Main Street; 517–652–3281) includes a room with free tastes (for those twenty-one and older) of the fruits of the state's largest vineyard as well as a small on-site winery. Free tours are offered weekends at 1:00 and 3:00 P.M.

While much of Frankenmuth is oriented to the thousands of tourists who flock here annually, there are still places where the original German small town can be seen. Off the beaten path, these places give you the chance to experience the "real" town behind the Bavarian facades.

Satow's Drug Store (308 South Main Street; 517–652–8001) is a popular local hangout with homemade soups and great prices. Most of the regulars still speak German. Those who aren't at Satow's are probably over at the **Main Street Tavern** (310 South Main Street; 517–652–2222), a plain bar owned by an ex-baker at Zehnder's. All the bread and buns are made on the premises and filled with things such as local beef and cheese or tangy bratwurst. Finally, don't leave Frankenmuth without a stop at **Willi's Sausage**

Haus (316 South Main Street, 517–652–9041), where this master sausagemaker cooks up sausages, hams, and bacon as well as some ninety-two other fragrant items. The beef jerky is famous. This is also the place to stop if you want to pick a picnic; Willi will grill your choice of meats to eat in the park across the street.

Dinner. If you find you're hungry again on the way home, a good place to stop is **Salvatore Scallopine's** just off the Miller Road exit on Interstate 75 (3227 Miller Road; 810–732–1070) in Flint. If you're sick of chicken, you can indulge in a great Caesar salad and a plate of pasta covered with one of six signature sauces. Inexpensive.

There's More

Art. Marshall Fredericks is one of the state's best known sculptors. Saginaw Valley State University is home to Marshall M. Fredericks Sculpture Gallery (2250 Pierce Road; 517–790–5667), the only gallery honoring his work. It's open Tuesday through Sunday from 1:00 to 5:00 P.M. and is free. This light-filled gallery includes models for more than two hundred of Fredericks's most famous works, including the landmark *Spirit of Detroit*. An adjacent sculpture garden and fountain also feature works by Fredericks.

Golf. The Fortress (950 Flint Street; Frankenmuth; 517–652–9229) is considered one of lower Michigan's best courses. Call for tee times and more information.

Teahouse. Nearby Saginaw is a surprising place to find a Japanese Cultural Center and Tea House (Ezra Rust Drive and South Washington Avenue; 517–759–1648). It offers insights into Japanese culture and to the ritual and ceremony of tea service. The nearby Friendship Garden and many of the trees, bridges, and stones used in the garden came from Japan. The adjacent teahouse has tea and sweets and a full tea ceremony every second Sunday.

Wildlife. The Shiawassee National Refuge is one of only four refuges in Michigan and contains the Shiawassee Flats, known as "Michigan's Everglades." For more information, call (517) 777–5930.

Special Events

January. Zehnder's Snowfest, Frankenmuth
March. Arts & Crafts Show, Frankenmuth
May. Cinco de Mayo, Saginaw
June. Bavarian Fest, Frankenmuth
July. Sidewalk Sales, Birch Run and Frankenmuth
August. Summer Music Fest, Frankenmuth
September. Oktoberfest, Frankenmuth
November. Holiday Lighting Ceremony, Frankenmuth

Other Recommended Lodgings

Bavarian Inn Lodge (1 Covered Bridge Lane, Frankenmuth; 517–652–2651) is just behind the Bavarian Village Restaurant and features 354 rooms decorated in—what else??—Bavarian style. There are also three pools, whirlpools, an exercise room, a family fun center, children's play village, eighteen-hole miniature golf, tennis courts, and nightly entertainment. Rates: $69–$99 per night.

Zehnder's Bavarian Haus (1365 South Main Street, Frankenmuth; 517–652–6144) has 137 rooms, as well as an indoor pool and game room. Rates range from $79 to $175 per night.

For More Information

Frankenmuth Convention and Visitors Bureau, 635 South Main Street, Frankenmuth, MI 48734; (800) 386-8696.

Ann Arbor

Ann Arbor's Hands-On Museum is popular with the young and the young at heart.

"Go Blue" Getaway

—————————— 2 NIGHTS ——————————
Galleries • Nightlife • Shopping • Restaurants

Sounds from a nearby gristmill allegedly inspired the local American Indians to name this area *kawgooshkawnick*. Luckily for modern tongues, later settlers preferred Ann Arbor, named for a local grape arbor and the first white pioneer wives, both named Ann. Not long after, in 1837, Ann Arbor bid for and was chosen as the new site for the University of Michigan, which was looking to leave already bustling Detroit for greener pastures.

Today the well-known university is an integral part of the fabric of the city—providing it with jobs, a young (and young at heart) population and a high quality of life (so high, in fact, that in 1996 *Money* magazine named Ann Arbor as the fifth-best place to live in the United States.)

From its original 40 acres, U of M has grown to cover more than 2,600 acres. The university has also spawned a wealth of museums, restaurants, shops, and nightlife. Here you'll find trendy Euro-style eateries as well as Old World German restaurants, tony art museums as well as the largest collegiate football stadium in the country, seating ten thousand Wolverine fans at a time. Many consider Ann Arbor the liveliest city in the state. It's been home to singers Bob Seger, Madonna, and Iggy Pop, Pulitzer prize–winning poet Robert Frost, President Gerald Ford, playwright Arthur Miller, director Lawrence Kasdan (of *Big Chill* fame), actor James Earl Jones, and comedienne Gilda Radner.

For those Detroiters who complain that Motown is comatose after hours, Ann Arbor is the perfect close-to-home getaway. You won't spend the weekend driving; the State Street exit is just 45 minutes west of the Motor City on Interstate 94.

Day 1

One of the charms of an Ann Arbor weekend is that Motown residents won't even have to leave work early to enjoy it. Ann Arbor is just 38 miles west of Detroit on Interstate 94. Plan on being in town early enough for dinner the first night, however, because the city is known for its restaurants (more than two hundred) and offers some of the most diverse dining experiences in the state.

Dinner: Housed in a huge former theater, trattoria-style **Gratzi** (326 South Main Street; 313–663–5555) is considered the liveliest spot in town. It still stages spontaneous productions nightly, although today the emphasis is on people-watching. The surprisingly good Italian food runs the gamut from classic (veal Saltimbocca, fried calamari) to nouvelle (smoked salmon pizza, butternut squash ravioli in walnut sauce). For dessert, don't miss the rich "Chocolato Ultimato." There are strolling musicians Thursday through Saturday and crowded patio dining in season. Moderate to expensive.

Lodging: If you're traveling sans kids, the **Bell Tower Hotel** (300 South Thayer Street; 800–999–8693) is an elegant, European-style inn in the heart of downtown. It's conveniently located across from the popular Hill Auditorium, the site of performances from pop to Puccini (most other hotels are clustered off the freeway). With a huge paneled fireplace in the lobby, sixty-six gracious guest rooms decorated in a clubby English style, the hotel offers a quiet retreat in the middle of campus. Nice touches include thick oversize towels, free valet parking, and a free continental breakfast. If you'd like a nightcap or a bite to

eat, the hotel's Escoffier restaurant offers an extensive menu as well as a respected wine list. Rates: $104–$217 per night.

If you've brought the family (and there are plenty of reasons to do so), the
best place to stay is the **Courtyard by Marriott** near Briarwood Mall (3205
Boardwalk; 800–321–2211). Although not as centrally located as the Bell
Tower, it's the best of the economy chains in the area, with 160 rooms, free
coffee and newspaper, an indoor pool, hot tub, and even—a mixed bless-
ing—, free Nintendo in the guest rooms. Rates: $69–$95 per night.

Day 2

Morning

Breakfast: The Bell Tower serves a nice complimentary continental spread
in the conference room, including fruits, juices, coffee and tea, breads, bagels,
and more. But if you want to try a local favorite, **Angelo's Restaurant** (1100
Catherine Street; 313–761–8996) is considered the city's best place for breakfast.
College students and professional types queue up on weekends for the waffles
and homemade breads and toasts (try the cinnamon raisin). Inexpensive.

You'll have to get up early, however, if you want to catch the real action at
the **Farmers Market** on Fifth Street. The dealers come as early as 5:00 A.M.
laden with fruits, flowers, crafts, and just about everything in between. The
market is one of the highlights of historic **Kerrytown,** a restored nineteenth-
century district of more than thirty shops and restaurants north of the campus.
The area is lined with brick buildings and cobblestone streets, with lovely
courtyards, and is perfect for walking and wandering. It's named after County
Kerry, Ireland, ancestral home of one of the original developers.

Kerrytown shops worth exploring include **Kitchen Port** (313–665–9188),
with an extensive array of goodies for foodies; **Mudpuddles,** with creative
toys for kids, innovative **Workbench** furniture (313–668–4688), ("For Homes,
Not Museums," the brochure claims); and **Vintage to Vogue** (313–665–9110),
a chic clothing shop. If you need a snack, consider the **Moveable Feast Cafe**
(313–663–3331), which has a well-known bakery and—as the name would
imply—"totable" cuisine that's perfect for picnics or for enjoying while bench-
sitting and watching the world go by.

Afternoon

Lunch: Although Kerrytown has lots of tempting places for lunch, save
them for another trip and head for **Zingerman's Deli** (442 Detroit Street;
313–663–3354), a city landmark and one of its best-known eateries. Zingerman's is the kind of deli that makes even New Yorkers jealous. This haven for
foodies is jam-packed with gourmet foods for sale as well as an extremely

popular counter business (although the staff is efficient, be prepared to wait in line). Ann Arborites line up around the clock for the more than one hundred sandwich varieties, including the Reuben, corned beef on rye, and others with more intriguing names such as Nate's Nosh, Pat & Dick's Honeymooner, Randy's Routine, and the Helen Have Trotter. Whatever your choice, you'll end up with a sandwich that's big enough for two. Zingerman's also serves Caesar and pasta salads and specialty coffees in the converted house next door known as "Zingerman's Next Door" and bakes its own breads. Inexpensive.

Ann Arbor is divided into two distinct areas: downtown (the area along Main Street, west of the campus) and the central campus area. Both offer distinct shops and attractions. After lunch, head for Main Street to explore the rest of downtown. While you walk, pick up a cappuccino or Italian soda at **Espresso Royale** (313–668–1838), about halfway down the street. They have great biscotti, too.

Unlike other small downtowns, Ann Arbor thrives, with a mix of funky shops, art galleries, great bookstores (so great, in fact, that Ann Arbor is the number one city in America in per-capita book buying), and restaurants. A few worthwhile stops include **AfterWords** (219 South Main; 313–996–2808), which features a wide selection of remaindered books; **FallingWater Books** (213 South Main; 313–747–9801), which appeals to the city's metaphysical community; the **Selo/Shevel Gallery** (335 South Main; 313–761–6263), a small space featuring hand-blown glass objects and fine contemporary American jewelry; and the **Peaceable Kingdom** (210 South Main; 313–668–7886), with folk art, crafts, and "fun stuff from here and far."

If you've brought the kids (or even if you haven't), be sure to stop at the **Ann Arbor Hands-On Museum** (219 East Huron Street; 313–995–5439), which is housed in a former fire station. Spread out over four floors, it includes fascinating exhibitions and displays such as "The Subject Is You," which teaches all about the human body, and "The Discovery Room," where kids can make waves, build an arch, even fly a hot air balloon and get inside a soap bubble. The upper floors include "Crane's Roost," with holograms, strobes, and lights, and "How Things Work," which includes the opportunity to communicate via computer and play three-dimensional tic-tac-toe. The museum's Explore Store has lots of fun and educational stuff the kids can spend their allowance on. Admission is $4.00 for adults; $2.50 for kids ages three to twelve. The museum is closed Mondays.

Not far away is another city landmark—the **Treasure Mart** (529 Detroit Street; 313–662–1363). The legendary resale store is huge, with fast-moving and wide-ranging stock that includes a number of antiques at bargain prices. It's a favorite of students, city bargain hunters, and interior designers.

Dinner: Head back to Kerrytown for dinner at **Sweet Lorraine's** (303 Detroit Street; 313–665–0700). One of the newest restaurants in Ann Arbor, it's a friendly yet chic bistro (the original is in Southfield, a Detroit suburb) that has quickly acquired a loyal clientele who willingly stand in line on weekends for the veggie burgers, salmon with maple syrup glaze, daily specials, and desserts such as Sinful Chocolate Decadence Cake. Moderate.

Afterward, if you're looking for music, you can't do better than the **Ark** (316 South Main Street; 313–761–1800), which has hosted both obscure and famous folk artists and other musicians for more than three decades.

Day 3

Morning

Brunch: Few brunches compare with the **Gandy Dancer** (401 Depot Street; 313–769–0592) in fare or atmosphere. Housed in a restored train station on the outskirts of town, it's the flagship of the renowned Chuck Muer seafood chain. The extensive brunch spread includes made-to-order omelettes, great apple dumplings, fresh fruit, fish dishes, the restaurant's signature homemade rolls, and a separate table laden with rich desserts. The Gandy Dancer is also crowded at dinner, when diners feast on specialties such as bluefish pâté bouillabaisse, yellowfin tuna, and soft-shell crabs. Reservations recommended for dinner on weekends; not taken for brunch. Moderate to expensive.

Afterward, walk off some of that meal with a tour of the U of M campus and the rest of downtown you missed yesterday. One of the most picturesque campuses in the country, it's famous for being a hotbed of liberalism (the annual Hash Bash is still well frequented by college students and others who favor legalizing marijuana) and for sites such as the Diag and the Union, where students congregate, and the Law Quad, which was modeled after Cambridge University in England.

State Street runs right through the heart of campus and is the anchor of the nearby shopping district. On State are the university's top attractions. The **University of Michigan Museum of Art** (313–764–0395; 525 South State) is among the top ten university art museums in the country, with more than twelve thousand works by Dürer, Delacroix, Rodin, Picasso, Rembrandt, Monet, and Miro. There's also an excellent Asian collection. More than fifteen changing exhibits are featured annually. Then there's the **Kelsey Museum of Archaeology** (434 South State; 313–764–9304). Part of the Kelsey's attraction—besides the intriguing collection of art and artifacts that dates back almost to the beginning of time, all products of university-sponsored digs in the Mediterranean and Near East—is the 1891 fieldstone building that holds it (don't miss the large Tiffany window). State Street is also the site of the famous Ann Arbor Art Fair, held each July, which encompasses twenty-two blocks, features one thousand artists, and draws more than four hundred thousand people.

If you're looking to exercise your credit cards, many of the city's best shops are found on State Street and the area surrounding it. One of the best is **Borders Books** (612 East Liberty Street; 313–668–7652), the new location of an Ann Arbor institution. Borders may have gone national, but it was born on State Street, where it became known as one of the country's best full-service bookstores long before it branched out around the country. Many prefer the old location, but the new East Liberty Street store, housed in a former Jacobson's, is still one of the city's best places to see and be seen. It still has the same wide selection that made the original location famous, as well as a great coffee bar. Other shops and galleries in the neighborhood worth a stop include **Chris Triola** (5 Nickels Arcade; 313–996–9955), located in the small arcade of worthwhile shops next to Espresso Royale. Known for her bold and breathtaking (also expensive) knitwear, Triola's shop is a favorite of Ann Arbor's fashion conscious. **Middle Earth** (1209 South University; 313–769–1488) is an Ann Arbor institution, with everything from obscene greeting cards and more than twenty thousand postcards to Elvis troll dolls and inflatable pink Cadillacs. If recordings are your thing, you won't want to miss **Schoolkids** (523 East Liberty Street; 313–994–8031), known for its wide array of alternative music and its great selection of imports.

There's More

Antiques. The Ann Arbor Antiques Market (5055 Ann Arbor/Saline Road; 313–913–8890) is one of the premiere antiques events in the state. Now in its twenty-eighth season, it's held the third Sunday of the month from April through November at the county fairgrounds (exit 175 off Interstate 94, then south for 3 miles). More than three hundred high-quality dealers from all over the country bring every kind of imaginable antique to show and sell. It's also one of the few shows that guarantees its merchandise as represented. Admission costs $4.00.

Dinosaurs and More. The Exhibit Museum of Natural History (1109 Geddes Avenue; 313–764–0478), also part of U of M, has more than three hundred displays on four floors. Highlights include the Prehistory Life exhibits on the second floor (including the ever-popular dinosaurs), the Peruvian collection on the fourth floor, and the displays exploring the life of the Michigan timber wolf on the third floor.

Football. The Wolverines inspire some of the fiercest loyalty in the state, with hundreds of "Go Blue" fans converging on the stadium each fall. Many games are sold out far in advance, but tickets can often be had at the gate for surprisingly affordable prices. For information call (313) 647–2583.

Gardens. When the concrete and the city get to be too much, urbanites retreat to Matthaei Botanical Gardens (1800 North Dixboro; 313–998–7061). Owned and operated by the university, it's a quiet and serene oasis of walking trails, display gardens, and a conservatory of exotic flora. The more than 600 acres include four nature trails, wetlands, a woodland wildflower garden showcasing Michigan and Great Lakes wildflowers, and a charming Herb Knot garden. The adjacent gift shop sells an unusual variety of gardening goodies as well as plants.

Golf. Golf enthusiasts can tee off at one of eight area courses, including Stonebridge Golf Club (5315 Stonebridge Drive South; 313–429–8383), an eighteen-hole championship course by Arthur Hills; Leslie Park Golf Course (2120 Traver Road; 313–994–1163), rated one of the top ten municipal courses in Michigan, and the Huron Golf Club (1275 South Huron Street in Ypsilanti; 313–487–2441), one of the most challenging courses in Southeast Michigan.

Shopping. If you haven't had enough shopping, Ann Arbor's Briarwood Mall, at the State Street exit off Interstate 94, has more than two hundred stores, including Jacobson's, Hudson's, Williams Sonoma, the Coach Store, Godiva, Banana Republic, the Disney Store, Gymboree, Gap and Gap Kids, and more.

Chelsea. The nearby town of Chelsea, about 10 miles west along Interstate 94, is known as home of both the Purple Rose Theater, owned and operated by actor Jeff Daniels, and the wonderful Common Grill (112 South Main Street; 313–475–0470), a great restaurant known for its innovative cuisine and casual atmosphere. Both are worth a side trip.

Special Events

January. Ann Arbor Folk Festival
March. Pow Wow
April. Flower and Garden Show
June. Summer Festival
July. Art Arbor Art Fairs
September. Blues & Jazz Festival
October. Winter Art Fair
November. Domino's Farms Christmas Lights Display

Other Recommended Restaurants and Lodgings

Restaurants

Amadeus (122 East Washington Street; 313–665–8767) is one of the only places in the city you can partake of Central European fare such as Hungarian goulash and pierogi with the background of nightly classical music. Moderate.

Blue Nile (317 Braun Court; 313–663–3116), an outpost of a popular downtown Detroit eatery, serves up Ethiopian-style buffets in an exotic setting. Moderate.

The **Earle** (121 West Washington; 313–994–0211) is one of the city's premiere dining spots. Appetizers include a tasty baked garlic and shrimp pesto pizza; poached salmon and breast of duck are popular entrees. Reservations recommended on weekends. Expensive.

Kerrytown Bistro (415 North Fifth Street; 313–994–6424) serves mostly country French cuisine in a casual setting accented with brick walls and wooden tables. Try the Cassoulet de Carcassone, a house specialty. Reservations recommended Friday and Saturday nights. Inexpensive to moderate.

Middle Kingdom (332 South Main Street; 313–668–6638) serves up tasty Chinese specialties such as General Tso's chicken, hot and sour soup, and Bali Maki. Inexpensive.

Moveable Feast (326 West Liberty Street; 313–663–3278) has spawned several take-out shops, but that doesn't dull the shine of the original location. The main eatery serves American specialties with a French accent, including chicken with walnuts and gorgonzola, poached salmon Hollandaise, and a bevy of delicious desserts, including chocolate pave with raspberry sauce, Kahlua cheesecake, and more. Moderate to expensive.

Seva (314 East Liberty Street; 313–662–1111) is the city's best-known vegetarian restaurant and a favorite of students and health-conscious others. Menu highlights, most based on Mexican, Italian, and Oriental cuisines, include *tempeh* fajitas, meatless nachos, and more.

Lodging

Crowne Plaza Hotel (610 Hilton Boulevard; 800–344–7829) has more than two hundred spacious rooms (all with iron and ironing boards, hair dryers, coffeemakers, and free Nintendo) as well as coffee and afternoon tea delivered to your door. Rates: $99–$175 per night.

For More Information

Ann Arbor Convention & Visitors Bureau, 120 West Huron Street, Ann Arbor, MI 48104-1318; (313) 995–7281 or (800) 888–9487.

Marshall

Marshall's collection of vintage architecture is one of the country's finest.

The Town That Time Forgot

_____ 2 NIGHTS _____

Antiques • Architecture • Shopping • Museums • Magic

Tiny Marshall, Michigan, has had many claims to fame through the years. In the early 1840s, this Calhoun County town was confident of being chosen to replace Detroit as the state's capital. Marshall, which sits almost dead center between Michigan's east and west coasts, lost out—incredibly, by just one vote—to Lansing, also centrally located but farther north (and today's home to Michigan State University).

In 1846 Marshall was once again in the news when Adam Crosswhite, an escaped slave living in the town, was taken by force by his former owner. Townspeople rose up and arrested the slave hunters, sending them back to Kentucky empty-handed and focusing national interest on the subject of fugitive slaves (some say this incident fanned sentiments leading to the Civil War). Later the town grew again, this time as an important shipping point and stop on the Michigan Central Railroad. In the early 1900s, it also served as home to popular patent medicines such as "Lydia Pinkham's Pink Pills for Pale People."

Today's Marshall has once again reinvented itself. Ironically, it owes its current livelihood to its past—and, thanks to a forward-thinking mayor in the 1920s, to its reputation as one of America's best-preserved historic towns. Indeed, there are so many nineteenth-century homes and businesses (roughly eight hundred) that the city was designated the country's largest National Historic District, the highest honor passed out by the National Park Service. The city's big event is the historic homes tour, held each year on the weekend after Labor Day. Townspeople pitch in to offer food, arts and crafts, and tours of more than a dozen local residences and structures. And while residents are proud of their past, Marshall is no ghost town. It's a charming mix of young and old, antiques stores and new-wave cybercafes, a perfect getaway for architecture or antiques buffs or anyone who is looking to escape the modern world.

Day 1

Afternoon

From Detroit, Marshall is about 100 miles west on Interstate 94. Worth a stop along the way is the Common Grill (112 South Main Street; 313–475–0470) in Chelsea, a surprisingly cosmopolitan cafe lined with Edward Hopper–style murals that depict old town scenes. Seafood specialties, fresh pastas, and tasty signature rolls draw crowds from nearby Ann Arbor and beyond (for more on Chelsea, see the subsequent section "There's More").

Lodging: No visit to Marshall would be complete without a stay at the charming **National House Inn** (102 South Parkview Street; 616–781–7374). The state's oldest inn, it was founded in 1835 as a stagecoach stop between Detroit and Chicago. In 1975 the inn was completely restored; it opened in 1976 as a bed and breakfast. Rooms are furnished with impressive wooden beds and comfortable country-style antiques. Rates: $66–$130 per night, including continental breakfast.

Day 2

Morning

Breakfast: Your accommodations include a tasty breakfast of fresh breads and pastries, hot egg strata, cereals, and more. If you'd like something heartier or have a hankering for hash browns, head for the cozy **Coffee Pot** (228 West Michigan Avenue; 616-781-7477), just across the square from the inn. This friendly diner-style eatery serves classic breakfast fare such as thick cinnamon French toast, golden brown pancakes, and fluffy "Good Ole Omelets"—from the plain-Jane variety to western. You can also get steak and eggs with American fries or toast for $8.00. At lunch or dinner, locals graze on favorites such as meatloaf sandwiches, chicken-fried steak, and homemade pie. Inexpensive.

So fortified, head out on a walking tour of the town's distinctive architecture (before doing so, pick up a copy of the self-guided walking tour available at the hotel and at the town's shops or chamber of commerce). It lists more than 130 buildings, with short descriptions of style, as well as notable architectural elements and former owners.

First stop: the fascinatingly eccentric **Honolulu House** (107 North Kalamazoo Street), across from your hotel and the Brooks Memorial Fountain. The house was built in 1860 by Abner Pratt, a Marshall judge who became U.S. consul to the Sandwich Islands (now Hawaii). Forced to return to Michigan by an ill wife, he chose to bring the islands with him in the form of this unusual piece of architecture. Pratt topped his house with a pagoda-shaped tower and filled it with Polynesian souvenirs, but he died soon after returning to the mainland (it may have had something to do with the fact that he chose to wear white linen suits even during frigid Michigan winters). Today the distinctive building functions as a museum and as home to the city's historical society. *The New York Times* called it "a tropical fantasy... the architectural equivalent of a four-rum cocktail served in a coconut." Highlights inside include tropical murals from 1885, with more than 120 paint colors, an elaborate made-in-Michigan dining room suite from the 1876 Philadelphia Centennial Exposition, and the Marshall Folding Bathtub, a relic of the city's patent medicine era. Be forewarned, however: The house is only open daily from mid-May through October from noon to 5:00 P.M.; from November to mid-May it's open weekends only from 1:00 to 4:00 P.M. Admission is $3.00.

After leaving the Honolulu House, wander Marshall's other streets and ogle many the fine homes. You'll get a lesson in nineteenth-century architecture—everything from Queen Anne to Italianate to Greek Revival. Even if you don't care about architecture, you'll go away impressed by the obvious love and care lavished on each of these historic structures.

The best houses are found spread out along the area known as **Prospect Hill**, 2 blocks north of Main Street. An easy hour or so walk gives you a good look at some thirty or more fine homes and gardens (be sure to peek behind the houses, too, as many sport fashionable carriage houses). Notable homes include the 1839 Greek Revival "Governor's Mansion" built by Governor James Wright Gordon before the capital was moved to Lansing; the 1857 Italianate Adams-Schuyler-Umphrey House, built on land that was once owned by James Fenimore Cooper; the 1907 Sears-Osborne House, ordered from the Sears catalog at the turn of the century for $1,995; the 1886 Queen Anne Cronin-LaPietra House, one of the city's most ornate, designed by the Detroit firm best known for the Michigan Central Railroad Terminal; and the 1843 Greek Revival Camp-Vernor-Riser House, once home to the founder of Vernor's Ginger Ale.

Lunch: **Malia** (130 West Michigan Avenue; 616–781–2171), housed in a renovated storefront, is a recent addition to the city's restaurant scene. Open just three years, it features nouvelle Italian cuisine and delectable homemade pastas in a Tuscan-style setting with daily blackboard specials, glazed ocher walls, and an original tin ceiling. Try the grilled Portobello mushroom sandwich, the pesto linguine, or the refreshing *orchiette primavera*. Moderate.

Afternoon

Time for some shopping. The pineapple, the symbol of hospitality, flies on colorful flags all over downtown. That warm welcome is evident in many of the city's charming boutiques and antiques shops, where you'll find owners who are happy to chat, find out where you're from and what you're looking for, and linger over a little good-natured bargaining.

Fittingly, this historic enclave is also an antique-lover's dream. Along Michigan Avenue, the main drag, you'll find about a dozen antiques shops and mini-malls. Even the local dentist's office is full of antique dental equipment. It's sure to make you happy you live in the twentieth century.

Downtown is full of terrific Italianate architecture and old-fashioned institutions such as a "variety" or dime store and a good hardware store. Other favorite stops include the **Kids' Place** (106 North Jefferson; 616–781–3853), a small but choice children's bookstore that also stocks a number of books on Marshall; **Keystone Antiques** (110 East Michigan Avenue), where owner Denny Hughes has a large selection of salvaged architectural elements (none from local houses, he swears) as well as general goodies; and **Horace Higgby** and the adjacent **Serendipity** (106 and 108 East Michigan Avenue, respectively), with sophisticated country-style gifts and other stylish home wares.

The **J. H. Cronin Antique Center** (101 West Michigan Avenue; 616–789–0077) features the offerings of more than twenty-five local dealers. If you've got kids in tow, head for **Tunes & Toons** (102 South Eagle; 616–789–1000), where Paul Braggeman buys and sells classic comics, discs, and more, and **Pineapple Lane** (209 West Michigan Avenue), which has a staggering selection of heirloom teddy bears as well as a wide array of general antiques. Nearby, **McAuliffe's** (203 West Michigan Avenue) has locally made ice creams that are a bargain at 50 cents for a mini dip, $1.25 for a sundae. Go ahead—indulge.

Marshall is also home to one of the country's most unique and little publicized museums. The **American Museum of Magic** (107 East Michigan Avenue, next to the chamber of commerce; 616–781–7674), is a passionate fan's tribute to the world of professional magic and magicians. It's a mecca for modern masters such as David Copperfield, who has called it "one of my favorite places on earth." Founder Robert Lund was a longtime fan of the "conjuring culture." Even if you're not interested in magic, you'll be won over by this intriguing museum housed in an 1868 building with a handsome cast-iron front, once a saloon, billiard hall, and bakery. The Lunds restored the building themselves and opened it in 1978. The memorabilia inside dates to 1584 and include "notional whimsies, cabalistic surprises, phantasmagorical bewilderments, and unparalleled splendors." Roughly translated, that means anything and everything remotely related to the practice of magic. The extensive collection spans four centuries and six continents and includes advertising and promotional posters, beautiful antique props, a carrying case once used by Harry Blackstone, even posters celebrating Marjorie Waddell, one of the few successful women magicians. Although Bob recently passed away, his wife Elaine carries on in his memory and keeps the museum open only on summer weekends, when guided tours are offered at 2:00 and 4:00 P.M. Saturday and 1:00 and 3:00 P.M. Sunday. Admission is $4.00 for adults, $2.00 for kids ages eight to twelve. If you're there in other seasons, you can catch a glimpse of the collection through the front window.

If you haven't had enough museums, check out the **Postal Museum** (616–781–2859) inside the town's small post office (202 East Michigan Avenue). Built of locally quarried sandstone, it includes interesting artifacts such as the old post office boxes that once graced general stores as well as unusual see-through glass mailboxes and canceled stamps. Tours by appointment or by chance.

Dinner: By now, you should be ready to eat. No visit to Marshall would be complete without a stop at **Schuler's** (115 South Eagle Street; 616–781–0600), an area institution. Signs in the Centennial Dining Room include one that reads: THE DIFFERENCE BETWEEN GOOD AND GREAT IS A LITTLE EXTRA EFFORT. Extra effort is a specialty here, where the Schuler family has been serving up comforting fare such as Swiss onion soup, barbecued meat balls, and prime rib for more than eighty-five years. The first Schuler's opened in Marshall in 1909 as a combination cigar store and restaurant. The restaurant recently added lighter cuisine to its menu, including Sicilian grilled chicken pizza, Calico Bay scallops with angel hair pasta, Caesar steak salad, woodgrilled Texas bay shrimp with black bean quesadilla, and almond-crusted orange roughy. Moderate.

The clubby **Winston's** is a great place for a post-dinner drink.

Afterward, you might take in a movie at the old-fashioned **Bogar Theater** (223 East Michigan Avenue), which features first-run films in a vintage movie house. More local color can be had at the **Copper Bar** (133 West Michigan Avenue), which has stuffed and mounted animal trophies and a quirky local clientele; it looks like a scene from the now-defunct television series *Northern Exposure*.

Day 3

Morning

Linger over breakfast at the National House Inn. After a leisurely start, you might choose to head to the Calhoun County Fairgrounds south of downtown, where the **Marshall Antiques Market** is a popular hunting ground for enthusiasts from all over the Midwest. Held weekends from May through October, the market includes more than one hundred quality dealers. All merchandise is guaranteed. Admission is $4.00; if you're obsessive enough to want to be there first, you can pay $20.00 and get in Friday night. There has been talk of discontinuing the market, however, except for select weekends, so be sure to call ahead. For more information call 616–789–0990.

Before heading back onto Interstate 94, fuel up with a stop at the **Hi-Lite Drive In** (1005 East Michigan Avenue; 616–781–6571). Home of local Elvis sightings (remember, he supposedly hides out in nearby Kalamazoo) and super-thick shakes, it's a popular hangout for all ages on the eastern city limits. Inexpensive.

There's More

Albion

Just 11 miles east of Marshall, Albion is the birthplace of Albion College, one of the state's best private institutions. The classic tune "Sweetheart of Sigma Chi" was penned and first sung here. The town's downtown is one of the last all-brick main streets; Victory Park is considered one of the most picturesque sights in the state and has good fishing to boot. Nearby Riverside Cemetery has an unusual mix of monuments, from simple Russian crosses to ornate Victorian tributes. A walking-tour guide is available at the office. Hiking fans flock to the 135 acres at the Whitehouse Nature Center (517–629–2030), which unlike many other attractions, is open year-round. For information call or write the Albion Chamber of Commerce, 416 South Superior, Albion MI; (616) 629–5533.

Battle Creek

Famous as the "Cereal City," Battle Creek is just 15 miles west of Marshall. The city's sanitarium made Battle Creek famous as the "health city" (it was also featured in the recent film *The Road To Wellville*). Today the city's industries are more diverse, with a minor-league class A baseball team, a fine arts center with a unique Michigan artworks shop, a respected zoo, the Kellogg Bird Sanctuary, McCamley Place mall, and much more. For information call or write the Battle Creek/Calhoun County Visitors Bureau, 34 West Jackson Street, #4B, Battle Creek, MI 49017; (616) 962–2240.

Special Events

February. Moonlight Madness
March. Quilter's Weekend
July. Old-Fashioned Fourth
August. Calhoun County Fair
September. Marshall Historic Home Tour
November. Annual Christmas Parade
December: Christmas Candlelight Walk

Other Recommended Restaurants and Lodgings

Restaurants

Cornwell's Turkeyville U.S.A.(18935 15½ Mile Road; 616–781–4293) is a campy, country-style restaurant just north of Marshall. Wayne and Marjorie Cornwell introduced their first turkey sandwich at a county fair thirty years ago; today their restaurant has become a 180-acre turkey farm and a complex of buildings known as "Turkeyville." The menu includes everything from a classic buttered turkey sandwich and turkey hot plate to a piled-high Reuben sandwich or turkey stir fry. An adjacent 170-seat dinner theater gives afternoon and evening performances accompanied by a carved roast turkey buffet. A new Coffee Coop serves cappuccino and other specialty drinks. Open seven days a week; inexpensive to moderate.

Dug Out (107 West Michigan Avenue; 616–781–8373) has been a local favorite since 1928 (many residents have been making daily stops for years). Recently renovated, it still specializes in family dining, with classics such as egg salad sandwich and a side of macaroni salad or new additions such as turkey croissants and Irish-style omelettes (Swiss cheese and corned beef hash). Inexpensive.

Espresso Yourself (301 East Michigan Avenue; 616–789–1136) is a European-style coffeehouse on the outskirts of downtown. It serves light meals including low-fat pitas, bagels, and croissants as well as specialty coffee drinks. It's also a cybercafe, with access to the Internet. Inexpensive.

Lodging

Arbor Inn (15435 West Michigan; 800–424–0807) is a budget-minded chain hotel located along a strip of fast-food restaurants outside the historic downtown. It features forty-eight well-kept units with air-conditioning and an outdoor pool. Rates: $42–$49 per night.

McCarthy's Bear Creek Inn (15230 C Drive North; 616–781–8383) once was the home of a wealthy agricultural inventor (his claim to fame was the automatic milking machine). Just 1 mile from downtown, it's now an elegant bed and breakfast, with seven rooms in the original house and seven in a renovated dairy barn. The property overlooks charming Bear Creek and is ringed by fieldstone fences. Rates: $65–$98 per night, including breakfast.

For More Information

Marshall Area Chamber of Commerce, 109 East Michigan Avenue, Marshall, MI 49068; (800) 877-5163.

Saugatuck

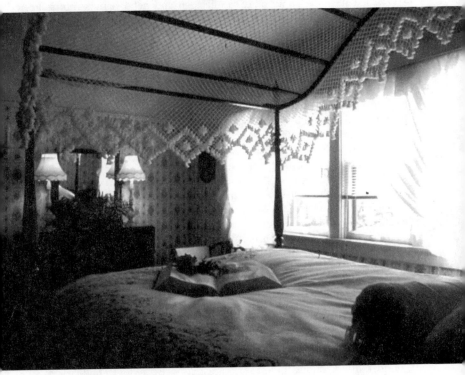

With more than thirty bed and breakfast inns (including the romantic Fairchild House), Saugatuck is known as the State's B&B capital.

Michigan's Art Coast

<hr />

2 NIGHTS

Art Galleries • Shopping • Sand and Sun • Fishing • Golf

<hr />

There are two sides to Saugatuck. The city is home of world-famous Broward Marine, where multimillion-dollar yachts are assembled for well-heeled clients around the world. It's also home to the Saugatuck Drug Store, with a soda fountain that has served up cream sodas, phosphates, and malted milks for more than seventy years. That contrast is seen downtown, where quiet city parks coexist with sophisticated urban restaurants and where midwestern families share the picturesque streets with members of Chicago and Detroit's gay elite.

Nestled near the shore of Lake Michigan and defined by steep, rolling dunes to the west and lush, green orchards to the east, Saugatuck ("river's mouth," in the parlance of the American Indians who originally lived in the region) was settled in the mid-1800s by lumber interests, which produced a thriving mix of sawmills, factories, and enough people to support them. Saugatuck, in fact, produced the majority of the lumber used to rebuild the Windy City after the Great Fire of 1871.

When the trees disappeared, however, so did much of the city. The lack of trees proved especially fateful to a neighboring village known as Singapore. Without the windbreak the trees provided, blowing sand eventually buried the village. Today this "ghost town" lives on in local lore and in stories told by area tour guides and is a popular stop on the area's free-wheeling dune rides.

Saugatuck, however, survived and found new life as an art colony. In 1914, the Art Institute of Chicago, less than 130 miles away, began sponsoring a summer camp at nearby Ox-Bow. Lured by the warm breezes and picturesque location, other creative types and eventually tourists soon followed, earning Saugatuck a reputation as Michigan's "art coast" (Ox-Bow is still open to the public from mid-June through mid-August with galleries, demonstrations, and changing exhibitions in one of the most scenic spots in the area.)

Today Saugatuck is one of Michigan's most popular resort towns. Art still plays a major role and is one of the main draws. (In Saugatuck, even the public restrooms are artistic—they're painted with scenes from Impressionist painter Georges Seurat's *Sunday Afternoon on the Island of La Grande Jatte*). Art is so popular, in fact, that in summer the streets of Saugatuck become overwhelmingly crowded. If you do go in summer, try midweek. Otherwise, consider visiting during the off-season, when prices are lower and crowds are smaller. Or consider combining a.few days in Saugatuck with a few in Holland (Michigan Escape Ten) or Southwestern Michigan (Michigan Escape Eleven) for a longer vacation.

Day 1

Saugatuck is 190 miles west of Detroit. (It's also just 127 miles from Chicago, which explains the proliferation of Illinois license plates in the town's parking lots.) To get there, take Interstate 94 west from Detroit to Interstate 196 north into the city. Plan on arriving in time for lunch.

Afternoon

Lunch: The **Loaf & Mug** (236 Culver Street; 616–857–2974) is a comfortable, casual eatery, winery, and bakery that serves breakfast and lunch daily. The airy backyard terrace has garden furniture where you can rest awhile and partake of fresh salads, hearty muffins, or the restaurant's signature hollowed-out round loaf of bread filled with steaming soup du jour. Inexpensive to moderate.

Saugatuck has some of the best shopping in West Michigan. An eclectic mix of more than fifty stores and twenty-five art galleries—most housed in picturesque nineteenth-century storefronts—hawk stylish twentieth-century merchandise. Stores range from highbrow antiques and a year-round Christmas store to a campy boutique that lures browsers and buyers with a pair of female mannequin legs dangling from a second-story window. Depending on your interests, you can easily spend a weekend exploring the town's varied offerings.

Most of the shops and boutiques are clustered along Butler Street, the main drag. Here you'll find everything from funky jewelry to fine art. A few highlights are **American Spoon Foods** (308 Butler, 616–347–9030), for gourmet made-in-Michigan treats; the **Old Post Office Shop** (238 Butler; 616–857–4553), with fine imported papers and stationery; the **Singapore Bank Bookstore** (317 Butler; 616–857–3785), saved from the sands when it was moved here; and **East of the Sun** (252 Butler; 616–857–2640), a large and eclectic gift shop. **Bentley's** (616–857–5416) features English art and antiques. If trendiness threatens to overwhelm you, however, duck into the town's old-time hardware store, **Wilkins** (439 Butler; 616–857–7501), where you'll find reassuring necessities such as fertilizer, mailboxes, and garden gloves as well as wicker and wind socks. It's been in business since 1864.

It was the area's reputation as an art coast that initially attracted galleries here. And they're still coming—between 1994 and 1996 the number jumped from fourteen to twenty-five. Strolling the city's galleries is a pleasant pastime whether you're a browser or a buyer. Highlights include the **Button Gallery** (955 Center Street; 616–857–2175), with its spectacular outdoor sculpture garden; the **Cain Gallery** (322 Butler Street; 616–857–4353), specializing in Midwestern artists; and **Good Goods** (106 Mason Street; 616–857–1557), housed in a restored Victorian boardinghouse. Good Goods is also the only place in town where you can pick up a one-of-a-kind piece by one of the area's founding artists, Sylvia Randolph Bekker, still prolific at age ninety-one.

Three other galleries in nearby Douglas ($^1/_2$ mile east of Saugatuck) are worth a special trip. The **Joyce Petter Gallery** (161 Blue Star Highway; 616–857–7861) has been West Michigan's largest marketplace for fine art for more than twenty years and is housed in a landmark building. Not far away, the **Out of Hand Gallery** (36 Center; 616–857–1420) showcases regional artists in all media, and **Australian Galleries** in Douglas (95 Blue Star Highway; 616–857–6022) imports aboriginal art, landscapes, and wearables.

For a midafternoon snack, don't miss **Saugatuck Drug Store Soda Fountain** (201 Butler Street; 616–857–2300). Here visitors take a trip back in time at the 1913 counter tucked in back of more modern necessities such as video games and a souvenir shop. (With movie rentals, an arcade, and more, this is a also a good place to remember for rainy days.)

Dinner: Friday nights are generally less crowded than Saturday at Saugatuck's many restaurants. A good one to try is **Toulouse** (248 Culver Street; 616–857–1561), which features French country cuisine in a relaxed Provençal setting. If you're lucky, you'll get a table for two by one of the cozy fireplaces. Specialties include classic cassoulet, rack of lamb, veal scallopini, and a sinful chocolate fondue for dessert. Moderate.

If you're looking for something more casual, consider **Chequers** (220 Culver Street; 616–857–1868) down the street. It's a comfy, English-style pub with a classic British menu that includes fish and chips and a famous shepherd's pie as well as a wide selection of beer and ales. Be fore-warned, however: Reservations aren't accepted, and lines can be long on weekends. Moderate.

Lodging: Saugatuck, with thirty bed and breakfasts, is fast becoming the B&B capital of the Midwest. It would be a shame not to enjoy one while in town.

Where you'll be most comfortable depends on whether you're traveling with or without children. If you've got kids in tow, head for the **Twin Oaks Inn** (227 Griffith Street; 616–857–1600). Jerry and Nancy Horney, who have owned Twin Oaks since 1989, welcome children with wide smiles and open arms. Spacious rooms in the 1860 English-style inn have portable cribs and pull-out beds. A large basket in the common room is full of well-loved and well-used toys. There's even a resident "grandma"—Nancy's mother, Kay, who oversees the property. Rates: $65–$95 per night.

If romance is your goal, few places compare to the **Fairchild House** (606 Butler Street; 616–857–5985). Felicia Fairchild—who also happens to run the Saugatuck/Douglas Area Convention & Visitors Bureau—has furnished the three bedrooms in her white, two-story 1919 inn with European feather beds, Battenburg lace linens, down comforters, and on-request bathrobes. Fairchild is as well known for its elegant champagne breakfasts (with great eggs-crab Benedict and raspberry nut bread) as for its elegant accommodations. Rates: $125 per night, double occupancy.

Unlike many resort towns, Saugatuck has a lively nightlife scene. If you're in the mood for a nightcap, head for one of the popular late night spots such as **Coral Gables** (220 Water Street; 616–857–2162), which has four different bars under one roof. If ice cream's more your style, you won't do better than a lick at **Around the Corner** ice-cream parlor (134 Mason Street; 616–857–8851), a town landmark that boasts more than fifty delicious flavors.

Day 2

Morning

Breakfast: Enjoy the complimentary breakfast at your B&B or head for **Ida Red's Cottage** (645 Water Street; 616–857–5803), considered by many locals to have the best breakfasts in town. Breakfasts are served all day; specialties include entrees with a Greek and Italian flair, such as the Italian sausage omelet. Inexpensive.

Morning is the best time to head to 1,100-acre **Saugatuck Dunes State Park**, one of the best-kept secrets in West Michigan. Just 3.5 miles north of downtown, it boasts a remote location and an early-morning serenity that's hard to beat. Families appreciate the 2 miles of Lake Michigan beachfront and 14 miles of hiking trails with breathtaking dune-top views. Uncrowded even in the heat of summer, it's also a great place to for a picnic. Stop at one of the area grocery stores and pack your own, or pick up the fixin's at the Loaf & Mug or at **Pumpernickel's Eatery** (210 Butler Street; 616–857–1196), known for its sandwiches, its hearty daily specials served with homemade bread, and its gooey sticky buns; inexpensive. Be sure to bring along a bottle of local Michigan-made wine.

Afternoon

If you've had a taste of the dunes and want to see more, hop aboard one of the sixteen-seat open-air "schooners" (actually, a converted pickup) for a traditional half-hour thrill, the **Saugatuck Dune Ride** (6495 Washington Road; 616–857–2253). You'll travel over shifting sands and take in a number of the area attractions. Along the way, the driver is likely to suddenly yell, "We've lost the brakes!" But don't worry, it's all a planned part of the adventure.

The **S. S. *Kewatin*** (616–857–2107) is an easy landmark to spot and another local favorite. Docked near the bridge that separates Saugatuck from neighboring Douglas, it had to be cut in half to fit through the narrow channel linking Lake Michigan and the Kalamazoo River. Now reassembled, it's the last of the classic Great Lakes steamships and a fascinating maritime museum that recaptures a lost era.

If you're looking to use your sea legs, the ***Star of Saugatuck*** (716 Water Street; 616–857–4590) is a two-level stern-wheeler that offers cruises along the Kalamazoo River. Along the way, it passes beautiful homes (including one that once belonged to Al Capone) as well as the city's famous boatyard and other points of interest.

Dinner: The **Global Bar & Grill** (215 Butler Street; 616–857–1555) is a rustic bistro that's one of those rare restaurants that are popular with both families and singles. It has brown-papered tables with crayons and an avant-garde menu that features many southern specials such as grilled shrimp with mango salsa. Moderate.

Afterward, you may want to check out what's on stage at the **Red Barn Playhouse** (3657 63rd Street; 616–857–7707), Saugatuck's popular summer stock venue and the third-largest playhouse in the state. Performances such as "Ain't Misbehavin" and "Born Yesterday" are offered May through October. Next door is the **Belvedere Inn and Restaurant** (3656 63rd Street), which has a restaurant as well as a wonderful new dessert and cappuccino bar. It's the perfect place to top off your day with a creamy café latte.

Day 3

Morning

Breakfast: Depending on your appetite, you have two choices. You might grab a bite at your B&B. But if you have something heartier in mind and don't feel like stopping for lunch (or dinner!) on the way home, head for the brunch at the **Clearbrook Golf Club & Restaurant** (6494 Clearbrook Drive; 616–857–2000), just a few minutes outside of town. Many residents consider this the city's best restaurant. The brunch features the well-known 1912 breakfast (just $8.50), which includes a frittata, redskin potatoes, fruit, and your choice of French toast or pancakes.

Afterward, check out any shops or attractions you may have missed earlier, or head to neighboring Fennville, about 6 miles away. Here you'll find one of West Michigan's landmarks, also known as the **Crane Orchards and Pie Pantry Restaurant** (6054 124th Avenue; 616–561–2297). This is one of the best orchards in the state, with a cider mill, great-tasting pies to take home, and U-pick fruit orchards. It's also the site of the Crane House, the 1872 family homestead that's now a charming five-bedroom bed and breakfast. If you're here at lunch or dinnertime, don't miss the chance to sample the old-fashioned cooking in the adjacent farm-style restaurant. Inexpensive.

There's More

Amusements. Blue Star Playland (6069 Blue Star Highway; 616–857–1044) has go-kart rides, bumper boats, miniature golf, a driving range, moon walk, and more.

Antiques. If the prices in the downtown antiques shops are a bit steep for your budget, try to snag a bargain at the Allegan Antique Market (616–453–8780), about 40 miles away. The market is held at the Allegan County Fairgrounds and features more than three hundred dealers on the last Sunday of each month from April through September.

Ballooning. Its up, up, and away with one of the fastest-growing sports in western Michigan. For information, call 616–335–3363.

Blueberries. Krupka's (2647 Sixty-eighth Street, Fennville; 616–857–4278) was the first blueberry farm in Michigan. It's been offering U-pick fun since the 1930s. If you're here during harvesttime—traditionally between July 4 and Labor Day—this is great, if messy, fun for the whole family.

Canoe Rental. Old Allegan Canoe Rental (2722 Old Allegan Road, Fennville; 616–561–5481) offers three- and five-hour canoe trips through the scenic Allegan State Forest.

Fishing. Looking to bag the big one? From April through November a number of charters will take sport fishers out after chinook and coho salmon and lake, brook, and steelhead trout. Popular charter operators include Can't Miss Charters (616–857–6007) and Best Chance Charters (616–857–4762). A few even clean your catch and provide a box lunch.

Golf. West Shore Golf Club (14 Ferry Street, Douglas; 616–857–2500) was founded in 1917 and is the second-oldest golf course in the state. Mi-Ro (Blue Star Highway and 130th Street, Douglas; 616–857–6161) has a nine-hole course and a driving range.

Horseback Riding. Triple R Ranch (1861 Fifty-Second Street, Fennville; 616–561–2970 or 616–561–5661 on weekends) offers horseback riding in the Allegan State Forest. Closed Mondays.

Jet Skis. Surf Slammers in Saugatuck (360 Water Street; 616–857–5387) rents jet skis for enthusiasts.

Skiing. Cross-country trails are available in Saugatuck Dunes State Park as well as the Allegan State Game Area. Call (616) 399–9390 for information.

Wineries. The Fenn Valley Winery (6130 122nd Avenue, Fennville; 616–561–2396) offers free tastings, direct discounts on products and a picnic area. Tabor Hill, another local award-winning vineyard, maintains a wine tasting room in downtown Saugatuck (214 Butler Street; 616–857–4859).

Special Events

February. Midweek Winterfest, Saugatuck
　　　　Mardi Gras Celebration, Douglas
May. Memorial Day Parade, Saugatuck
　　　　Sauga-Duck Festival, Saugatuck
July. Fourth of July Celebration, Saugatuck
　　　　Harbor Days/Venetian Night, Saugatuck
August. Sidewalk Sale, Saugatuck
　　　　Taste of Saugatuck/Douglas
September. Allegan County Fair, Allegan
　　　　Clown Festival, Saugatuck
October. Gallery Stroll Weekend, Saugatuck
　　　　Halloween Harvest, Fennville
November. Moonlight Madness Sale, Saugatuck
　　　　Holiday Lights of Saugatuck

Other Recommended Restaurants and Lodgings

Restaurants

Auction House (8 Center Street, Douglas; 616–857–4292) is known for its huge breakfasts and low prices (you can get pancakes smothered in strawberries for less than $3.00). The homemade biscuits and gravy are also a big draw. Inexpensive.

Douglas Dinette (11 Center Street, Saugatuck; 616–857–4240) features low-fat and vegetarian meals as well as weekend breakfast specials in a smoke-free setting. Inexpensive to moderate.

Maplewood Hotel (428 Butler Street, Saugatuck; 616–857–1771) has fifteen antique-filled bedrooms in the heart of Saugatuck's shops, galleries, and restaurants. The 1860s Greek Revival inn was a former home; breakfast is served in the Burr Tillstrom Dining Room, named for former Saugatuck resident and creator of the TV puppet show *Kukla, Fran, and Ollie.* Rates: $85–$155 per night.

Restaurant Su Casa (306 West Main Street, Fennville; 616–561–5493) has surprisingly authentic Mexican eats and atmosphere for a West Michigan town and has been written up in both the *Detroit Free Press* and the *Chicago Tribune.* Moderate.

Lodgings

Kingsley House (626 West Main Street, Fennville; 616–561–6425) features six rooms in an 1886 mansion built by the man who introduced fruit trees to the area. Not surprisingly, spacious Victorian-inspired rooms are named after a variety of apple. Rates: $65–$145.

Wickwood County Inn (510 Butler Street, Saugatuck; 616–857–1097) is probably Saugatuck's best-known (and most expensive) bed and breakfast. It's owned and run by Julee Rosso-Miller, a New York expatriate and the author of the *Silver Palate Cookbook.* The European-style inn is filled with French and English antiques, overstuffed chairs, fresh flowers, and original art. Guest rooms are equally attractive. Rates: $140–$190 per night.

For More Information

Saugatuck/Douglas Area Convention and Visitors Bureau, 303 Culver Street, P.O. Box 28, Saugatuck, MI 49453; (616) 857–1701.

Holland

Tulip Time is Holland's largest festival and a real "Dutch Treat."

Dutch Treat

—————————————— 2 NIGHTS ——————————————

Flowers • Dutch Village • Discount Shopping • Museums

If a trip to the Netherlands is out of your travel budget this year, you can still enjoy a touch of Dutch in Holland, Michigan. Nestled in the state's tulip country, the village is full of nostalgia for the Old World, with wooden-shoe dancers, authentic windmills, and other Dutch treats.

For years, people of Dutch ancestry dominated the city. Holland, in fact, remained 90 percent Dutch for more than a century. While the ethnic makeup is a bit more varied today (the area is also home to the state's largest Hispanic community), there are still local families who can trace their roots back to the 1840s, when Dutch separatists settled in this part of the Midwest. Whatever their original heritage, Holland residents know that it's the city's Dutch traditions that attract thousands each year, and all are pleased to roll out the *welkom* mat for visitors.

Many people head for Holland in May (reason enough, for some, to go at other times), when the annual Tulip Time Festival is in full bloom. At that time, downtown's scrubbed streets are full of flowers, costumed *klompen* dancers, local bands, parades, and thousands of tourists. There's even an inspector—called the *burgemeister*—to make sure everything is in top shape. If Holland's amusement-park quality wears thin or you start longing for all-American attractions, head for Grand Haven, about 20 miles north, which has a great lakefront and a new 3-mile boardwalk. Together, the two cities make a great quick getaway.

Day 1

Afternoon

From Detroit, Holland is about 172 miles. To get there, take Interstate 94 west to Interstate 96 north into Holland. Plan on leaving in midafternoon and arriving in time for dinner.

Dinner: After the three-hour ride from Detroit, you should be ready to eat. To get into the Holland spirit, head for **Queen's Inn** (U.S. Highway 31 at James Street; 616–393–0310), which claims to be the only town eatery serving authentic Dutch fare. A top choice is the Pigs in a Blanket, the thick pea soup, and a helping of Dutch apple pie. Reservations recommended for dinner on weekends. Moderate.

Lodging: The **Parsonage 1908** (6 East Twenty-fourth Street; 616–396–1316) was the area's first bed and breakfast, and it's still one of the best. It offers three spacious rooms in a former 1908 parsonage (hence the name) near Hope College and features a full breakfast of freshly baked breads, muffins, and egg specialties served in the formal dining room. The finely landscaped backyard has a croquet set; in summer, guests choose to enjoy the view with breakfast on the outdoor patio. Rates: $90–$100 per night. Note: Children are allowed, but adults are preferred. Most families go to the Holiday Inn (see page 85).

Day 2

Morning

Breakfast: Parsonage 1908 will fill you up for a busy day. If it's April or May, you'll be overwhelmed by the spectacle at **Veldheer Tulip Gardens** (12755 Quincy Street at U.S. Highway 31; 616–399–1900). Veldheer's is Holland's only tulip farm and perennial gardens. Tulips take center stage in the spring, followed by perennials, such as lilies and peonies, and annuals from June through October. Green thumbs are in their glory; you can also pick up bulbs and flowering plants for your at-home garden. Beds are numbered to correspond with mail-order catalogs so you can place orders for bulbs after seeing the real thing. A tip: Locals recommend visiting at dusk, when the tour buses are gone and the sunset casts a warm glow on the thousands of beautiful blooms.

Adjacent to the tulip gardens is **DeKlomp Wooden Shoe & Delft Factory**, the only production Delft factory in the United States. You can watch the crisp blue-and-white china made by hand. Artisans carve wooden shoes on authentic Dutch machinery, and you can try on a pair to take home.

Just 2 miles from downtown is **"De Zwaan"** (The Swan), a 230-year-old working Dutch windmill. It's part of the **Windmill Island Municipal Park** (Seventh Street and Lincoln Avenue; 616–396–5433). Shipped to Holland in 1964, it's the last windmill the Dutch government allowed to leave the Netherlands. At 12 stories high, its steel beams and sails span 80 feet and crank out a fine graham flour, which is available for purchase within the park. Costumed guides escort visitors through the mill. Other park highlights include the **Posthouse Museum,** a charming replica of a 200-year-old Dutch country inn, with an interesting collection of Dutch furniture, free rides for kids on an authentic Dutch carousel, a miniature display of Dutch life in the "Little Netherlands," and the ubiquitous gift shop. Admission is $5.00 for adults and $2.50 for children ages five to twelve.

Afternoon

If you're ready for some all-American shopping, downtown Holland has both small boutiques and a large outlet mall. Wander along the restored nineteenth-century storefronts in the central business district, where shops range from the whimsical **Sand Castle Toys** (2 East Eighth Street) to the literary minded **Center Aisle Books** (77 East Eighth Street). Downtown's **Centennial Park** is an old-fashioned shady downtown square with a canopy of century-old trees. It's a good starting point for walking tours of downtown, nearby Hope College, and the historic district. Good walking-tour brochures are available at the Herrick Public Library on River and Twelfth streets.

Also worth a stop is the gallery shop of the **Holland Area Arts Council** (25 West Eighth Street), which has an eclectic collection of interesting stuff, including jewelry, games, and art by local artists and craftspeople. If you're looking for bargains, the **Horizon Outlet Center** (800–866–5900) has more than thirty-five stores including Carter's Childrenswear, Barbizon Lingerie, Eddie Bauer, and Royal Doulton in a—what else?—re-created Dutch village.

Dinner: **Sandpiper** (2225 South Shore Drive; 616–335–5866) in nearby Macatawa (ten minutes from downtown Holland), was named the best restaurant in southwestern Michigan by *Grand Rapids* magazine. It overlooks Lake Macatawa and features a menu of nouvelle cuisine, including a sixteen-ounce pork chop topped with arugula, roma tomatoes, and goat cheese, oregano-seared Atlantic salmon, and for dessert the rum-vanilla-caramel flan or chocolate Chambord cake. Moderate to expensive.

If it's summer, you might want to take in a performance at the **Hope Summer Repertory Theater** (141 East Twelfth Street; 616–395–7600). Besides staging three musicals and two plays in a rotating repertory from mid-June through mid-August, the group also mounts an annual Christmas celebration. Plays are held at DeWitt Center, part of Hope College.

Day 3

Morning

Breakfast: On Sunday, **Calypso's** in the Holiday Inn (U.S. Highway 31 at Twentieth Street; 616–396–0709) is the place to be. From 10:00 A.M. to 2:00 P.M., the hotel serves the area's biggest Sunday brunch, with more than 70 feet of breakfast and lunch entrees, including chicken, fish, roast beef, eggs, baked goods, and more for just $10.95 per person. Moderate.

Today's the day to hit the beach and relax before heading home. Sun and sand can be found at Holland State Park or at one of the many spots in nearby Grand Haven. **Holland State Park** (2215 Ottawa Beach Road; 616–399–9390) is one of the state's most popular parks, with Victorian gingerbread cottages (part of a beach development that dates back to the 1880s), 1,800 feet of sugary sand, and a full gamut of water sports, from boating and pier and charter fishing to jet skis and windsurfing. There are also a number of picnic tables that face the channel, good spots to relax and watch the world go by.

Before heading home, be sure to stop at the **Crane's Orchards Pie Pantry and Restaurant** (6054 124th Avenue, Fennville; 616–561–2297) , an attraction in its own right and a West Michigan institution. Crane's U-pick farms are popular with families, as are the famous pies and the adjacent inexpensive country-style restaurant. There's even a B&B in the original mid-nineteenth-century homestead.

There's More

Academia. Serene Hope College (141 East Twelfth Street; 616–395–7000) is a great area in which to wander. The institution traces its roots to the same Dutch expatriates who founded the town. Today, Hope is a nationally recognized liberal arts college affiliated with the Reformed Church in America. Guided tours are available by appointment, but you can easily take in the campus on foot.

Antiques. The Tulip City Antique Mall (1145 South Washington Street; 616–396–8855) has more than eighty dealers with collectibles that range from oak furniture and imported Dutch wares to old advertising and maritime paraphernalia.

Bicycling. Holland State Park (616–399–9390) has more than 100 miles of scenic paths. Bring your own wheels or rent some at Papa Donn's (2250 Ottawa Beach Road). They're open seven days a week from Memorial Day through Labor Day.

History. City residents are justly proud of two local museums, the Holland Museum (31 West Tenth Street; 616–392–9084) and the Cappon House (228 West Ninth Street, 616–392–6740). Together they contain more than 400 years of Dutch and American heritage, with displays that cover Holland's 150-year history. Interesting exhibits include an 1866 Amsterdam dollhouse, a display of items from the 1939 New York World's Fair, a section on the area's Great Resort era in the nineteenth century, and a display on Lake Michigan's maritime lore.

Water Sports. Holland Water Sports (2212 Ottawa Beach Road; 616–786–2628) rents jet skis, parasailing paraphernalia, and other watery family fun.

Special Events

February. Valentine's Day Gallery Stroll
April. Cambodian New Year's Celebration
May. Cinco de Mayo Fiesta
      Tulip Time Festival
June. Celebration of the Arts
July. Ottawa County Fair
      Fourth of July Fireworks
August. Art in the Park
September. Fall Color Tours
November. Gallery Stroll
December. Dutch Winter Festival
      Vietnamese New Year's Bash

Other Recommended Lodgings

Dutch Colonial Inn (560 Central Avenue; 616–396–3664) has five elegant guest rooms in a 1928 colonial home best suited to adult guests. All have private bath; some have whirlpools. Rates: $85–$115 per night.

North Shore Inn (686 North Shore Drive; 616–394–9050) is the city's only lakeside B&B and is located near downtown shops and restaurants. It features lush gardens, a gracious decor, and friendly service. Rates: $90–$120 per night.

Holland Holiday Inn and Conference Center (650 East Twenty-fourth Street; 616–394–0111 or 800–465–4329) is the place for you if you don't like B&Bs or if you've brought the kids along. It has 168 rooms, an indoor pool, exercise and game rooms, as well as a restaurant and nightclub. Rates: $89–$100 per night.

For More Information

Holland Area Convention and Visitors Bureau, 171 Lincoln Avenue, Holland, MI 49423; (800) 822–2770 or (616) 296–4221.

Southwestern Michigan

Harbor Country's Lake Michigan shoreline attracts visitors from across the Midwest.

Harbor Holiday

_____ 3 NIGHTS _____

Antiques • Shopping • Sun and Fun • Nature • Wineries

A weekend visit to West Michigan's Harbor Country reveals as many Chicago natives as Detroiters. Just an hour from the Loop, this has become the summer community of choice for Windy City expatriates such as movie critics Gene Siskel and Roger Ebert, novelist Andrew Greeley, and scores of others who build and inhabit the pricey condos and glass-fronted luxury homes that line Lake Michigan.

Located along the lakefront in the most southwestern corner of the state, Harbor Country (a Chamber of Commerce nickname) includes eight communities that form the gateway to Michigan: Michiana, Grand Beach, New Buffalo, Union Pier, Lakeside, Harbert, Sawyer, and Three Oaks. As a destination, the area is sometimes called (most often by its Convention and Visitors Bureau and local public relations efforts) the "Riviera on Lake Michigan" and the "Hamptons of the Midwest." The area also encompasses nearby towns such as Baroda, Buchanan, Bridgman, and Berrien Springs.

Behind its silver-spoon facade, however, much of the area's sleepy old charm remains. Tony shops may line the main streets, but the sand, surf, and sunsets are still famous—and still free. Hotels exist in all price ranges, as do restaurants. While you can easily drop $100.00 for dinner for two at one of the city's tony restaurants, you can also easily enjoy a huge breakfast of thick French toast slices, two eggs, and two slices of bacon for just $3.00 at Rosie's in downtown New Buffalo. And there are plenty of things to keep you busy, whether you're a solo sojourner, a curious couple, a fun-loving family, or any other type of traveler.

Day 1

Afternoon

Harbor Country is about 200 miles from Detroit, roughly a three-hour trip west along Interstate 94. Plan on leaving early enough to arrive in time for dinner.

Dinner: The **Red Arrow Roadhouse** (15710 Red Arrow Highway; 616–469–3939) is a quintessential Harbor Country eatery. Located in Union Pier, it's a laid-back place with fresh fish, pastas, and salads that won't break your budget, along with more than thirty varieties of beer. Good people-watching too, with a colorful mix of locals and landed gentry.

Lodging: Harbor Country is a haven for bed-and-breakfast fans. One of the best and most popular in the area is the **Pebble House** (15093 Lake Shore, Lakeside; 616–469–1416), run by Chicago expatriates Ed and Jean Lawrence. Ed also runs the East Road Antiques in nearby Lakeside. Unlike many B&Bs, the Pebble House is appropriate for children as well as adults. Travelers without kids may choose one of the rooms in the 1912 main house, while families often opt for the three–bedroom Coach House or the two-bedroom Blueberry House. The main house has seven rooms and suites in three guest buildings connected by wooden walkways and pergolas. Guests are encouraged to use the tennis courts and the nearby beach. Everyone enjoys the public areas filled with arts-and-crafts-style antiques and Mission furniture, as well as Jean Lawrence's hearty Scandinavian breakfasts. Rates: $100–$145 per night, including breakfast.

Day 2

Morning

Breakfast: The Pebble House will fortify you for the day ahead. Now it's time for a little exploring. Harbor Country's towns offer a wide variety of personalities, from simple to sophisticated. Your first stop will probably be New Buffalo, the area's historic hub. Now a seaside boomtown, it's been almost overrun with development that threatens to obliterate its small-town charm. Tiny summer cottages that once sold for almost nothing now command six-figure prices. The town's the outpost of choice for most wealthy Windy City residents, as well as the center for most of the area's shopping. Nonetheless, the town still maintains vestiges of its former self, including the hundred-year-old **Barbie's Department Store** and a number of friendly neighborhood taverns that serve up simple fare such as fresh fish and fries.

Wander New Buffalo's Whittaker Street and you'll find wares that run from small collectibles to major home furnishings. You'll also find the most sophisticated clothing stores this side of the Magnificent Mile, with favorites including **Trillium** (30 North Whittaker; 616–469–1400), the high-fashion selection at **Whittaker House** (26 North Whittaker; 616–469–0220), and ready-to-wear from classic to trendy at **La Grande Trunk** (447 South Whittaker; 616–469–2122). If you're looking to update your house instead of your wardrobe, ideas and inspiration can be found at **Le Panache** (122 North Whittaker; 616–469–4610) and **By Design** (427 South Whittaker; 616–469–1930), both run by local designers, and **Hearthwoods At Home** (110 North Whittaker; 616–469–5551), which specializes in hand-crafted furniture made from Michigan logs and twigs as well a wide selection of rustic accessories, including candlesticks, frames, mirrors, and whimsical wares. Other shops worth a stop include The **Shop Across the Street** (126 North Whittaker; 616–469–0669), with an eclectic collection of antique pillows, furniture, robes, jewelry, and other goodies; **Michigan Thyme** (107 North Whittaker), a foodie's fantasy; the **Clipper Ship Gallery** (116 North Whittaker), the place for marine-inspired art; and the **Art Barn Gallery North** (419 South Whittaker), which sells fine art, jewelry, sculpture, and pottery and features an open-air art market each third weekend in summer, when you can watch artists at work under sunny skies.

More sunny skies can be enjoyed at the **New Buffalo Lakefront Park and Beach,** located at the north end of Whittaker Street across the bridge. While it can be crowded on a really hot day, families enjoy the dune climb and resulting panoramic views as well as feeding the ducks, geese, and gulls. Another popular place is the **Warren Dunes State Park** (616–426–4013), where the massive dunes encourage climbing and, later, resting along the beautiful sandy beach. On a clear day you can see the Sears Tower and other Chicago landmarks across the way.

Afternoon

Lunch: **Redamak's** (616 East Buffalo Street; 616–469–4522) is known as the home of "the hamburger that made New Buffalo famous." This casual eatery with a range of food is perfect for the whole family—and has two game rooms if the kids (or you) get restless. Try the "workingman's special" during the week, when burger and fries are just $3.00. In good weather, there's dining on the open-air patio. Inexpensive.

Had enough shopping? If not, more can be found along the Red Arrow Highway. If antiques are your passion, you'll be in heaven here. Harbor Country is one of the state's major antiques centers, with an assortment of shops and malls spread out across the picturesque countryside. Wandering through the shops, kibitzing with dealers, and browsing and buying is a great way to spend an afternoon—or longer.

Most shops are spread out along the Red Arrow Highway. If you like what you see at the Pebble House and want to take a few similar pieces home, don't miss the **East Road Gallery** (14906 Red Arrow Highway; 616–469–5995). Like the Pebble House, Ed Lawrence's shop is filled to the brim with furnishings and decorative items from the Arts and Crafts Movement. Nearby **Rabbit Run Antiques & Interiors** (15460 Red Arrow Highway; 616–469–0468), displays antiques in homey roomlike settings and also sells accent pieces, plus folk and fine art. Owners and brothers Ken and Tom Gosh are happy to give free advice or consult on your collection through their design service. **Vintage Pine** (15980 Red Arrow Highway; 616–469–6252) specializes in what you'd expect from the name—imported pine furniture. The cozy shop has armoires, tables, bookcases, sideboards, and accessories.

If you prefer the wide selection at antiques malls, Harbor Country has those as well. **Dunes Antique Center** (12835 Red Arrow Highway; 616–426–4043 in Sawyer) is the newest. With more than 20,000 square feet and sixty dealers, it presents a broad selection of antiques and collectibles, from heirloom quality through funky 1950s furniture and more. In Harbert you'll find the **Harbert Antique Mall** (13887 Red Arrow Highway; 616–469–0977), with more than forty dealers with a constantly changing inventory of goods. But the most unusual antiques mall in the state—possibly in all the Midwest—is the **Antique Mall and Village** in Union Pier (9300 Union Pier Road; 616–469–2555). In addition to a main building housing a variety of dealers, there is a chapel with a (surprisingly good) copy of the ceiling of the Sistine Chapel, a diner, a pottery emporium, and a log cabin full of Native American artifacts.

Dinner: Rest your feet over a meal at **Miller's Country House,** not far from the antiques malls along the Red Arrow Highway in Union Pier (616–469–5950). Depending on your mood, you can choose to eat in the rustic dining room and watch chefs prepare food in the exhibition kitchen or opt for the more formal dining rooms that overlook a beautiful woodland garden (wherever you choose, dress is strictly casual). Entrees range from gourmet pizzas and steakburgers to more creative cuisine such as grilled Portobello mushrooms and New Zealand rack of lamb with mango chutney, the house specialty. Moderate.

Day 3

Morning

Breakfast: If you're opting to eat out, consider a stop for an impromptu breakfast at **Harbert Swedish Bakery** (Red Arrow Highway; 616–469–1777) in Harbert. Traditional Swedish breads and cakes are the draw; tables inside and out are usually crowded. Inexpensive.

Not far from the Red Arrow Highway is the area's other big attraction—rolling hills covered with lush grapevines that yield award-winning wines. Talented local wine makers attribute their success to the area's sandy, well-drained, fertile soil, the hilly terrain, and Lake Michigan's weather-tempering influence. Whatever the cause, you'll enjoy the results. Area wineries offer free tasting and tours as well as fine dining and specialty food items. Depending on the time of day you visit, you can enjoy picturesque picnic sites and scenic lookouts as well as great gift shops. One winery—Tabor Hill—is also home to a gourmet restaurant, the only such eatery of its kind in the state.

Start your vineyard tour at **Heart of the Vineyard Winery** in Baroda (16024 Red Arrow Highway; 800–716–9463). The winery is housed in a restored 1881 post-and-beam-plank barn, and sampling is done inside at the hand-hewn bar or outside on an open-air veranda. The Moersch family takes pride in the their product and is happy to share their secrets. After a tour and tasting, you can opt to stay longer in the vineyard's adjacent bed and breakfast. Heart of the Vineyard also has a tasting room and gift store adjacent to Riviera Gardens on Red Arrow Highway in Union Pier.

St. Julian Winery (9100 Union Pier Road; 616–469–3150) is the state's oldest and largest-selling winery. It has a wine-tasting center near Interstate 94 in Union Pier, where oenophiles can stock up on more than thirty-five varieties of wine, nonalcoholic juices, and the vineyard's famous Italian dressing. The vineyard has won a number of national and international awards.

Top off your day with a tour of **Tabor Hill Winery** (185 Mt. Tabor Road; 800–283–3363). A vineyard visit takes guests through the rows of huge vats and small oaken casks that hold the aging wines. Afterward, enjoy the wines at the winery on Mt. Tabor Road in Buchanan or at the Tabor Hill Champagne Cellar on the Red Arrow Highway in Bridgman.

Lunch: **Tabor Hill Winery & Restaurant** (800–283–3363) is the perfect place to end your Harbor Country weekend. Lunch and dinner are served Wednesday through Sunday from April through November. From December through March, it's open only weekends. Entrees include specialties such as mesquite-grilled shrimp, Maryland soft shell crab, and raspberry chicken. Not surprisingly, the dining room overlooks the surrounding vineyards and breath-taking countryside. Moderate.

There's More

Family Fun. Pee-Wee golf, go-karts, bumper boats, and batting cages are just a few of the thrills for small fries found at Captain Mike's Fun Park on Red Arrow Highway in Sawyer (616–465–5747).

Flora and Fauna. Fernwood, located not far away between Berrien Springs and Buchanan (13988 Range Line Road; 616–465–6101) is a relaxing, six-acre botanical garden and nature facility. A pleasant sidetrip, it includes a lilac garden, a boxwood garden, a fern trail, a perennial garden, and a rock garden. There's also a new Visitors Center, with a tea room that's a great place to take a break before hitting the interstate.

Golf. The Harbor Country area is home to five courses, including Pebble-wood (9794 South Jericho Road, Bridgman; 616–465–5611), the new Whittaker Woods (12620 Wilson Road, New Buffalo; 616–469–1313), Grand Beach (48200 Perkins Grand Beach; 616–469–4888), Brookwood (1339 Rynearson, Buchanan; 616–695–7817), and Briar Leaf, in nearby La Porte, Indiana (3233 North State Road; 219–326–1992).

Orchards. Tree–Mendus Fruit Farm (East Eureka Road, Berrien Springs; 616–782–7101) is one of the largest orchards in the Midwest, with a delightful one-hour harvest tour, 560 acres of U-pick orchards, a nature park with hiking trails and swings for the kids, even a picnic area and chapel in the woods.

Special Events

March. Other Side of the Lake Art Exhibition, New Buffalo
April. Art Attack, areawide
June. Flag Day, Three Oaks
July. Lakeside Arts and Crafts Festival, Lakeside
August. Ship and Shore Festival, New Buffalo
      Berrien County Youth Fair, Berrien Springs
September. Apple Cider Century Bike Tour, areawide
November. Antique Trek, areawide

Other Recommended Restaurants and Lodgings

Restaurants

Bilgewater Bar & Grill (244 North Whittaker Street, New Buffalo; 616–469–5323) is Harbor Country's only waterfront restaurant. Specialties include the breakfast buffet and seafood, and most guests opt to sit outside when weather permits. This is also one of the few spots to feature regular live entertainment, from rock and roll to jazz. There's also a comedy club, big-screen TV, and game room for the kids. Moderate.

Hannah's Restaurant (115 South Whittaker Street, New Buffalo; 616–469–1440) serves lunch and dinner daily, with an extensive menu that features everything from pot roast to an award-winning apple-brandied pork chop. There's also a children's menu. Reservations recommended. Moderate.

Jenny's (16220 Lakeshore Road, Union Pier; 616–469–6545) is regarded by many as the best restaurant in the area. On weekends, it's also incredibly crowded, with reservations a necessity. Specialties include Cornish hens with raisins and almonds, anything with Portobello mushrooms, and the profiteroles for dessert. Housed in a restored 1920s inn, it's also open for lunch. Expensive.

Skip's Other Place (Red Arrow Highway between New Buffalo and Union Pier; 616–469–3330) is Harbor Country's oldest fine-dining restaurant and is known for its prime rib and steaks. There's also a children's menu. Reservations are suggested. Moderate to expensive.

Lodgings

Bauhaus on Barton (33 North Barton Street, New Buffalo; 616–469–6419) is a stylish B&B with three suites and one double room, all decorated in hip 1950s furnishings and accessories (even the in-room magazines are from the period). Rooms are named for 1950s television shows; ask for the "Jetsons" room, with skypad furniture and a comet rug. All include private baths, cable TV, full breakfast, and terry cloth robes. Rates: $80 and up per night.

Harbor Grand Hotel & Suites (111 West Water Street, New Buffalo; 616–469–7700) is the newest addition to New Buffalo and the only hotel in Harbor Country. Just steps from the marina, beach, shops, and restaurants, its architecture and fifty-seven guest rooms were inspired by Frank Lloyd Wright. There are also an indoor pool and spa with sundeck, gym, and harbor and lake views. Rates: $155–$175 per night.

The **Inn at Union Pier** (9708 Berrien, Union Pier; 616–469–4700) has sixteen spacious guest rooms that are just two hundred steps from Lake Michigan and the beach. The charming inn also has the largest private collection of *kakelugns*—antique Swedish ceramic fireplaces—in the country. Rates: $115–$185 per night.

Lakeside Inn (15281 Lake Shore, Lakeside; 616–469–0600) is reminiscent of another area, with a 100-foot-long front porch lined with rockers. There's also a private beach. Breakfast is included in the rates for the thirty rooms, and children are welcome. Rates: $75–$150 per night.

The **Pine Garth Inn & Cottages** (15790 Lakeshore Road, Union Pier; 616–469–1642) was built in 1905 as a summer home. There are seven bedrooms and five romantic cottage suites with private hot tubs that are surrounded by wooden fences. Located on a high bluff, six of the seven rooms and all of the suites offer vistas of Lake Michigan. The inn also has a private beach. Rates: $130 per night.

For More Information

Harbor Country Chamber of Commerce, 3 West Buffalo Street, New Buffalo, MI 49117; (616) 469–5409.

Southwest Michigan Tourist Council, 2300 Pipestone Road, Benton Harbor, MI 49022; (616) 925–6301.

Illinois Escape

Chicago

Chicago's famous skyline attracts architecture buffs from all over the world.

Windy City Weekend

_____ 3 NIGHTS _____
Shopping • Restaurants • Museums • Sports • Theater

Chicago has so many things to do, the famed "City of Big Shoulders" could easily be called the "City of Big Decisions." Like to shop? Head for the Magnificent Mile or Oak Street. Into architecture? Sign on for one of the tours offered by the city's renowned Architecture Foundation. How 'bout sports? You won't find more loyal fans than those who cheer for the Bulls, the Bears, the Cubs, and the White Sox.

Chicago is all Detroit aspires to—a big midwestern city that's both friendly and sophisticated, with a mix of elegance and economics. While known for its hard-working mentality, it's also incredibly beautiful, with the blue infinity of Lake Michigan edged by curling swaths of parks and beaches. Downtown's gleaming towers meld gracefully with the high-rises of the Gold Coast and the flatter surrounding prairie. When summer finally arrives, all of the city moves outdoors, where you'll find residents enjoying the legendary 29 miles of lakeshore and twenty-nine beaches.

There is no way to do the city justice in a weekend, and entire guidebooks are dedicated to exploring its many facets. Two worth picking up before you go are Marilyn J. Appleberg's *I Love Chicago* guide and Paul Engleman's *Chicago Access*. Both offer great ideas for putting together your own Chicago adventure; consider the following itinerary just a starting point for a lifetime of weekends spent exploring the Windy City.

Day 1

Chicago is roughly a six-hour drive along Interstate 94 west. To squeeze the most into your trip, plan on skipping work on Friday so you can hit the road early. Chicago is known for its variety of great restaurants, so try to arrive in time for dinner.

Afternoon

Dinner: Need something meaty after the long drive? **Morton's of Chicago** (1050 North State Street, 312–266–4820) is famed for catering to carnivores, with huge porterhouse steaks and a wide variety of beef entrees. There are also veal and chicken dishes, as well as wonderful dessert soufflés. Moderate to expensive.

Lodging: The Windy City has dozens and dozens of hotels to choose from, many catering to the convention crowd. If you're looking for something a little more personalized, the **Whitehall** (105 East Delaware Place; 312–944–6300 or 800–323–7500) is an intimate hotel with 221 English–style rooms. Just a block from the Magnificent Mile, the stretch of tony shops along Michigan Avenue, it's surprisingly quiet and makes a welcome retreat at the end of a hectic day of sight-seeing and shopping. From it, you can "toddle" anywhere quite easily. Room rates for two people start at a relatively reasonable $139 per night on weekends.

Day 2

Morning

Breakfast: **Lou Mitchell's** (565 West Jackson Boulevard; 312–939–3111) has been a city institution for more than seventy years. It's the kind of place that attracts diners who range from chauffeur-driven CEOs to tourists. The restaurant is famous for its double-yolked fried eggs, served in skillets along with huge glasses of freshly squeezed orange juice. If you're not into eggs, try the malted milk Belgian waffles. Inexpensive.

Saturday is the best day to shop the Magnificent Mile, when the stores have extended hours (some are closed on Sunday) and the people-watching is prime. This high-rent district between the Chicago River and the Drake Hotel is home to **Saks Fifth Avenue** (700 North Michigan Avenue; 312–944–6500), Neiman Marcus (737 North Michigan Avenue; 312–642–5900), and Bloomingdale's (900 North Michigan Avenue; 312–440–4460), as well as the limestone **Water Tower,** one of the few major buildings to escape the Great Chicago Fire of 1871. Just about every designer boutique and upscale store in the country has a presence here. But there are also stores for more everyday budgets, including **Banana Republic** (835 North Michigan Avenue; 312–642–7667) and a huge, sparkling glass-sided **Crate & Barrel** store (646 North Michigan Avenue; 312–787–5900).

Shopping the "Mag" Mile can take up the better part of the day if you let it. If, however, you're looking for an alternative to Michigan Avenue's crowds, take your credit cards to Oak Street, a quiet street of tony boutiques housed in vintage brownstones, or State Street, the city's old retail center, where you'll find institutions such as beautifully renovated and huge **Marshall Field's** (111 North State Street; 312–781–1000) and the classic **Carson Pirie Scott** (1 South State Street; 312–641–7000). State has been a famous urban thoroughfare for more than a century, and people continue to meet under Marshall Field's landmark corner clock as they have since the late 1800s.

South of the river is the **Loop,** the old heart of the city, where the world's first skyscraper (the 9-story Home Insurance Building, now long demolished) was erected in 1885. Today the Loop boasts the nation's tallest building, the 110-story **Sears Tower** (233 South Wacker Drive; 312–875–9696) as well as a host of other famous buildings by architects such as Louis Sullivan, Ludwig Mies Van der Rohe, Helmut Jahn, and others.

Afternoon

Lunch: You've been looking up all morning, so now look down on the city from the Signature Room on the ninety-fifth floor of the **John Hancock Center** (875 North Michigan Avenue; 312–787–9596). Huge, floor-to-ceiling windows offer an amazing view of the Chicago cityscape and the Lake Michigan shore. On a really clear day you can see all the way across the lake to Michigan. The lunch buffet is a pleasing array of salads and pastas—all at just $8.95 per person. When you consider that admission to the observatory deck is about $5.00, it's also an incredible deal.

If you'd prefer not to navigate the city on your own, sign on for one of the walking tours offered by the excellent **Chicago Architecture Foundation** (312–922–3432) or the **ArchiCenter** (330 South Dearborn, 312–782–1776).

Stops along the way include the turn-of-the-century mansions along the Gold Coast, the Frank Lloyd Wright home in suburban Oak Park, the Gothic towers of the University of Chicago, native son Louis Sullivan's cast-iron classic, the Carson Pirie Scott department store at the corner of State and Madison, and more. The ArchiCenter also has a great design shop and gallery, so leave some browsing time at the end of your tour.

If you'd rather rest your feet, the foundation also offers the **Chicago from the Lake** cruise, a ninety-minute ride on the river that highlights some of the city's glittering gems. Cruises leave at 10:00 A.M. and noon Wednesday through Sunday; 10:00 A.M., noon, and 6:00 P.M. Monday and Tuesday. Admission is $15 per person. You can also stow away on one of the sight-seeing tours offered by boats. **Wendella Sightseeing Boats** (312–337–1446) ply the Chicago River and Lake Michigan several times each day and depart from the Chicago River from the lower level of Michigan Avenue at Wacker Drive. Cruising season runs from mid-April through mid-October.

Dinner: Looking to splurge? The five–star **Everest** (440 South LaSalle Street; 312–663–8920) is on everyone's list of the city's best restaurants. Located on the fortieth floor of the Chicago Stock Exchange, it has dramatic city views and light-as-a-whisper French cuisine, the creation of the Alsatian chef Jean Joho. Entrees include dishes such as a salmon soufflé or sautéed elk with wild mushrooms. Try to get one of the few tables at or near a window for an incredible view of downtown. Closed Sunday and Monday. Very expensive.

Day 3

Morning

Breakfast: Enjoy breakfast in bed or head for the **Oak Tree** (900 North Michigan; 312–751–1988), where you can join other diners in the Sunday morning ritual of noshing a bagel and perusing a copy of the thick weekend edition of the *Chicago Tribune.* Inexpensive.

Sunday is a great day to explore the city's museums. The **Art Institute of Chicago** (111 South Michigan Avenue; 312–443–3600) is the city's answer to New York's Metropolitan Museum of Art and one of the finest institutions in the world. Inside these hallowed halls are masterpieces that range from the earliest civilizations to modern times. Among the most famous are the works by the always popular French Impressionists, including Monet's haystacks and water lilies series, Renoir's *Two Sisters (On The Terrace),* and Seurat's pointillist canvas known as *Sunday Afternoon on the Island of La Grande Jatte,* later inspiration for the successful Broadway play *Sunday in the Park with George.* Other works of note include Grant Wood's pioneer father and daughter in *American Gothic,* Picasso's *Old Guitarist,* and important works by more modern masters. You can easily spend the entire day here. When museum feet hit, however, be sure to take a break in the cafe or the cavernous gift shop, where you can pick up a few reprinted masterpieces for your walls at home as well as books, note cards, jewelry, and more.

The stunning new **Museum of Contemporary Art** (MCA) debuted in 1996 in new lakefront digs (220 East Chicago Avenue; 312–280–2660). You won't want to miss the lake views from the terraced sculpture garden or the mind-bending exhibitions of contemporary culture. If you've brought the family, there's no better place to spend the day than **Navy Pier** (600 East Grand Avenue; 312–595–7437), a renovated festival marketplace of shops, parks, restaurants, and entertainment on Lake Michigan. Reopened amid great fanfare in 1995, the huge lakefront playground features a 150-foot-tall Ferris wheel, a musical carousel, and the new **Chicago Children's Museum** (312–527–1000), an exciting mix of hands-on exhibits for the young and young at heart.

Afternoon

Lunch: The **Berghoff** (17 West Adams Street; 312–427–3170) has been a city institution for almost a century. This crusty, oak-paneled beer hall has served up some of the most authentic German food in the city along with foamy steins of home-brewed, Dortmunder-style beers. The specialties are the huge platters of sausage, succulent Wiener schnitzel, crisp potato pancakes, and bowls of smooth creamed spinach. Be sure to leave room for the strudel. Moderate.

Walk off your lunch with an afternoon visit to **River North,** the heart of Chicago's art district. To get there, head north 4 blocks on either Clark or Adams streets. Along the way you'll pass the controversial **James R. Thompson Center,** named after a former longtime Illinois governor and also known as the State of Illinois Center (100 West Randolph Street; 312–814–6660), an ultramodern glass and steel structure designed by modernist architect Helmut Jahn. Inside is a tempting artisan center with quilts, carvings, textiles, and other works by the state's best artists. As for the building, locals either love it or hate it. You decide.

If you were inspired by the works at the Art Institute, you can take a few River North paintings and other goodies home and support local artists at the same time. Dozens of River North galleries showcase painting, sculpture, and the decorative arts. Some of the best are **Objects Gallery/Ann Nathan Gallery** (210 West Superior Street; 312–664–6622) and the southwestern-style **Mongerson Wunderlich** (704 North Wells Street; 312–943–2354). If you prefer, you can do some power shopping at the **June Blaker** boutique (200 West Superior Street; 312–751–9220), **Mig & Tig** (549 North Wells Street; 312–644–8277), and **Sawbridge Studios** (406 North Clark Street; 312–828–0055). The **Paper Source** (232 West Chicago Avenue; 312–337–0798) has a great collection of rubber stamps.

Dinner: **Kiki's Bistro** (900 North Michigan Avenue; 312–335–5454) is a cozy, French–style bistro with great onion soup and a stylish, unpretentious atmosphere. Other specialties include the steak and *frites* and the silky custard *crème caramel,* the perfect ending to a memorable meal. Moderate.

Looking for some late night action? **Gordon** (500 North Clark Street; 312–467–9780) is an eclectic restaurant that serves innovative American cuisine and has dancing on weekends. Or you can head for the Loop, where you'll find **Yvette Wintergarden** (311 South Wacker Drive; 312–408–1242). This is where pianist Harry Connick Jr. heads to tinkle the ivories when he's in the Windy City. The mood is decidedly 1940s—diners even get up and take a few dips and twirls on the dance floor in between courses.

Other good options include the clubby **Gold Star Sardine Bar** (680 North Lake Shore Drive; 312–664–4215) for piano music, the legendary **Pump Room** (1301 North State Street; 312–266–0360), **Jazz Showcase** (59 West Grand Avenue; 312–670–2473), or **Buddy Guy's Legends** (754 South Wabash Avenue; 312–427–0333). Guy plays only in January, but he drops in often and jams the rest of the year.

Fans of alternative rock head for the **Empty Bottle** (1035 North Western Avenue; 312–276–3600), a funky club in the Ukrainian Village neighborhood that features cutting-edge music on weekends and experimental jazz on Wednesdays.

The ninety-fourth-floor observatory at the **John Hancock Center** (875 North Michigan Avenue; 312–751–3681) offers a spectacular nighttime view of the city, including a look down on the four glowing towers of the Bloomies building at 900 North Michigan Avenue.

Day 4

Morning

Breakfast: Since this is your last day, have something special sent up from room service and eat it in bed. If you want to go out, a good choice is the **Park Avenue Café** in the Doubletree Guest Suites (199 East Walton Street; 312–944–4414). This New York import made an initial sensation because of trademarked entrees such as Pastrami Salmon and Swordfish Chop. It's also known for its American dim sum Sunday brunch, which features a full array of appetizers and entrees for $28.50 per person. Don't plan on eating for the rest of the day.

Try to squeeze anything you missed into your last day here. You might choose to experience the Great Chicago Fire or let the kids climb on the city's first locomotive at the **Chicago Historical Society** (Clark Street and North Avenue; 312–642–4600), or take in a manageable museum such as the **Terra Museum of American Art** (666 North Michigan Avenue; 312–664–3939), where works by Sargent, Chase, and Wyeth are exhibited in a soothing, dove-gray interior. The museum is a great antidote to the teeming crowds outside.

End your Windy City weekend with a bit of Great Britain. Indulge in a "veddy" English–style tea at one of the city's exclusive hotels. They all have one, but the scones, sandwiches, cakes, and pastries at the **Drake** (Michigan at Lake Shore Drive; 312–787–2200) are the closest to the real thing. If they're crowded, your next best choice is the **Four Seasons** (120 East Delaware Place; 312–280–8800), where you can sink into a plush couch by the fire.

There's More

Cycling. Zoom along the lakefront on rented bikes or Rollerblades from Bike Chicago (800–915–2453), which has six locations, including Buckingham Fountain, Navy Pier, and Oak Street Beach. Rates start at $7.00 an hour, protective gear included.

Natural History. The Field Museum of Natural History (Roosevelt Road at Lake Shore Drive; 312–922–9410) is a hands-on, science-oriented museum that has succeeded admirably in transforming itself from a dusty institution into an innovative learning center for all ages. The stuffed animals and dinosaurs are perennially popular; special exhibitions aim at expanding visitors' knowledge of critters from bats to spiders. You'll pay about $5.00 admission for adults, $3.00 for students and seniors; free on Wednesday.

Science. The Museum of Science and Industry (Fifty-seventh Street and Lake Shore Drive; 312–684–1414) is a longtime city favorite, with everything from a German submarine to a re-created coal mine. While the old favorites are still popular, the museum is poised for the twenty-first century, with the Crown Space Center, a state-of-the-art approach to space exploration. There's also an awe-inspiring Omnimax theater with a 76-foot screen, a newly refurbished "Curiosity Place" for kids up to age sixteen, and a Transportation Gallery, where you can engineer virtual car wrecks and view antique cars in the new "Auto Gallery." Admission is roughly $5.00 per person, less for kids; free on Thursdays. The Omnimax costs extra, even on Thursdays.

Sky Shows. Adler Planetarium (1300 South Lake Shore Drive; 312–322–0300) gives you the chance to look up at one of the planetarium's sky shows and look down at the lake as well as all around at the panoramic view of the city skyline.

Sports. Chicago is a big sports town, with the Cubs playing on the North Side at Wrigley Field (312–404–2827) and the White Sox on the South Side at Comiskey Park (312–924–1000) in the summer as well as the Bulls (312–455–4000), the Bears (708–615–2327), and the Blackhawks (312–455–7000) when the legendary Chicago winter winds blow.

Television. One of the city's most unusual—and probably most fun—museums is the Museum of Broadcast Communications in the Chicago Cultural Center (Michigan Avenue at Washington Street; 312–629–6000). Here you'll find everything from classic commercials to the infamous Nixon-Kennedy debate.

Water World. The John G. Shedd Aquarium (1200 Lake Shore Drive; 312–939–2438) has a wonderful Oceanarium, where families can watch the antics of dolphins, beluga whales, and perky penguins. Admission to the aquarium costs about $4.00 per person; free on Thursdays. Oceanarium admission costs extra every day.

Special Events

January. Skate on State
February. African-American History Celebration
　　　Navy Pier County Fair
March. Chicago Flower and Garden Show, Navy Pier
April. Chicago Latino Film Festival
May. Asian Heritage Month Celebration
　　　Cinco de Mayo, Navy Pier
　　　Viva! Chicago Latin Music Festival
June. Gospel Fest, Grant Park
　　　Blues Festival, Grant Park
　　　Taste of Chicago, Grant Park
July. Chicago Air and Water Show
August. Gold Coast Art Fair
September. Jazz Festival, Grant Park

Other Recommended Restaurants and Lodgings

Restaurants

Ambria (2300 North Lincoln Park West; 312–472–5959) is the place to go when you've won the lottery. Prices are expensive (entrees start at $21 a la carte) but worth every penny. Housed in a turn-of-the-century hotel, the restaurant is the dream of chef Gambino Satelino, who specializes in fresh seafood and changes the menu seasonally. Prix fixe dinners are available and often offer a good deal. Note: the dining room is nonsmoking only. Very expensive.

Arun's (4156 North Kedzie Avenue; 312–539–1909) is the city's top Thai restaurant, with a lavish decor and beautiful presentation that turns dishes into works of art. Specialties include stuffed noodle rolls, Thai noodles, and stuffed pork in hot pepper sauce. Closed Monday. Expensive.

Billy Goat Tavern (430 North Michigan Avenue; 312–222–1525) is famous for its role in *Saturday Night Live*'s "cheezburgah, cheezburgah" skit. The walls are papered with the articles by the city's hard-nosed journalists, who still pack this famous lower-level bar after work. Moderate.

Bistro 110 (110 East Pearson Street; 312–266–3110) is a bustling restaurant with wood-roasted meats, chicken and fish and staples such as baked onion soup, crusty baguettes, and *steak frites*. Expect waits at peak periods Moderate.

Brasserie Jo (59 West Hubbard Street; 312–595–0800) is one of the hottest restaurants to open in recent years and is run by Jean Joho, of Everest fame. The food has a number of Alsatian specialties as well as good baguettes and cheeses, affordable wines, and house-brewed beer. Try the "shrimp bag"—a phyllo purse filled with shrimp, wild mushrooms, and leeks in a lobster sauce. Moderate to expensive.

Carson's—the Place for Ribs (612 North Wells Street; 312–280–9200) helped put Chicago on the map with its chewy baby back ribs, slow cooked with a tangy, slightly sweet sauce. Moderate.

Charlie Trotter's (816 West Armitage Avenue; 312–248–6228) is one of the most unusual restaurants in the city and a must for serious food lovers. Housed in a tastefully renovated townhouse, it features food that is both appetizing and artfully arranged. Patrons order from two tasting menus for either $65 or $85 per person; each includes six to eight courses. Dinner only. Expensive.

Prairie (500 South Dearborn Street, 312–663–1143), in the Hyatt on Printer's Row, evokes the midwestern landscape in an atmosphere inspired by Chicago native Frank Lloyd Wright. Regional cuisine with fresh heartland ingredients and creative presentation is featured; try the chilled tomato soup, sturgeon with horseradish crust, or the buffalo steak in shallot sauce. Expensive.

Lodgings

Days Inn (644 North Lake Shore Drive; 312–943–9200) is the best choice when you're on a budget. It has 578 rooms and an excellent location on the lakefront within walking distance of Michigan Avenue. Rates: $95–$130 per night.

The **Drake** (140 East Walton Place; 312–787–2200) is the favorite of kings, queens, and presidents, with 535 rooms. It's famous for its turn-of-the-century charm and for its marble lobby and lavish tea rooms. Guest accommodations are equally plush, and go for $235 to $325 per night, although weekend packages are sometimes available for less. Ask for a room that faces north; they have the best views.

Ritz Carlton Chicago (160 East Pearson Street; 312–266–1000) is an elegant and understated inn with magnificent flower arrangements in the public rooms and a two-story greenhouse lobby on the twelfth floor with a fountain, wicker, and palms. The guest rooms are spacious, furnished with mahogany, armoires, and wing chairs. The dining room has a French-inspired menu and rates four Mobil stars. Water Tower Place shopping is just across the street. Rates: $155 and up per night.

Stouffer Renaissance (1 West Wacker Drive, 312–372–7200) has 553 rooms and forty suites in a hotel that evokes the ambience of the nineteenth century. It has multiple fountains, crystal chandeliers, lots of marble, and a grand staircase. Rooms can be small, but all have sitting rooms and many offer dramatic river views. Rates start at $200 per night.

For More Information

Chicago Office of Tourism, 78 East Washington Avenue, Chicago, IL 60602; (800) 487–2446.

Chicago Convention and Tourism Bureau, 2301 South Lake Shore Drive, Chicago, IL 60616; (312) 567–8500.

Ohio Escapes

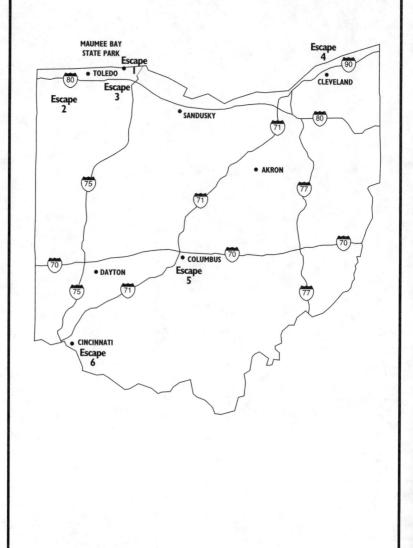

OHIO ESCAPES

MAUMEE BAY
STATE PARK

Escape
1

TOLEDO

Escape
3

Escape
2

SANDUSKY

Escape
4

CLEVELAND

AKRON

COLUMBUS

Escape
5

DAYTON

CINCINNATI

Escape
6

Maumee Bay State Park

Maumee Bay State Park is just an hour from Detroit.

Beauty by the Bay

1 NIGHT
Beaches • Birds • Winter and Water Sports

You need to get away but don't have a free full weekend until the turn of the century. Is there someplace nearby—no more than an hour away—that offers a relaxing one-day respite from the city's fast pace and frantic lifestyle? Stop looking—and start driving. Just across the Ohio border is Maumee Bay State Park, a dream of scenery and serenity on Lake Erie. It's just one of seventy-two great parks—eight with deluxe resorts—in the Buckeye State.

Ohio boasts what many consider the best park system in the country. From the sandy shores of Lake Erie to the wooded banks around the Ohio River, the 207 acres of parkland offer a wide range of activities and experiences. More than seventy million visitors pass through the parks' gates each year, making Ohio's the most used park system in the United States.

Unlike in some other states, entrance to all of Ohio's parks is free. And each park has its own distinct personality. You'll find flatlands and forests, wilderness and wildlife, waterfalls and wetlands, pristine streams and prairies as well as lakes both big and small. You can visit a working farm, see a canal lock in operation, rough it in a primitive camp, or pamper yourself in deluxe resort cabin with all the comforts of home. Along with all that scenic splendor and the welcome chance to chill out for awhile, you'll also find opportunities for dozens of outdoor adventures, including backpacking, bicycling, horseback riding, swimming, boating, canoeing, skiing (both water and cross-country), and more.

Day 1

Afternoon

Although all of the eight Ohio parks with resort-style accommodations are within driving distance for Michiganders, only Maumee Bay is within an hour's drive from Detroit. Luckily for us, it's also the most luxurious of the state's parks, with a classy Cape Cod lodge, a challenging Scottish links golf course, and cozy yet elegant cabins.

To get there, take Interstate 75 from Detroit. Along the way, you may want to stop and shop at the **Horizon Outlet Mall** (313–241–4804) in nearby Monroe, Michigan, with some three dozen stores offering discounts and deals on everything from kitchen gadgets to children's wear. Once in Toledo, follow Interstate 280 south to State Highway 2 east for 6 miles to North Curtice Road. Watch for signs from there. Try to get to the park in time to watch the sun set over Lake Erie; it's a sight you won't soon forget.

Lodging: Depending on your taste (and family size, if you've brought the kids), Maumee Bay has two options. You may choose to stay in the showpiece **Quilter Lodge** (Maumee Bay State Park; 419–836–1466), named for state Representative Barney Quilter. Overlooking Maumee Bay, it has 120 guest rooms, all with modern conveniences such as coffeemakers and blow-dryers. Lodge rooms also allow easy access to the facility's racquetball courts, game room, saunas, exercise rooms, whirlpool, indoor and outdoor pools, snack bar, and restaurants. *Tip:* Ask for a room at the end of the north wing—they're more isolated and have the best views. Loft rooms with a refrigerator are also available. High-season rates in the lodge start at $130 per night.

If you're lucky, however, you'll be able to book one of the twenty modern beach house–style cottages, known simply to park employees as "the cabins." There's nothing simple about them, however. Forget your experiences at state park cabins as a Boy or Girl Scout—these are nothing short of luxurious by those standards. Each is equipped with a gas fireplace, central heat and air-conditioning, television, telephones, even a microwave. Two- or four-bedroom units are available, all with views of either the surrounding swamp woods or the resort's golf course. Two bedrooms will accommodate six people; up to eleven friends or family members can stay in one of the four-bedroom units. Favorites include No. 16, a two-bedroom unit that sits on a picturesque pond; No. 12, a four-bedroom unit near a small peninsula; Nos. 13, 14, and 15, set against the woods, or Nos. 3, 7, 17, and 19, all opposite the golf course. Cottage guests, of course, have use of all resort facilities. Note, however, that cottages are rented by the week only from Memorial Day through Labor Day. They're available on a nightly basis the remainder of the year. High-season rates are $165 per night for the two-bedroom cabins, $225 for the four-bedroom.

Dinner: The lodge's full-service dining room has a varied menu, featuring soups, salads, steaks, lighter fare, and kid cuisine. If you're looking for something a little spicier, however, head into downtown Toledo, just a ten-minute drive away. In one of the older neighborhoods near the river you'll find **Tony Packo's** (1902 Front Street, 419–691–6054), an area institution. Native son Jamie Farr, better known as the quirky, cross-dressing Corporal Klinger on the TV series *M*A*S*H,* grew up in this neighborhood bordering the river and brought this Hungarian-style eatery to national attention when he starred on the long-running hit series in the 1970s and early 1980s. The cafe had been a local favorite for decades before it was "discovered" by the sitcom's audiences. Despite recent additions to the menu, visitors of all ages still opt for the house specialties: stuffed cabbage smothered with tomato sauce, tangy chicken paprikash, or the signature chili dog, made with sausage and Packo's famous chili. While there, don't miss the chance to peruse the hot dog buns signed by past visitors—from avant-garde musician Frank Zappa to President Bill Clinton—framed throughout the inside. Inexpensive to moderate.

Day 2

Morning

Breakfast: Linger over toast and coffee in your cottage kitchen or head for the moderately priced dining room for something heartier. You have a full day ahead of you, so be sure to fuel up.

Maumee Bay has 1,850 acres in a section of the state once known as the corn capital of the world. It was once dominated by huge coastal marshes and by area known as the Great Black Swamp, a once impenetrable barrier and one of America's most forbidding forests. These marshes once teemed with waterfowl, wildlife—even wild rice. The Black Swamp was also among the state's last strongholds for elk, bison, wolf, black bear, and mountain lion. You'll find evidence of that swampy past throughout the park, where wildlife and flora and fauna are still found in abundance.

Today's the day to enjoy all the park has to offer. Like to fish? Many anglers opt to fish from the park's sandy shore for largemouth bass, bluegill, and catfish. As a result of a connection to the bay, small walleye can also be found in Inland and Canoe lakes. If you're a hiker or horseback rider, easy trails are available off Cedar Point Road west of the park entrance. For walkers, joggers, or cyclists, a 6-mile asphalt walkway connects park facilities. There's also a 7-mile system of grass paths and two other popular trails, a 2.8-mile loop known as **Mouse Trail** (a great place to observe owls in winter) and the 1.9-mile **Boardwalk Trail**, which starts by the Nature Center and traverses both marsh and swamp forest along the way. Bikes—from toddler-size to tandem—are available at the boat rental or the lodge or you can bring your own.

Afternoon

Lunch: The **Surfside Snack Bar** near the amphitheater serves up All-American burgers, fries, and hot dogs during the summer. If it's off-season or you're not into fast food, pack a picnic lunch. The nearby city of Oregon and State Highway 2 offer plenty of places to stock up for some al fresco adventure. Picnic areas are concentrated around the beach and at the base of Big Hill. Or hike up the paved walkway to the small shelter above the amphitheater, where you'll find a small open area with a fine view of the bay.

Resist the urge to stretch out on the picnic blanket afterwards and take an afternoon siesta. There's a lot more to do after lunch. You might want to soak up some sun on the 2,000-foot beach, where guests are entertained by free performances—from solo artists to symphonies—on summer weekends. Or you might peruse the displays at **Trautman Nature Center,** where interactive displays concentrate on area nature, history, research, and wildlife. If it's winter, the park also boasts a network of cross-country trails, with skis available for rent at the lodge, as well as some breathtaking (literally!) sledding on Big Hill. Big Hill is also a great lookout point in the summer.

If you're a nature lover or bird-watcher, you won't want to miss the park's 2-mile elevated walkway. It wends its way through the freshwater marshes, punctuated by 20-foot-high scanning towers and lovely seating areas. The marshes are teeming with life, from muskrat and red fox to more than a dozen species of ducks, including mallards.

If you visit in the fall, nothing beats the tundra swan migration for sheer drama. This is Ohio's greatest expanse of coastal marsh and a favorite staging area for birds traveling south on the Great Lakes flyway. If you're really lucky, you'll be rewarded with the sight of a bald eagle nesting nearby.

If you're a golfer, **Maumee Bay Golf Course** is well worth playing. The eighteen-hole par seventy-two championship course was designed by Arthur Hill, who has attempted to re-create a Scottish course with moors, low, rolling, grass-covered mounds, bent-grass fairways, banks of sand bunkers, lots of water, and, in the true Scottish style, no trees. Tee times are available by calling the pro shop at (419) 836–9009.

Enjoy a leisurely dinner in the **Dining Room** before heading home. Or hit the road in time for a stop and an early meal at the **Toledo Museum of Art** (2445 Monroe; 419–255–8000), which has an airy and art-filled cafe that serves appetizing entrees such as Caesar salads, fresh deli sandwiches, and daily specials. Afterward, wander through the many excellent galleries. Local residents are justifiably proud of this small but choice collection, which includes works by all the big names: El Greco, Rubens, Van Gogh, Picasso, Monet, Matisse, and more. If you've brought the kids, skip the museum and top off your escape with a trip to the respected **Toledo Zoo** (419–385–5721). Located a few miles from downtown, the zoo houses more than three thousand animals representing 525 species on 51 acres. Highlights include the world's only "Hippoquarium," where you'll come nose-to-nose with a hippo, the "Diversity of Life" exhibit, winner of a Significant Achievement Award from the American Zoological Association, and the recently renovated Carnivore Cafe, once home to the zoo's primates and large cats, where *you're* the species behind bars as you nosh on hamburgers, hot dogs, and deli-style snacks.

There's More

Ohio State Park Resorts are located throughout the state. If you're looking for something more rustic and are willing to travel a little farther afield, consider one of the following seven other parks with resorts.

Burr Oak State Park Resort & Conference Center (Route 2, Box 159, Glouster, OH 45732; 614–767–2112) is northeast of Athens in the southern part of the state. Not far from picturesque Athens University, it borders part of the huge Wayne National Forest and the Sunday Creek Wildlife Area. The sixty-room Burr Oak Lodge is one of the older state park lodges, but its modern glass-and-beam construction keeps it comfortably up-to-date. The cathedral-ceilinged sitting area is a great place to relax by the fire. The park is also known for its Cardinal Dining Room, with great views and a warm country atmosphere. It's a popular eating place for local residents as well as hotel guests. All rooms have great views, but no balconies as in other state parks. There are also thirty family-style two-bedroom cabins, many of which are booked up to a year in advance, and a number of theme weekends. Rates: $80–$108 per night.

Deer Creek Resort & Conference Center (22300 State Park Road, Mt. Sterling, OH 43143; 614–869–2020) is just a thirty-minute drive from Columbus. It's the second-newest facility in the state park system, with 110 luxurious guest rooms, including lofts, king-size beds, and suites. Cradled by the main section of the lodge is an outdoor recreation area that includes a pool, shuffle-board, children's area, basketball, and practice putting green. There are also twenty-five two-bedroom cabins, an eighteen-hole championship golf course, indoor and outdoor pools, and more. For something really different, try the Harding Cabin, a rustic 1½-story cabin built in 1918 that overlooks the lake. It was built by William Daugherty, attorney general in the Harding administration, and was once used by President Warren Harding. It sleeps up to nine people in three upstairs bedrooms and also has a screened-in porch, dish-washer, and private dock. Rates: $111–$157 per night.

Hueston Woods State Park (Rural Route 1, College Corner, OH 45003; 513–523–6381) is 5 miles north of Oxford, Ohio, and north of Cincinnati. It's one of the oldest parks in the Ohio system and dates back to 1797 and Matthew Hueston, the state's first conservationist, who held the land until 1941. It has a variety of amenities, including hiking, horseback riding, a historical museum, and a wildlife rehabilitation center. The lodge is located on Acton Lake in an unusual building that was originally a council site for the Western Ohio Indian tribes. Today that theme is carried through the resort in the 110-foot-tall sandstone fireplace and ninety-four guest rooms. There are also sixty one- or two-bedroom cabins as well as an eighteen-hole golf course, sauna, hiking trails, and cross-country skiing. Rates: $104 per night.

Mohican State Park Resort & Conference Center (Rural Route 2, Perrysville, OH 44864; 419–938–5411) is in southern Ashland County, about halfway between Cleveland and Columbus. Its main focus is the Mohican, a rare "reversed stream" that was formed a as result of glacial activity twelve thousand years ago. The lodge has ninety-six guest rooms with private balcony as well as twenty-five cabins and a dining room with a sparkling lake view. There are also an Olympic-size pool, a sauna, and a charming fireplace in the round, a great place to relax with a glass of wine or cup of hot cocoa on chilly fall and winter weekends. Rates: $115–$132 per night.

Punderson Manor Resort & Conference Center (11755 Kinsman Road, Newbury, OH 44065; 216–564–9144) is just 30 miles east of Cleveland and fifteen minutes from Sea World and Geauga Lake Amusement Park. Located on one of the few natural lakes in the state, it has a charming English Tudor lodge that was completely renovated in 1982. The thirty-one rooms share an Old English decor, including some suites with fireplaces and large windows overlooking the lake. There are also an eighteen-hole golf course, twenty-six cabins perched on the south end of the lake, and an outdoor pool, tennis and basketball courts, and a popular sledding hill. Rates: $106–$138 per night.

Salt Fork Resort & Conference Center (Route 22 East, Box 7, Cambridge, OH 43725; 614–439–2751) is a pleasantly hilly surprise with great golf and wonderful wildlife viewing. It has fifty-four modern cabins along the shore of Salt Fork Lake (try No. 20, by itself on the north end of the beach) as well as the Salt Fork Lodge and Conference Center, the largest in the park system. Guests in its 148 rooms have access to a number of recreation and dining options, including pools, tennis, volleyball, indoor and outdoor shuffleboard, and exercise and playground equipment. The modern resort is softened by huge wood-beamed ceilings, stone fireplaces, and paneled guest rooms. Ask about the special rates and theme packages. Rates: $114–145 per night.

Shawnee State Park (P.O. Box 189, Friendship, OH 45630; 614–858–6621) is located in the Appalachian foothills on the banks of the meandering Ohio River and is surrounded by the 60,000–acre Shawnee State Park. It's a dramatically hilly wilderness known affectionately as "the Little Smokies of Ohio" because of the foggy haze that sometimes descends on the forest. You can enjoy the forest on foot, on horseback, with a backpack, or from a car and, afterward, stay the night at the fifty-room Shawnee Lodge or one of twenty-five two-bedroom cabins. Built in 1973, the lodge has a rustic flavor that's complemented by the Native American motif throughout. Big stone fireplaces, timber framing, and a full-size birchbark canoe enhance the setting; even the menu in the dining room is full of Shawnee lore and legends. Rates: $94–$114 per night.

For More Information

Ohio State Park Information Center, 1952 Belcher Drive, Building C–3, Columbus, OH 43224–1386; (800) 282–7275. Information on the individual parks and surrounding attractions is also available directly from each park or lodge.

Kerr House Spa

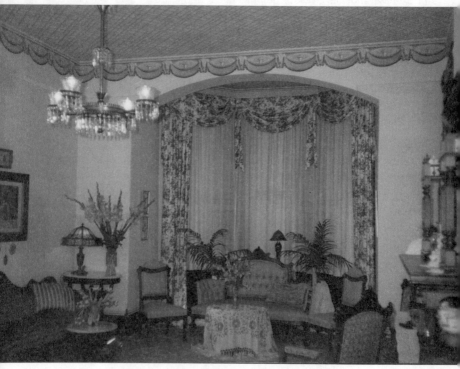

The Victorian Kerr House offers an atmosphere unmatched by any U.S. Spa.

Oasis in Ohio

_____ 2 NIGHTS _____

Health • Fitness • Pampering • Self-indulgence

It's hard to believe that a spa the quality of the Kerr House could exist just over an hour from Detroit. There is no desert sun, mineral springs, or hotshot aerobics instructors. What the Kerr House does have, however, is Laurie Hostetler. A determined dynamo, it was her dream to buy a run-down Victorian mansion in Grand Rapids, Ohio, and transform it into one of the Midwest's most exclusive health retreats.

Some say the Kerr House is the best spa in the country. It consistently ranks up there with more famous sun-filled getaways such as Canyon Ranch and the Golden Door. What makes a weekend at the Kerr House so special, however, is the personal attention each guest receives. Hostetler takes no more than eight guests at a time for a weekend full of personal pampering. This getaway is designed for adults.

Day 1

Afternoon

The Kerr House is a twenty-minute drive southwest of Toledo. To get there from Detroit, take Interstate 75 south and then Interstate 475 west; then follow U.S. Highway 24 into Grand Rapids. From Ann Arbor, take U.S. Highway 23 to Highway 24 and on into Grand Rapids.

Plan on leaving late Friday afternoon. The Kerr House requests that guests arrive between 6:30 and 7:30 P.M., so eat at home or grab something quick along the way. Just about every exit between Detroit and Grand Rapids has restaurants, if only fast-food. Later arrivals are okay too; just let the staff know in advance. You'll be tempted along the way to stop and shop in nearby Waterville and downtown Grand Rapids, both charming river towns, but save that for Sunday afternoon. There's also some free time for wandering on Saturday.

Whenever you arrive, you'll be given a warm welcome from Hostetler and her staff, who will show you to your room. All rooms are spacious and decorated, like the house, in a high Victorian style. Filled with antiques and items from Laurie's vast collections, they manage to be both elegant yet cozy, with imposing wooden beds covered with crisp cotton sheets and homey quilts. After a chance to relax, guests are invited downstairs to meet other guests, some of whom come from as far away as Australia and Saudi Arabia, says Hostetler. The majority, however, are from the United States, with a number from Detroit, Chicago, and the East Coast.

Friday night is casual. You can relax in your room and recover from the drive or enjoy the whirlpool and sauna in the whitewashed basement. Everything is flexible, but recommended lights-out time is 11:00 P.M. Bring a good book if you're a night owl; there is no television.

Day 2

Morning

Breakfast: If you've never been served breakfast in bed, you're in for a treat. Anywhere from 7:30 to 8:30 A.M. (depending on the number of guests and the day's schedule), a gentle knock rouses you before a staff member enters with a tray full of homemade granola, fresh fruit, juice, and (if you want it) coffee or tea (Hostetler insists that while she will try to teach you healthy habits during your stay, she's not a fanatic).

After breakfast, a full day of pampering awaits. During the day you'll enjoy three "treatments"—generally an herbal wrap, a one-hour massage, and a finger facial. In between sessions (all are given in the treatment rooms in the house's former basement, now a whitewashed space full of chintz and wicker), guests are encouraged to use the whirlpool or sauna. Two of the treatments precede lunch.

Afternoon

Lunch: Served in the cheerful basement cafe, lunch consists of healthy yet satisfying vegetable soup and a crunchy salad made from Amish-grown chicken, celery, nuts, and Dijon mustard. While you may come expecting only carrot sticks, food here is surprisingly flavorful and ample. Hostetler makes a point of telling you that it's more important that you relax during the weekend than reform. That means that if you really want a pizza from the in-town pizzeria during your stay, she'll deliver.

There's a third treatment after lunch, then guests are free to relax, nap, read, or wander into Grand Rapids's one-block downtown, just a block from the Kerr House. First settled in 1833, the town is perched on the scenic banks of the Maumee River and is full of shops that carry antiques and collectibles. Highlights include the **Olde Gilead Country Store** (419–832–7651), a one-hundred-year-old mercantile with a sophisticated mix of gifts, books, toys, and more than one hundred varieties of old-fashioned candy; **Angelwood Gallery** (419–832–0625), a recent addition to the townscape, with abstract and avant-garde works by local artists, and **Nan-tiques** (419–832–0124) full of collectible dolls and gifts for the young and young at heart. If you're feeling deprived, there's also an old-fashioned ice-cream parlor.

Downtown is small, so there's plenty of time to explore and still be back in time for the 4:00 P.M. yoga class in the house's renovated attic, now an airy, light-filled exercise studio. Don't miss the framed blueprints of the house that line the walls—a lucky find during renovation.

Another thing that sets the Kerr House apart from other, more regimental, spas is its attitude toward exercise. You won't be bombarded with strenuous step classes or power aerobics. In fact, on weekends, you'll attend just two classes, both of them yoga—and even those are optional. The first is a two-hour beginning class. During the class, Hostetler teaches breathing, philosophy, and proper movement—you'll be surprisingly winded afterward. She also gives fascinating demonstrations of the mind-body connection that'll be enough to turn you off French fries forever—or at least for a few weeks, anyway. The second class comes tomorrow.

Dinner: Served in the elegant, high-ceilinged dining room, dinner is a more formal affair, served with silver and glowing candlesticks and accompanied by a harpist. An appetizer of meatless minestrone soup is followed by an Amish chicken breast, crunchy brown rice pilaf, and freshly steamed broccoli. Dessert is a fabulous frozen whipped banana that tastes remarkably like ice cream, topped with plump raspberries and blueberries. Afterward, teas (herbal or otherwise) are served in the parlor, where guests can chat and further enjoy the elegant strains of the harp.

Day 3

Morning

Breakfast: Breakfast in bed again? After a few days of being waited on, you'll find it hard to go back to the bagel-and-coffee-on-the-run way of life. Today breakfast is yogurt and bananas topped with chewy granola, sliced apples, juice, and (because I'm a wimp) coffee.

So fortified, it's time for your second yoga class. This one is just an hour and contains more of the same from the day before as well as more discussion of nutrition, body performance, and Hostetler's general philosophy of health and life. Depending on how much you want to learn (or reform), Hostetler also sells related books in the small basement gift shop.

Time is quickly running out. After class, it's time to don the white robe again and head to the basement for (sigh), one last full-body massage. Afterward, there's time to soak in the hot tub or heat up in the sauna before joining Hostetler and the other guests for a farewell lunch in the cafe.

Afternoon

Lunch: After eating here for a few days, you'll be requesting Hostetler's recipes. She's working on a book but is happy to share her secrets with interested guests in the meantime. Sunday lunch includes a tasty couscous with chopped-up vegetables and a creamy veggie-based soup. Most guests leave after lunch (if you're flying here, the limo will pick you up and take you back to the airport), although there is no set checkout time. Either way, you'll want to say good-bye to the staff and your newfound friends and promise to keep in touch.

There's More

Antiques. Waterville, Ohio, is a charming community about 10 miles from Grand Rapids with a couple of good antiques malls. In Grand Rapids, there's also the Warehouse (Mill Street next to the Bluebird Train; 419–832–0397), which houses fifty dealers.

Canals. The Maumee River is very scenic and a great place for a stroll. The Isaac Ludwig Mill (419–832–8934) on Highway 24 gives you an idea of a working mill, with free tours Wednesday through Sunday as well as Sunday afternoon milling demonstrations.

Train. On weekends in season, the Bluebird takes passengers on scenic routes from Grand Rapids through the surrounding countryside. For tickets and schedules, call (419) 878–2177.

Special Events

You may want to time your visit to coincide with one of the Grand Rapids area events and enjoy it during or after your Kerr House stay.

April. Spring Fling
May. Colonial Lost Arts Festival
July. Rapids Rally Days
August. Community Garage Sale
September. Canal Days
October. Applebutter Fest
November. Christmas Open House

For More Information

Rates at the Kerr House range from $575 for a weekend to more than $2,000 for a weeklong stay. For more information, contact the Kerr House, P.O. Box 363, 1777 Beaver Street, Grand Rapids, OH 43522; (419) 832–1733.

Cedar Point

Soak City at Cedar Point invites plenty of wet and wild fun.

Family Fun

1 NIGHT

Roller Coasters • Rides • Water Park • Historic Hotel

When I was a kid, summer didn't start until the day we went to Cedar Point. Thirty years later, the annual trek to this amusement park west of Detroit is still one of the highlights of my summer, although more now because of my children's excitement than my own. The weather is barely above fifty degrees when they start badgering me about setting a date. And they don't let up until we're in the car and heading east.

Now in its 125th year, Cedar Point has changed since the days when its biggest attraction was a dance hall. Today it's best known for its eleven scream machines, including the 205-foot-tall Magnum XL-200, the soaring Raptor, the wicked 13-story Demon Drop, the new Mantis, and fifty-six more down-to-earth rides spread out over more than 364 acres.

Although much larger than it was when I was a child, the park still holds much of what drew us all those years ago—snow cones, sun, and fun. If you're not the type for roller coasters, there are many options to being spun, twisted, dropped, or turned upside down. Check out the IMAX film in the cinema. Come nose-to-nose with performing sea creatures at the Oceana Stadium. Wander the Lake Erie beach and boardwalk. Dance to live stage shows. Record your kids' fleeting childhoods with a $10 crayon sketch.

While many metro Detroiters choose to make this a one-day pilgrimage (exhausing for both parents and offspring), smart families stay over at least one night, which lets you add the watery fun of the adjacent Soak City and maybe some of the family-style attractions in nearby Sandusky. Either way, adding time to your trip means you can pack as much pleasure as possible into a visit to the park and make the trip a mini-vacation for the whole family. A tip: The park is less crowded early and late in the season. Plan on visiting anytime in June or late August and September if you tend toward claustrophobia.

Day 1

Morning

Rise at the crack of dawn so you can get there when the park opens at 10:00 A.M. Cedar Point is about two and one-half hours from Detroit. To get there, take Interstate 75 south to State Highway 2 and then continue straight east to Cedar Point. Highway 2 skirts Lake Erie and although it's just two lanes, is much more scenic than the anonymous Ohio Turnpike (it also generally has less construction). If your brood gets hungry once you're on the road, there are a number of fast-food restaurants along Highway 2 in Oregon, just outside Toledo. We usually stop at the McDonald's on Alexis Road just inside the Ohio border.

From Oregon you can't miss the signs to Cedar Point. You'll pass lots of restaurants and budget-level hotels in Sandusky, all good options if you're just looking for a place to sleep after a busy day. The Sandusky Visitors Bureau can supply you with a guide that lists the hotels if you opt not to stay within the park.

If you've got preschoolers, your first stop at Cedar Point will be the **Kiddy Kingdom** just past Main Street. With seventeen miniature rides, including a small-scale roller coaster, bumper boats, and drive-it-yourself four-by-four trucks that look just like the grown-up models, the kids will think they're in heaven. If that's not enough, there's barnyard fun at the petting farm; the popular Berenstain Bear Country with tree houses, sand boxes, miniature train rides, and other themed fun; and an area with ball crawls, ropes, slides, and other playground favorites.

Afternoon

Lunch: If you're smart, you'll pack a picnic lunch from home rather than buy the ubiquitous (and expensive) burgers, pizza, and chicken nuggets sold at stands throughout the park. (One exception is the French fries sold at a stand near the aquarium. They're good and greasy and best eaten smothered in malt vinegar.) An area near the park entrance has lots of tables on which to stow your stuff—most families leave their coolers covered in blankets while they explore the park and return throughout the day for breaks. You may also choose to bring something to tide the gang over until a late dinner so you can plan on eating outside the park grounds.

Dinner: The nicest restaurant in the Cedar Point complex is the **Breakwater Cafe** at Sandcastle Suites (419–627–2107). This popular eatery on the northern tip of the peninsula serves breakfast, lunch, and dinner—all with breathtaking views. The cafe's cocktail lounge and patio are choice locations to view Lake Erie pleasure boats and the evening sun setting across Sandusky Bay. Moderate.

Lodging: If you're just staying one night or if money's no object, splurge with a stay at the historic **Breakers Hotel** (419–627–2106). The 1905 hotel underwent a $10 million facelift in 1995, adding 206 new units to this resort that once housed luminaries such as Abbott and Costello, Annie Oakley, and six U.S. presidents. With a sandy Lake Erie beach, two outdoor pools, whirlpools, and on-site restaurants, it's an elegant and convenient location. It also offers easy access to the adjacent park, so you can come and go as you please throughout the day or be the first ones at the park each morning. Rates: $90 to $260 per night.

The park also operates the new **Sandcastle Suites** (419–627–2107), which sit on a beach at the very tip of the Cedar Point peninsula facing Sandusky Bay and Lake Erie. Rates: $115–$265 per night. Both the Breakers and the Sandcastle Suites hotels offer getaway packages, which include discounted rates on accommodations as well as admission to the park, meals, and more.

Day 2

Morning

Breakfast: Fuel up for another fast–paced day with breakfast in one of the Breakers restaurants. Head back to the park if you missed some of the rides or if lines were too long the first day. Otherwise, plan on spending the second day enjoying the wet and wild fun at the adjacent **Soak City Water Park**.

Soak City was added to the park in the late 1980s, partly as a way of keeping families at Cedar Point longer. It was recently doubled in size, with three new rides, including a gigantic, high-action water slide, featuring six-person rafts, an inner-tube river adventure, and two new playgrounds. (Note: The two parks charge separate admission).

Afternoon

Lunch: Head back to the hotel or grab something to tide you over at one of the concessions inside Soak City. Spend the afternoon in Soak City or in the adjacent **Challenge Park,** where you can live out your fantasies of being a race car driver as you speed your go-kart to victory on the Grand Prix Raceway, tee off on two 18-hole miniature golf courses, or even experience the new RipCord, a bungee-jumping-like activity where you'll fall 150 feet and swoop through the air like a bird—all while safely anchored to a support structure, of course.

Dinner: **Perkins Family Restaurant and Bakery** (1530 Cleveland Road, Sandusky; 419–625–9234) is just outside the park grounds in the Best Western hotel. It's a family-style national chain but doesn't taste like a chain, with an on-site bakery, tasty sandwiches, salads for grown-ups, and an extensive kids' menu. Inexpensive.

There's More

Animals. Nearby Sandusky is also home to **Lagoon Deer Park** (off U.S. Highway 269; 419–684–5701), open mid-April through mid-October. Here your family can get up close and personal with more than 250 animals from Europe, Asia, and North and South America. Hand-feed hundreds of deer and other tame species, feed fish, or cast your line in stocked lagoons and fishing lakes. Don't miss the famous "Dancing Chicken." There's also an attractive picnic area.

Carousels. The old-fashioned merry-go-round may seem a little tame after a day at Cedar Point, but it has a nostalgic charm that's perennially appealing—especially to toddlers and smaller children who may be a bit overwhelmed by Cedar Point's crowds and pace. The **Merry-Go-Round Museum** (Sandusky; 419–626–6111) lets you relive the glory days of the carousel and other classic Americana with a tour of the museum, housed in the city's former 1920s post office. Highlights include a working Allen Herschel carousel from the 1930s (a free ride is given as part of the tour), a small turn-of-the-century English carousel, and a great gift shop that carries virtually every known carousel-related souvenir. There's also a charming full-time carver-restorer on the premises.

Caves. Not far from Sandusky is Bellevue, where you can visit **Seneca Caverns** (Highway 269; 419–483–6711). This 110-foot-deep cave—technically considered an earth crack—was discovered in 1872 by two boys hunting rabbits; it opened to the public in 1933. Today's visitors descend steps 110 feet underground through seven levels on hourlong tours. The cavern is fairly rugged—kids love it—and is one of the few in the country kept in its original natural condition. Don't leave without panning for gems at the Sandy Creek Gem Mining.

Cruises. Sandusky is also home to a number of companies that offer day cruises in and around the Lake Erie Islands. Many offer meals as part of the package. The *Emerald Empress* (800–876–1907) is a 150-foot, three-deck cruise ship that accommodates up to six hundred people on twelve different itineraries. "Lazy Day" cruises head for Put-In-Bay and Kelley's Island, with continental breakfast and lunch en route. Lunch and dinner cruises include a one-and-one-half-hour sight-seeing cruise around the islands and Sandusky Bay and feature an on-board buffet. "Saturday Prime-Time" cruises include a hand-carved prime rib dinner and a dance band. There are also Sunday brunch cruises and "Lakebreak" sight-seeing cruises. Prices range from $5.25 to $29.95 per person. Popular island cruises are also offered on the **MV *City of Sandusky,*** (800–426–6286), docked at the foot of Columbus Avenue downtown, and the *Goodtime I* (800–446–3140), docked at Jackson Street Pier. Both include full bar service, dance floor, and snack bar.

Inventions. About 13 miles south of Sandusky is **Thomas Edison's Birthplace** (419–499–2135). Would-be inventors find the simple seven-room, $2^1/_2$-story home built in 1841 fascinating. The inventor of the phonograph and the lightbulb lived here from the time he was born in 1847 until he was seven years old, when the family moved to Port Huron, Michigan. Today the museum is still run by his great-grandson and furnished with many original family pieces. Don't miss the room honoring his many inventions, including phonographs, lightbulbs, and models of his movie studio and Menlo Park laboratory. The adjacent Milan Historical Museum has old-fashioned dolls and glassware, a blacksmith's shop, and a vintage general store.

Toft's Dairy. A must-stop on any visit to Sandusky, this local dairy (3717 Venice Road; 419–625–4376) has been serving up creamy confections since 1900, when it was founded as a small farm with a respected herd of dairy cattle. Since then it's moved three times and is the only locally owned and operated dairy on Lake Erie between Lorain and Toledo. Tours are offered daily. Afterward, sample favorite ice-cream flavors such as butter pecan and vanilla or newer additions such as Moose Tracks and Mother Lode, full of chocolate and caramel (kids may prefer the chewy Dinosaur Crunch).

Special Events

April. Spring Bounty of Arts, Crafts, and Collectibles, Vermilion
June. Free Fishing Days, Lake Erie
    Festival of the Fish, Vermilion
July. Arts and Crafts Show, Sandusky
October. Woolybear Festival, Vermilion
November. Santa's Arrival, Sandusky

Other Recommended Restaurants and Lodgings

There is no dearth of family-friendly restaurants and lodgings around the park, from bare-bones basic to top-of-the-line top-dollar. Restaurant highlights include T.G.I. Friday's, McDonalds, and other classic family favorites; lodging includes **Holiday Inn–Sandusky/Cedar Point** (5513 Milan Road; 419–626–6671), **Comfort Inn–Sandusky** (5909 Milan Road, 419–621–0200), **Ramada Inn–Sandusky** (5608 Milan Road, 419–626–9890), and other dependable—if predictable—chain hotels. There are also a number of hotels and bed and breakfasts in nearby downtown Sandusky. For information, contact the Sandusky Area Chamber of Commerce at 231 West Washington Row, Sandusky, OH 44870; (800) 255–3743.

For More Information

Cedar Point Amusement Park & Resort, P.O. Box 5006, Sandusky, OH 44871–5006; (419) 626–0830.

Cleveland

The Cleveland Museum of Art is one of the country's top museums.

Renaissance in the Rust Belt

2 NIGHTS
Theater • Restaurants • Rock and Roll Museum • Nightlife

Ohio's second-largest city, once jokingly referred to as "the mistake by the lake," is having the last laugh these days. Urban pioneers and envious city officials around the country—and especially in Detroit—are pointing to Cleveland as the comeback city of the century.

Today the city is a sophisticated midwestern metropolis and a fascinating family destination. Despite an admitted industrial bent, you'll find more than 19,000 acres of parkland and 90 miles of scenic Lake Erie shoreline, one of the country's finest art museums, and a renowned group of professional theaters for drama enthusiasts of all ages.

Clevelanders are proud of their city—a five-time recipient of the prestigious All-American City award. And they know how to have a good time—1996 was the city's two-hundredth birthday, and the entire population got into the swing with fireworks, parties, special events, even a giant traveling birthday card donated by American Greetings. Whenever you visit, however, you'll find a spirit of celebration that characterizes the new Cleveland.

Day 1

Afternoon

Cleveland is about a two-and-one-half-hour drive from Detroit. You can take Interstate 75 to the Ohio Turnpike or take the more scenic State Highway 2 east. Either way, plan on arriving in town in time to relax over dinner and a little nightlife. Few areas of the city are as lively as **"The Flats,"** a renovated area located not far along the Cleveland Memorial Shoreway. Once the home of hundreds of heavy industries, the Flats is now the city's premier entertainment district. An interesting mix of converted warehouses dots the east and west banks of the area where the Cuyahoga River meets Lake Erie.

Here you'll find the popular **Nautica Entertainment Complex,** which covers some 28 acres on the river's west bank and includes an amphitheater, a riverfront boardwalk, and a floating restaurant. Anchored by two dramatic jackknife bridges, the complex has attracted millions of people since it opened in 1987.

Dinner: If you've brought the kids, check out downtown's **Spaghetti Warehouse** (1231 Main Avenue; 216–621–9420), where you can pig out on pasta and even dine in a trolley car. If you were hoping for something a little less predictable, try **Watermark** (1250 Old River Road; 216–241–1600). It has what many consider the best seafood in town as well as riverfront patio dining in the summer. Moderate.

Afterward, consider a nightcap and some jazz at **Sammy's in the Flats** (1400 West Tenth Street; 216–523–5560) or a rousing sing-along at the rollicking **Howl at the Moon Saloon** (2000 Sycamore Street; 216–771–4695). Dueling baby grands and TV theme songs make this a popular spot.

Lodging:

The **Wyndham Cleveland Hotel** (1260 Euclid Avenue; 216–615–7500) was built in 1995 and is the city's newest hotel. Centrally located, the 205-room upscale hotel cost $28 million to build and is just steps away from the city's theater district. The spacious rooms all sport cable TV, voice mail, coffeemaker, and ironing board. Because of the hotel's proximity to the theater district, the hotel was voted "The Place Most Likely to See Stars" by *Cleveland*

Magazine. For a special treat, ask for one of the circular corner rooms, which feature a king-size bed and six floor-to-ceiling windows that overlook the theaters below. **Winsor's,** the hotel's restaurant, has a clubby, theater motif and is named after Winsor French, a popular 1920s gossip columnist. Rates: $109–$179 per night.

Day 2

Morning

Breakfast: A great place for an impromptu and always fresh breakfast is the historic **West Side Market** located at West Twenty-fifth Street and Lorain Avenue in the neighborhood known as Ohio City. Duck inside the door of this vintage 1912 Old World–style market, one of the largest and last in the United States, and you'll be overwhelmed by the smells of fresh baked goods, exotic meats and cheeses, and more. Some one hundred indoor and outdoor merchants from a variety of ethnic groups serve up anything you desire in a friendly, carnival-like setting. Inexpensive.

Set aside the rest of the day for exploring downtown. Getting around is easy; most attractions are clumped together. Two good examples are the University Circle area and the North Harbor Coast. To get a better idea of what you can skip and what you won't want to miss, consider a swing around town on **Lolly the Trolley** (216–771–4484 for tickets and information). The bright red trolleys cover 20 miles and more than one hundred attractions.

If you'd rather go by sea (or, in this case, by lake), stow away on board the one-thousand-passenger *Goodtime III* (216–861–5110). The city's largest charter boat offers sight-seeing and entertainment cruises along the Cuyahoga and Lake Erie from May through October. The *Nautica Queen* (216–696–8888) also offers cruising and dining on its three-hundred- to four-hundred-passenger ships during warm-weather months.

Other would-be sailors head to the *William G. Mather* (216–574–6262), a restored steamship that was originally christened in 1925. The former flagship of the Cleveland Cliffs Iron Company is docked at downtown's East Ninth Street pier and is now a floating discovery center. At 618 feet, it was built in 1925 to carry ore, coal, and grain throughout the Great Lakes but now houses exhibits and displays that focus on the history and lore of these "iron boats." Visitors are escorted through the pilothouse, the crew and guest quarters, and the galley as well as the guests' and officers' dining room. Tours are offered daily from June through August and on weekends in May, September, and October. The ship was also the first landmark to open in the city's hot new "North Coast" district.

The *Mather* may have been the first, but it's certainly not the last, of the North Coast notables. The city's—some say even the country's—hottest ticket is the new, $92-million **Rock and Roll Hall of Fame and Museum** (1 Key Plaza; 216–781–7625). Put on your dancin' shoes and prepare to be swept off

your feet by the stunning design and the toe-tapping tunes. I. M. Pei's controversial creation is a dramatic structure that includes a 165–foot tower rising
from the water and a variety of geometric shapes exploding from the tower
along with a shimmering, 7-story triangular glass tent. Pei, best known for his
contemporary glass pyramid addition to the historic Louvre museum in Paris,
wanted to "echo the energy of rock and roll" when he designed the museum.
Opened in 1995, it houses 150,000 square feet of interactive exhibits, performance spaces, special programs, and displays and attracted more than a million visitors in its first year of operation.

City leaders claimed that Cleveland was the most appropriate site for the
new hall of fame since legendary disc jockey Alan Freed reportedly coined the
phrase *rock and roll* here during a 1951 broadcast. In the museum the orga-
nizers hope to tell the story of rock and roll from its roots in country, blues,
rhythm and blues, and jazz to the latest forms of hip-hop and rap. Among the
more than four thousand artifacts in the collection are Elvis Presley's black
leather outfit worn in his 1968 TV special; John Lennon's "Sgt. Pepper's Lonely
Hearts Club Band" uniform; handwritten lyrics by Chuck Berry and Jimmy
Hendrix, even Roy Orbison's sunglasses and Jim Morrison's Cub Scout uniform. Other exhibits let you "host" a "live" radio broadcast and explore the
recording booths where hit songs were made.

Lunch: If all that excitement and energy makes you hungry (or tired!), take
a break at the cafe on the museum's third floor. The menu changes monthly
but always includes sandwiches, salads, and a daily hot entree special. There
are also beer, wine, and gourmet coffee. Moderate.

Just steps away from the Rock and Roll Hall of Fame is the new $54.9 mil-
lion, 165,000-square-foot **Great Lakes Science Center** (601 Erieside Avenue;
216–694–2000). It opened in late 1996 and quickly earned a reputation as one
of the most innovative science centers in the world.

Designed to provide a comprehensive learning center, it features 50,000
square feet of exciting hands-on exhibits that encourage visitors of all ages to
learn and have fun. Features include a 20,000-square-foot gallery devoted to
traveling and seasonal exhibits; a huge, 320-seat Omnimax theater, and another
sure-hit: a riveting replica of the NASA mission control station in Houston.

From the North Coast, head back into the heart of the city's downtown.
Once a joke, Cleveland's downtown has made a startling comeback, with new
shopping, sports, and entertainment complexes. In the heart of it all is Public
Square, where the **Terminal Tower** (216–621–7981) rises fifty-two stories
above the city streets. The lower level, once a train depot, was renovated in
1989 into an upscale shopping mecca known as "The Avenue." It now houses
more than 120 shops, restaurants, and entertainment options. Don't leave the
Terminal Tower without stopping in at the beautifully restored **Stouffer Renaissance Hotel**, one of the city's finest. It's also the site of **Sans Souci**
(216–696–5600), an intimate restaurant that's always a good bet. It features
hearty country fare from the Provence region of France; delicious but expen-

sive. A forty-second floor observation deck in the hotel offers a spectacular view of downtown and the Lake Erie waterfront.

Dinner: Linger at Sans Souci or grab at early bite at **Parker's** (2801 Bridge Avenue, 216–771–7130). It's considered one of the best restaurants in the city and is Cleveland's only Mobil four-star restaurant. It's located in the recently resuscitated Ohio City neighborhood, about a five-minute ride from downtown. Pleasant and unpretentious, it features excellent Country French cuisine and an equally fine wine list. Try the five-course prix fixe menu, a bargain at about $40 per person. Moderate to expensive. Reservations recommended.

Afterward, take in a performance at one of the city's restored theaters. Cleveland is considered Broadway's home away from home, with many major shows either debuting or coproduced here. Recent productions have included *Phantom of the Opera, Grease,* and the family favorite *The Nutcracker.*

The cornerstone of Cleveland theater is **Playhouse Square** (1501 Euclid Avenue; 216–771–4444), now the third-largest performing arts center in the country. With more than seven thousand seats and nearly a million annual patrons, Playhouse Square boasts four renovated theaters, all of which are worth visiting for a tour even if nothing's on stage. The spectacular Ohio, State, Palace, and Allen theaters were all originally built in the 1920s as vaudeville palaces. They were converted in the 1950s into movie houses and fell into disrepair in the 1960s. After a long fund-raising drive, they became home to five resident companies, including the **Cleveland Opera**, the **Cleveland Ballet**, the **Ohio Ballet**, **Dance Cleveland,** and the **Great Lakes Theater Festival**. The Great Lakes Theater Festival was founded in 1961 to preserve classic theater and is one of only a few companies left in the United States that is dedicated to this art form.

If you're more into the roar of the crowds than the smell of the greasepaint, Cleveland is also a great sports town. Those traitor Browns may have moved to Baltimore, but there's plenty of all-star action left. From the excitement of a buzzer shot at a Cavs basketball game to the frigid frenzy of a Lumberjacks hockey game, Cleveland offers enough thrills to satisfy sportaholics of any age.

Catch an Indians major-league baseball game at the new **Jacobs Field** in the heart of downtown. This state-of-the-art facility holds forty-two thousand screaming fans who come to experience the thrills of America's favorite pastime while enjoying spectacular views of the field and skyline and the largest freestanding scoreboard in North America.

Jacobs Field is part of the city's world-class sports and entertainment complex that opened in 1994. The new **Gateway Sports Entertainment Complex** cost $362 million to build and is located on the site of the city's Old Central Market. It has gained international acclaim for the visionary design of its two arenas—the aforementioned $161-million Jacobs Field and a $118-million, twenty-thousand-seat indoor arena, home of the Cleveland Cavaliers NBA basketball team, the Lumberjacks hockey team, and the

Thunderbolts arena football team as well as concerts and special events. Young fans love the on-site Kidsland, with a retail store, children-only concessions, and a restaurant with an eagle-eye's view of the playing field.

The ballpark is a mere five–minute stroll from most downtown hotels and is connected by a walkway to Tower City Center. With panoramic views of the skyline, a restaurant that looks out over the playing field, food courts, tempting team gift shops, and a colorful collection of public art by noted regional artists, Gateway is sure to score with fans.

Day 3

Morning

Breakfast: It's Sunday, so plan on indulging yourself with brunch at the **Ritz Carlton Cleveland** (1515 West Third Street; 216–623–1300). The hotel's Riverview Room is an elegantly paneled oasis that overlooks the Flats. Its brunch includes both breakfast and lunch specialties, including waffles, eggs, smoked seafood, cheeses of all kinds, pastas, veggies, a carving station, and a delectable dessert bar. It's $32 per adult; $16 per child.

While the city has been historically known for its grimy industrial image, it's also long been a strong supporter of the arts. The majority of its cultural attractions are grouped in the **University Circle Area.** Just 4 miles east of downtown, it features the country's largest concentration of arts and cultural institutions—more than a half dozen in all. All are within easy walking distance of each other and situated in a relaxing, parklike setting.

Your first stop is the respected **Cleveland Museum of Art** (11150 East Boulevard, 216–421–7340). With more than thirty thousand works of art spanning some five thousand years, there's definitely something to suit every taste. The museum was founded by a group of civic–minded philanthropists "for the benefit of the people forever" and opened in 1916. True to the spirit of its founders, admission is always free—one of the few museums across the country to remain so.

Highlights of the collection include the ominous-looking swords, daggers, suits of armor, and other weapons of war (a favorite of young museumgoers), the exotic Egyptian galleries, with a rare statue of pharaoh Amenemhet III, a stunning collection of medieval art (including the famous golden Guelph Treasure), Old Master works from the thirteenth through the eighteenth centuries, and more modern masterpieces by David, Delacroix, Gauguin, Van Gogh, and Picasso. The surrounding 15–acre park has an outdoor sculpture court that's open to diners in season. There's also an indoor cafe when your feet and eyes get tired.

Afternoon

Lunch: You've feasted your senses, now treat your stomach at the museum's restaurant. It offers hearty fare that includes soups, sandwiches, hot entrees, and more. Inexpensive to moderate.

More into dinosaurs than Dali? The nearby **Cleveland Museum of Natural History** (1 Wade Oval Drive; 216–231–4600) is the state's largest natural science museum. Regarded as one of the finest in North America, the museum is located in a modern, 200,000-square-foot facility and draws some four-hundred thousand visitors annually.

Many come to see the Foucault Pendulum in the main lobby, which demonstrates the rotation of the earth. It's the world's only pendulum in which the electromagnet that keeps the 270-pound plumb bob moving is placed underneath rather than mounted on top. Rock hounds of all ages appreciate the Gem Room, with an impressive collection of quartz crystals, opals, and diamonds in a rainbow of colors. The Barney set loves the dinosaurs and other prehistoric creatures as well as the birds, botany, and geology displays and the fascinating Hall of Man, home to "Lucy," the three-million-year-old skeleton of the oldest known human being. You can also see stars in the state's oldest planetarium, come nose-to-nose with native animals and wildlife in an outdoor environmental courtyard and rustic wood garden, or browse in the well-stocked gift shop, cleverly named the "Ark in the Park." Admission is free on Tuesdays and Thursday afternoons; at other times it costs $6.00 for adults and $4.00 for young people ages five through seventeen. Children age four or younger always get in free.

More recent history can be found at the **Western Reserve Historical Society** (10825 East Boulevard; 216–721–5722), the city's oldest cultural institution. It was founded in 1867 to preserve and promote the area's rich heritage. Think you're a pack rat? You'll be amazed by the diverse collections here. Baseball, roller coasters, classic cars, bowling machines, airplanes, full-size log cabins, and more are crammed into this huge and fascinating space. Browse among the costumes, farming tools, manuscripts, and period rooms that recreate the area known as the Western Reserve from the pre–Revolutionary War era through the early twentieth century.

Centerpiece of the museum is the Hay-McKinney Mansion, built in 1911 and designed by the son of President James Garfield. The ornate Italian Florentine villa is filled with important period furniture and decorative arts and was once part of the city's "Millionaire's Row" that stretched along part of Euclid Avenue (the mayor's home located here even boasted an indoor ice–skating rink). Tours take you "downstairs" to the servants' quarters for a starkly different perspective of nineteenth-century life.

Car buffs of all ages flock to the society's **Crawford Auto–Aviation Museum**, which houses more than 150 streamlined, vintage, and classic automobiles and aircraft, including a rare collection of Cleveland-built cars. It's considered one of the finest collections in the nation. Clotheshorses get equal time at the Chisholme Halle Costume Wing, where they can stroll down a street of re-created turn-of-the-century shops and imagine themselves dressed in nineteenth-century finery.

Two other small museums in University Circle are worth mentioning—and visiting. "Please touch" could be the motto of the innovative **Cleveland Children's Museum** (10730 Euclid Avenue; 216–791–5437). More like an activity center than a museum, it houses more than one hundred displays that the whole gang will enjoy. Get wet—or at least learn about the properties of water in "Water, Water Everywhere," which explores the mysteries of water and its cycles as kids pour and pump, carve riverbanks, work waterwheels, and enjoy racing a boat down a replica of Lake Erie. Prefer heights? You can enter a deep forest to check out "Tales in Tall Trees," let your little hands work child-size bridges in the "Over and Under Bridges" area, or help them create a self-portrait in the "People Puzzle" area.

Looking for something really different? Check out the **Cleveland Health Museum** (8911 Euclid Avenue; 216–231–5010). This fascinating, 40,000-square foot museum is the first of its kind in the United States. More than two hundred permanent exhibits include Juno, the talking transparent woman; the world's largest tooth, which towers above your head at 18 feet; the family discovery center; and the theaters of Hearing, Sight, and Social Concerns. If you have kids and you've never been able to address the issue of the birds and the bees, check out the "Wonder of New Life" section, which tells the story of reproduction in an easy-to-understand cartoon style.

If you've brought the kids, let them stretch their legs a bit more before getting back in the car with a visit to the **RainForest at the Cleveland Metroparks Zoo** (3900 Brookside Park Drive; 216–661–6500). Just 5 miles south of downtown, it houses more than three thousand animals. The Rain-Forest is the big draw, however, with a simulated biosphere that features a two-story hydroponics plant wall, a 25-foot water curtain, and a tropical thunderstorm, complete with simulated lightning and melodic rain. After eight years of planning and nearly $30 million in expenses, the tropical netherworld opened in 1992.

There's More

Amish Community. Ohio has the largest Amish population in the world. About thirty-five thousand of these "plain people" live in the northeast part of the state, mostly in Holmes, Wayne, and Tuscarawas counties. The region is known for its working Amish farms, down–home restaurants, and country crafts. For more information on the area, call (800) 362–6474.

Amusements. Geauga Lake (1060 North Aurora Road, Aurora; 800–843–9283) is a classic summer park with one hundred wet and dry attractions as well as a new junior admission price that lets kids under 48 inches tall in for just $5.95. Located adjacent to SeaWorld (see "Wildlife" section below).

Fishing. Wave Walker Sport Fishing Charters (216–641–2549) offers anglers the chance to fish for trophy-size walleye and steelhead trout from downtown Cleveland.

Parasailing. Want to parasail over Lake Erie? Great Lakes Parasailing (3311 West 122nd Street, 216–771–4386) gives you the chance to try Lake Erie's only skyride. Open May through September only.

Skiing. Boston Mills/Brandywine Ski Resorts (7100 Riverview Road, Peninsula; 216–467–2242) operate seven slopes with six chairlifts and two surface tows, as well as a popular beginners' program.

Trees. The Holden Arboretum (9500 Sperry Road; Kirtland; 216–946–4400), east of Cleveland in Kirtland, is the United States's largest, with more than 3,000 acres of natural woodlands, horticultural collections, display gardens, walking trails, and open fields. Open year-round.

Wildlife. One of the top attractions in the Cleveland area is SeaWorld of Ohio (1100 SeaWorld Drive, Aurora; 800–637–4268), a wildlife-centered water park that's also a family favorite. Here you can touch the smooth skin of a dolphin, enjoy the synchronized swimming of killer whales, and come face-to-face with the razor-sharp teeth of a shark in Shark Encounter, the largest shark display in the Midwest. Open mid-May through mid-October.

Special Events

January. Winterscape
February. Autorama
    National Home & Garden Show
March. Cleveland International Film Festival
    World's Toughest Rodeo
April. Tri-C Jazz Fest
May. Great American Rib Cook-Off
June. Pepsi Country Music Festival
July. Cleveland Cook KidsFest
    Festival of Freedom
August. Cuyahoga County Fair
    Off-Shore Power Boat Races
September. Cleveland National Air Show
    Oktoberfest
November. Downtown Holiday Lighting Program

Other Recommended Restaurants and Lodgings

Restaurants

Great Lakes Brewing Company (2516 Market Street; 216–771–4404) has a friendly Midwestern atmosphere, casual grub, and lagers and ales brewed on the premises. Moderate.

Pearl of the Orient (20121 Van Aken Boulevard, Shaker Heights; 216–751–8181) has Northern and Szechwan Chinese food and is considered among the best ethnic eateries in the city. Moderate.

Lodgings

Omni International Hotel (Carnegie at East Ninety-sixth Street, 800–843–6664) is in the heart of the University Circle area and convenient to its museums and theaters. The 274 spacious guest rooms are comfortable and spacious. Rates: $119–$199 per night.

The **Ritz Carlton** (1515 West Third Street; 800–241–3333) is the city's only Mobil four-star hotel, with 208 rooms, china cabinets in the halls, and a classically elegant atmosphere. Rates: $150 and up per night.

Stouffer Renaissance Cleveland (24 Public Square; 800–468–3571) is a huge, 491-room historic hotel connected to all the major city sights. It's a member of the Historic Hotels of America and has been rated four stars by AAA. Rates: $129–$199 per night.

For More Information

Convention & Visitors Bureau of Greater Cleveland, 3100 Terminal Tower, Tower City Center, Cleveland, OH 44133; (800) 321–1004.

Columbus

The restored Ohio Theater was narrowly saved from the wrecking ball.

Hello, Columbus

2 NIGHTS

Historic Village • State Capitol • Avant-garde Arts • Sports • Shopping

To a University of Michigan Wolverine fan, suggesting a weekend getaway in Columbus, Ohio, home to the hated Ohio State Buckeyes, is akin to heresy. It's worth entering enemy territory, however, if you're looking for a weekend that offers the best of small-town America in a cosmopolitan city setting. Once a sleepy governmental cow town, today's Columbus is a thriving cosmopolitan city and the state's largest metropolis. And despite the fact that the Columbus area boasts the headquarters of thirty major American corporations and a total

of more than sixteen thousand hotel rooms, it has the pleasant feel of a much
smaller city. Here you'll find the best of urban living without the hassles of
modern urban life.

This is the place that *Newsweek* called "the gleam along the rust belt" and
listed on its roster of the nation's hottest cities. For visitors, that translates into a
suprisingly vibrant city, home of both German Village, one of the largest concentrations of restored historic structures in the state, and the mind-bending
Wexner Center for the Arts, known for its cutting-edge modern art exhibits.

Local author and cartoonist James Thurber once said that "Columbus is a
town in which almost anything is likely to happen and in which almost everything has." After a visit, you'll see what he meant.

Day 1

To reach Columbus from Detroit, take Interstate 75 to the Ohio Turnpike to
U.S. Highway 23 south, which cuts through downtown. It's a 186-mile drive,
most of it uneventful, although there are a few interesting places along the
way, such as the small town of Delaware, when you're ready to stretch your
legs or get a bite to eat.

Afternoon

Lunch: Fresh sushi in mid-America? If you like Japanese food, head for
Columbus's Sapporo Wind (6188 Cleveland Avenue; 614-895-7575), which
has been voted the area's best sushi as well as one of the city's top ten restaurants by the *Columbus Dispatch*.

Use the rest of the afternoon to explore downtown. It's compact, easy to
wander on foot, and boasts a number of things to see and do. For an
overview of the city and its history, consider a cruise on the ***Crystal Lady***
(614-224-1441). This 45-foot-long glass-topped sight-seeing boat, the city's
first privately operated vessel on the Scioto River since 1797, accommodates
up to forty-nine passengers and offers breathtaking views of the city skyline
from its deck. The 45-minute cruise covers the area's American Indian culture,
early settlements, and historic development. Besides daily river tours, the ship
also offers popular "Music in the Air" and "Laser Light" cruises nightly as well
as special moonlight tours and lunchtime excursions.

The waterfront is also home to two of the city's most popular parks. **Bicentennial Park,** at Rich Street and Civic Center Drive, is the site of the ex-
plosive "Red, White and Boom" fireworks display each July. The rest of the
summer, it's a quiet and serene oasis, with beautifully landscaped grounds, a
gurgling fountain, well-used bike trails, and the best skyline view in the city.
Battelle Riverfront Park is another great picnic spot and also home to the
flag-waving ***Santa Maria***, a full-size, carefully crafted replica of Christopher
Columbus's flagship. Built for the city's 1992 quincentennial celebration, the

vintage vessel lets you experience life on board a historic sailing vessel. Don't miss it—especially if you have kids.

Back on dry land, a good place to get a feel for the pulse of the city—and the state—is the **Ohio Capitol Square Complex** (614–752–6350) on Broad Street. First used in 1857, it's one of the oldest statehouses in continuous use in the United States and is affectionately known as the "Hot Box Capitol" because of its distinctive rotunda. It's considered one of the country's finest examples of Greek Revival architecture. Ironically, architect Frank Lloyd Wright considered it "the most honest of state capitols" although much of it was built by penitentiary inmates. This majestic structure was constructed of Columbus limestone after the city became the state's third capital in 1816. It's one of the few capitols that doesn't sport a dome and is decorated with twenty-four-karat gold leaf. It took six architects twenty-two years to complete it at a cost of $1,359,121. On a tour, you can climb the Senate Buildings 1901 Grand Staircase, watch restoration workers in more than sixty rooms, or sit a spell and just watch government in the making. The complex is open daily from 9:00 A.M. to 7:00 P.M.; tours are offered Monday through Friday from 9:00 A.M. to 3:00 P.M. On weekends, a guide is on-site from 11:00 A.M. to 4:00 P.M. for free impromptu tours.

If you're ready for a little all–American shopping, cross the street to the **Columbus City Center Mall** (111 Third Street, 614–221–4900), adjacent to the Hyatt Hotel. This downtown shopping center—one of the few in the country—has more than 150 stores for all budgets, including several of Columbus native and Limited founder Leslie's H. Wexner's stores. There are also a Marshall Field's, Jacobson's, and Ohio-based Lazarus department store as well as national restaurants and boutiques such as Gucci and Henri Bendel (the Columbus Bendel outpost is its first outside Manhattan). For something a little different, check out the ever-tempting A Show of Hands gallery, which features the best of Ohio-made arts and crafts. Kids love the Imaginarium and the Great Train Store, which is overflowing with train memorabilia of all kinds.

Dinner: The **Refectory** (1092 Bethel Road; 614–451–9774) has pulled in the awards (everything from "Best Restaurant" from *Columbus Monthly* and "Top Ten" from the *Columbus Dispatch*) since it opened. One reviewer says it "may well be the finest restaurant in Ohio." It serves the finest of French-inspired fare, including entrees such as sterling salmon and shrimp with mussel butter sauce. Expensive.

If you're a drama fan, check out the **Ohio Theater** (614–469–0939), a masterpiece on Broad Street. Lavishly restored by Loew's (one of the oldest theater families in the country) to the tune of $2 million, this 2,897-seat theater is adorned with gold-plated trimming and Tiffany chandeliers. Columbus residents raised funds to buy it just minutes—literally, as the bulldozer was driving down the street—before demolition began in the late 1960s. Since then, it's become a lively showcase for the performing arts, with a full schedule of events including the Columbus Symphony Orchestra, BalletMet

Columbus, a popular Broadway-style series, and a well–attended summer movie program. Today, it's the busiest performing arts facility in the state.

Lodging: The **Westin Hotel** (614–228–3800) is a beautifully restored downtown hotel located adjacent to the City Center Mall, the Brewery District, and German Village. It was formerly known as the Great Southern Hotel and was built in 1896 and renovated in time for its one-hundreth anniversary. The hotel's painstaking restoration is apparent as soon as you walk into the lobby. Marble floors, polished brass, and magnificent stained glass echo the opulence of the turn of the century, when the Great Southern Fireproof Building and Opera House was home to a theater, restaurants, shops, and apartments under its roof. Today, the 196 guest rooms and suites are decorated in traditional furnishings, with high ceilings and floral wallpaper. Rates: $165–$215 per night.

Day 2

Morning

Breakfast: **Juergen's Bakery and Kaffee Haus** (525 South Fourth Street; 614–224–6858) is a great place for a hearty omelettes, French toast, or other sweet treat and some strong coffee to go along with it. The restaurant is well-known for its German–inspired pastries and breads (don't miss the strudel) as well as for its sauerbraten, schnitzel, and bratwurst. There are also an on-site deli, gift shop, even a bed and breakfast. Inexpensive to moderate.

Juergen's is part of **German Village,** a friendly neighborhood just 6 blocks south of the State Capitol via Third Street. This friendly neighborhood earned a spot on the National Register of Historic Places in 1975 because of the quaint brick homes set along its narrow cobblestone streets. German immigrants settled the 230-acre area in the mid-1800s; it was narrowly saved from a freeway expansion and the wrecking ball in the 1950s. If you're curious about old-time Columbus, this is the place to get an idea of how city residents lived in the nineteenth century. Today German Village is home to young urban professionals and others who prize its heritage and historic charm. Chic coffeehouses sit side by side with quilt shops, neighborhood pubs, and authentic German bakeries.

Wanderers in German Village find well-tended cottages and stately mansions with flower-filled window boxes and wrought iron gates. Tours are offered in the summer from the **German Village Meeting Haus** (588 South Third Street; 614–221–8888), where volunteers are also available year-round to help you design self-guided tours.

Ideal for walking (but not always for parking), German Village is one of Columbus's major attractions and draws more than one hundred thousand visitors each year. More than just a pretty piece of restored Americana, this is a working neighborhood, with businesses that range from supermarkets and dry working neighborhood, with businesses that range from supermarkets and dry cleaners to antiques shops and bookstores. You can chew on some spicy bratwurst at **Schmidt's Sausage Haus und Restaurant** (240 East Kossuth Street; 614–444–6808), where they're also famous for their bet-you-can't-eat-it-all cream puffs. **Thurn's Bakery and Deli** (541 Third Street; 614–221–9246) is an old-fashioned and still popular lunch counter.

Another landmark is **Diebel's Restaurant and Bierstube** (263 East Whittier Street; 614–444–1139), where the spicy sausage and sauerkraut are legendary and where families get into the rollicking, good-time spirit of fun during weekly polka parties. It's also German Village's oldest restaurant. In the middle of it all is peaceful **Schiller Park,** 23 acres of greensward in the middle of the district's tree-lined streets and home to many of the area's bed-and-breakfast inns.

Afternoon

Lunch: Take a break from the streets with a picnic lunch from nearby **Katzinger's Deli** (475 South Third Street; 614–228–3354, an area landmark voted "Best Deli in America" by *Bon Appetit* magazine. You can't go wrong with the always popular Reuben or piled-high corned beef. If the weather's uncooperative, try Thurn's, Juergen's, or Schmidt's.

If you're looking for an unusual souvenir of your stay, check out the **Golden Hobby Shop** (630 South Third Street; 614–645–6329). Housed in a former school, the shop sells crafts made by area senior citizens, from wooden shelves and hard-to-find old-fashioned toys such as tops and airplanes to intricately pieced quilts and beautiful hand knits.

More goodies can be found in the nooks and crannies of the **Book Loft** (631 South Third Street; 614–464–1774), where the store takes up an entire city block and where negotiating the twenty-five rooms of discounted paperbacks and hardcovers can require a whole afternoon and a map—or at least an unlimited credit card. Another fun shop is the quirky **Hausfrau Haven** (614–443–3680), also on Third Street, with unusual greeting cards, fine wines, and a renowned homemade fudge. If you've got kids in tow, keep an eye on them while you're in the store. Playful signs warn that UNATTENDED CHILDREN WILL BE SOLD.

You might even see lederhosen on some natives during special events. The neighborhood is the spotlight of the annual Haus und Garten Tour the last Sunday in June as well as the Candlelight Garten Tour in August and a Merry Christmas Tour of Homes in December. It's also home to the city's wildly popular Oktoberfest, ironically held in September, where you can stomp along to oompah-pah music and sample local brews. For more information on German Village, contact the German Village Society, 588 South Third Street, Columbus, OH 43215; (614) 221–8888.

Dinner: The city's best seafood can be found at **Chuck Muer's Engine** house in German Village, it's lively and affordable, with fresh seafood, steaks, and Muer's signature rolls. Moderate.

Day 3

Morning

Breakfast: Skip the bagel and coffee this morning and save room for the brunch at the **Plaza Restaurant** in the Hyatt Hotel on Capitol Square (75 East State Street; 614–228–1234). Considered the best brunch in the city, it includes more than one hundred items, from eggs, waffles, hash browns, made-to-order omelettes, French toast, and more for $18.95 per adult, $9.95 for children, free for children under three.

Set Sunday aside for museum hopping. Had enough history for a while? It's back to the future at the popular **Ohio Center of Science and Industry,** affectionately known as COSI (280 East Broad Street; 614–228–COSI). It's hard to tell who's having more fun here, the kids or the so-called "adults." COSI is dedicated to the conviction that science can be fun. After a visit, you'll be convinced, too. Ohio's only science center is one of just twenty-two centers worldwide. Its action-packed exhibits are spread out over three floors in a former 1906 Memorial Hall, now refitted with modern solar addition. Visit the outer reaches of the solar system in the Planetarium. Lift a car... all by yourself. Touch a twenty-six-year-old concretion. Teach a computer to talk. COSI challenges people of all ages to explore, invent, imagine, probe, discover, and experiment with more than one thousand interactive exhibits. Where else can you climb aboard an authentic 1961 Mercury space capsule and prepare for launch, ride a high-wire bike to test the forces of gravity (with a protective net, of course), or pretend you're conducting laparoscopic surgery? Kids head for Familiespace, where they can play doctor at the COSI clinic, type in a make-believe office, walk on piano keys, even star in their own newscast or rock video (a concession sells videotapes so you can record the performance for posterity). Hours are Monday through Saturday 10:00 A.M. to 5:00 P.M.; Sunday noon to 5:30 P.M. Admission is $20.00 per family, $6.00 for adults, $4.00 for children two through twelve and for seniors.

After the excitement of COSI you may want to wind down with a visit to the peaceful **Franklin Park Conservatory and Botanical Garden** (614–645–8733), also on Broad Street. Located on 28 acres within the lush, 88-acre Franklin Park, the conservatory opened to the public in 1895. It underwent a dramatic change in 1992, when a $14 million expansion was built for AmeriFlora 92, a floral celebration marking Christopher Columbus's discovery of America.

This peaceful mix of glass and grace is home to approximately ten thousand plants representing more than twelve hundred species. Displayed in six climatic zones—the Himalayan Mountain Room, the Tropical Rain Forest, the Desert, the Pacific Island Water Garden, the Tree Fern Forest, and the Cloud Forest—it's a pleasant place to relax and regroup after a busy day. It also has a nice shop featuring everything for the green thumb.

If you're looking for a little inspiration for your own front lawn, head for the downtown Topiary Garden on East Town Street. This fanciful landscape created by sculptor James T. Mason depicts pointillist painter Georges Seurat's *Sunday Afternoon on the Isle of La Grand Jatte* and includes fifty-two larger-than-life human figures, eight boats, three dogs, and a monkey. It's the only topiary garden in the country to include human figures. Watch gardeners here snip and clip the figure into shape, and who knows what you'll decide to do with the bushes back home?

Lunch: A good place to grab a bite is the restaurant in the Columbus Museum of Art. While small, it's a relaxing cafe eatery with fresh soups, salads, and changing specials. Inexpensive to moderate.

Afternoon

A spot you won't want to miss is the **Columbus Museum of Art** (480 East Broad Street; 614–221–4848), Ohio's first museum. It's known for its innovative traveling exhibits and its small but excellent permanent collection, including the breathtaking $80 million Sirak Collection of Impressionist Art. The museum offers a relaxing respite from the city's streets and a well-rounded permanent collection that ranges from prehistory to modern times. While there, watch for works by two eminent Columbus natives, realist George Bellows and folk artist Elijah Pierce. The museum is worth a stop just for the well-stocked museum shop, which sells everything from unusual frames, greeting cards, and art books to innovative jewelry by local artists.

Not far from the museum is the **Thurber House** (77 Jefferson Avenue; 614–464–1032). Onetime home to James Thurber, it's now a lively writers' center and the popular site of summer "literary picnics" and the winter "Evening With Authors" series. You can wander in this modest home where Thurber lived during his college days with his parents, two brothers, numerous pet dogs, and an occasional relative. Artifacts and memorabilia from Thurber's long career fill the rooms. Many of Thurber's best-known stories (all available for sale in the small shop, once the dining room) are set here. It's open daily from noon to 4:00 P.M. for free self-guided tours.

Columbus prides itself on its strong support of the arts. One of the best places in the city to see cutting-edge visual arts is the 250,000-square-foot **Wexner Center for the Arts** (North High Street and Fifteenth Avenue; 614–292–0330). Located near the heart of the Ohio State University campus and dedicated to vanguard artistic activity, it opened in 1989 as a center for the presentation and study of contemporary arts.

With a multidisciplinary approach including exhibitions, media arts, performing arts, and education, the center encourages exploration. Four galleries host traveling exhibits from modern art museums around the world, including the Museum of Modern Art in New York, the Walker Art Center in Minneapolis, and the Georges Pompidou Center in Paris, as well as a popular avant-garde film series.

Dinner: Depending on how you late you want to stay, you may have time to squeeze in one more meal in Columbus before heading home. If so, check out **Rigsby's Cuisine Volatile** (698 North High Street; 614–461–7888). Located in the trendy Short North district, which is home to the city's most avant-garde arts community, its cuisine is a little Italian, a little French, a little Greek... but all good. Don't miss any of the fish dishes or the delectable homemade gnocchi. Moderate.

There's More

Academia. If you're visiting in the fall, you can't miss a tour of the Ohio State University campus. OSU is one of the country's largest universities and was designed by Frederick Law Olmstead of New York's Central Park fame. A free, two-hour tour departs from Drake Union and includes the residence hall, the main libraries, and the famous football stadium, long a home of gridiron glory. Tours depart from 1849 Cannon Drive; for more information, call (614) 292–3980.

Animals. The Columbus Zoo (9990 Riverside Drive, Powell; 614–645–3550) is one of the best in the country, with more than seven hundred species and more than eleven thousand animals and insects.

Bargains. Outlet shopping has become an American obsession. If you've been bitten, a good place to bag a bargain is the Ohio Factory Shops, about twenty-five-minutes' drive from Columbus. The intersection of Interstate 71 and U.S. Highway 35 is the location of the state's largest outlet mall, where you'll save 25 to 70 percent off retail prices at more than seventy-five stores. For more information and directions, call (800) 746–7644.

Baseball. Old-fashioned fun and the kind of baseball you remember from your childhood can be enjoyed at the city's Cooper Stadium, a 15,000-square-foot facility that's home to the Columbus Clippers, a AAA affiliate of the New York Yankees. Every night has a different special event, including kids' night, ladies' night, fireworks night, and a Sunday "family day at the ballpark," when the whole gang is admitted for just $8.00. For tickets and other information, call (614) 462–5250.

Beer. Visit the world's largest brewery and view the making of their famous beers at the Anheuser-Busch Brewery Tour and Gift Shop (700 East Schrock Road; 614–847–6465).

Caves. Olentangy Indian Caverns (1779 Home Road, Delaware; 614–548–7917) is a good side trip and a sure hit with families. It offers three levels of caverns and is a spelunker's delight.

History. The Ohio Village/Ohio Historical Center (1739 North High Street; 614–292–0418) is a museum and village complex that traces the fascinating history of the Buckeye State through acclaimed exhibits and costumed craftspeople.

Wet 'N' Wild. Wyandot Lake Amusement Park (10101 Riverside Drive; 614–889–9283) is the place to be in the summer, with thirteen water slides, kid and adult rides, and a million-gallon wave pool as well as go-karts, miniature golf, and a video arcade. Open May through September.

Special Events

May. Taste of Columbus, riverfront
June. Columbus Arts Festival, riverfront
     Haus und Garten Tour, German Village
July. Red, White and Boom!, riverfront
August. Candlelight Garten Tour, German Village
September. German Village Oktoberfest
December. Merry Christmas Tour of Homes, German Village

Other Recommended Restaurants and Lodgings

Restaurants

Dick Clark's American Bandstand Grill (100 Hutchinson Avenue; 614–785–1985) sports vintage photos, gold and platinum albums, rare posters, artists' contracts, and more from Clark's personal collection. You'll also see *American Bandstand* footage from the original TV series on screens around the restaurant. The cuisine in all-American, too—from Philly cheesesteaks and a classic burger and fries to spicy Santa Fe chicken fajitas. Open for lunch and dinner daily.

Handke's Cuisine (520 South Front Street; 614–621–2500) is in the city's Brewery District and built into the vaults of a nineteenth-century brewery. The restaurant, which has the state's only master chef, features American regional cuisine. Reservations suggested. Expensive.

Lindey's (169 East Beck Street; 614–228–4343) has been one of the city's top restaurants for fifteen years and was voted "the city's most popular restaurant" by the *Columbus Dispatch*. It features progressive American cuisine, including steaks, chops, pastas, and more. Expensive.

Spaghetti Warehouse (397 West Broad Street; 614–464–0143), always a good bet with families, features fast and friendly service and a reliable menu of kid's pasta favorites.

Lodgings

50 Lincoln (50 East Lincoln; 800–750–5056) is a small, urban inn in the budding Short North district, with friendly accommodations and an award-winning chef. Rates: $129–$139 per night, including breakfast.

Courtyard by Marriott (35 West Spring Street; 614–228–3200) is a good alternative for travelers on a budget who still expect attractive rooms and good service. The cheerful restaurant serves a hearty buffet breakfast with everything from cereals to croissants. Rates: $82–$94 per night.

Doubletree Guest Suites (50 South Front Street; 614–228–4600) is an all-suite luxury hotel that is rated four stars by AAA. It's located in Huntington Center just across from the state capitol. Rates: $99–$125 per night.

Embassy Suites (2700 Corporate Exchange Drive; 614–890–8600) offers spacious two-room suites with a refrigerator, microwave, wet bar, and coffeemaker as well as a free cooked-to-order breakfast each morning. A manager's reception nightly includes free beverages. Rates: $99–$149 per night.

Hyatt Regency Columbus (350 North High Street; 614–463–1234) has 631 newly decorated rooms in a location connected to the Greater Columbus Convention Center. Rates: $119–$205 per night.

Bed and Breakfasts. If you're a B&B fan, the city has a number of options. For a list of the more than twenty inns in the city, contact the Central Ohio Bed and Breakfast Cooperative (180 Lansing Street; 800–383–7839) for a list of facilities that range from urban active to country quiet.

For More Information

Greater Columbus Convention and Visitors Bureau, One Columbus, 10 West Broad Street, Suite 1300, Columbus, OH 43215–3424; (614) 221–2489 or (800)–345–4386.

Cincinnati

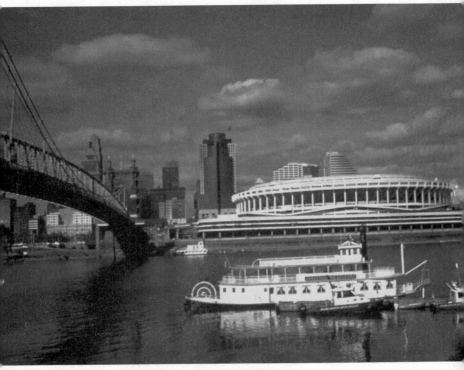

The river is an important part of the Cincinnati psyche.

Hail to the Queen (City)

2 NIGHTS

Chili Restaurants • Deco Hotel • Theater • Conservatory

English statesman Winston Churchill once dubbed Cincinnati "the most beautiful of America's inland cities." More recently, it was dubbed "North America's Most Livable City." This big city perched high on the bluffs of the Ohio River is known for its small-town charm. It also has a vibrant and exciting downtown, with a 20-block elevated skywalk system that connects department stores, specialty shops, hotels, and even a museum. Cincinnati is also renowned for its restaurants, with eateries that range from five-star French to the city's signature five-way chili.

Cincinnati is also as far south as you can go in Ohio without hitting the renowned bluegrass of Kentucky, located just across the river. It's so close, in fact, that Covington, Kentucky, located across the river, is considered part of Cincinnati and the two cities are marketed as one entity. And Cincy definitely feels more southern than midwestern—the pace is slower and accents are thicker. After a weekend in the Queen City, you're sure to agree with Churchill's assessment.

Day 1

Morning

Plan on getting an early start. From Detroit, Cincinnati is a straight shot (about 230 miles) south down Interstate 75. Most of the five-hour drive is an uneventful ride through flat Ohio farmland (watch for state troopers!), but there are a few places worth stopping along the way—including the **Neil Armstrong Museum** (500 South Apollo Drive; 419–738–8811) in Wapakoneta, which honors the first man on the moon and the history of space exploration—if you're looking to get out of the car and stretch your legs. You may also want to stop for a quick bite along the way (try Fazzoli's in Lima for quick yet tasty Italian specialties). Don't spend too much time lingering, however, as Cincinnati holds more than enough to fill a long weekend.

Afternoon

Dinner: Plan on arriving in town early enough for dinner. Cincinnati is known for its wonderful restaurants, and you won't want to miss the chance to sample as many as possible. A good one to try while you still have the car is **Grand Finale** (Sharon Road and State Highway 747; 513–771–5925), located north outside the city limits in historic Glendale. This once-dilapidated Victorian home was reputed to be haunted when owners Larry and Cindy Youse purchased it in 1975. Since then, it's racked up awards ranging from "Best Outdoor Dining" and "Best Sunday Brunch" to "Best Desserts." The atmosphere is relaxed, the food is great (try the homemade Coquille St. Jacques crepes or the signature lobster linguine), and the desserts are to die for. Forget the diet—go ahead and splurge. Moderate to expensive.

Lodging: The magnificent **Omni Netherland Plaza** (35 West Fifth Street; 513–421–9100 or 800–843–6664) is a local landmark and a stunning example of the French Art Deco style. It's worth spending a little extra to stay in this restored gem. Opened in 1931, the Omni antedated New York's Rockefeller Center by several years and was even compared to the grandeur of Solomon's temple. Pass through the impressive entrance of Roman Breche marble (look up and you'll see WELCOME TRAVELER inscribed in the ceiling in French) and you'll enter the elegance of another age. The hotel is also known for its Palm Court, with a ziggurat-shaped fountain made at the city's renowned Rookwood Pottery. Famous guests have included three presidents (Eisenhower, Truman, and Reagan) as well as Eleanor Roosevelt, Bing Crosby, and Winston Churchill, who was so taken with the yellow tile in his suite that he had it reproduced in his English country home. Rates: $99–$225 per night.

Day 2

Morning

Breakfast: **First Watch,** a popular suburban eatery, recently opened a downtown location (700 Walnut, at Seventh Street; 513–721–4744). Lines can be long on weekends (try to get there early), but it's worth the wait for gourmet pancakes (try the fresh apple cinnamon and oatmeal), raisin bread, French toast, and their signature *crepeggs*—thin, sweet crepes combined with whipped eggs. Inexpensive to moderate.

Set the day aside for strolling downtown. A good place to get a grip on the city's psyche is **Fountain Square,** where the Genius of Water sculpture atop the Tyler Davidson Fountain surveys a broad, open plaza. In sunny weather you'll find shoppers and businessfolk brown-bagging it on the square or enjoying some of the city's famous chili while being entertained by people-watching and the open–air pavilion stage. The plaza is also home to the **Cincy Shop** (513–579–1435), where you'll find maps, books, guides, and virtually any other Cincinnati-related item you could desire.

Paris has the Eiffel Tower, Chicago has the Sears Tower... Cincinnati has its own nosebleed section at the top of the **Carew Tower Observatory** (Fifth and Vine streets; 513–241–3888), where you'll be treated to excellent views of downtown as well as surrounding countryside from the top of the city's tallest building. Other great city views can be had in the stylish Mount Adams neighborhood, one of the city's liveliest. While much smaller, it's often compared to San Francisco, as much for its annoying one-way streets as its breathtaking hilltop views. Here you'll find narrow row houses restored to their nineteenth-century glory as well as funky shops and interesting restaurants. You could easily spend days here wandering through the many tempting shops and boutiques.

Afternoon

Lunch: The city's most unusual eatery must be the **Rookwood Pottery Restaurant** (1077 Celestial Street; 513–721–5456) housed in the former pottery of the same name. Rookwood, active around the turn of the century through the 1960s, is known for its intricate glazes and beautiful designs and is highly prized by today's collectors. Vintage photographs, original pieces of pottery, and the rare chance to dine inside one of the three huge brick kilns that once reached thousand of degrees make this place a treat. Entrees include everything from a tasty Potter's Salad to a burger voted the best in the city by *Cincinnati* magazine. Be sure to finish off your meal with a creamy concoction from the make-your-own sundae bar. Moderate.

Before leaving Mount Adams, trek over to **Eden Park.** When the skyscrapers and the bustle get to be too much, city residents of all ages retreat to this well–loved greensward. This sprawling park boasts many of the city's most popular attractions, including its renowned art museum, two professional theaters and miles and miles of trails perfect for walking, hiking, biking, or Rollerblading (be sure to wear pads!).

If you prefer a slower pace, consider a stroll around the eighty-eight galleries of the **Cincinnati Art Museum** (Eden Park; 513–721–5205). This was the first museum west of the Alleghenies built to be a museum; today its graceful halls house art dating back some five thousand years. Founded in 1881, the museum opened to world acclaim and was heralded as "The Art Palace of the West." Not content to rest on its laurels, the museum has recently completed an extensive renovation. Collection highlights include Mary Cassatt's *Mother and Child* from 1889, the colorful *Red Rooster* by Marc Chagall, the collection of Rookwood Pottery, Andy Warhol's tribute to Cincinnati Reds great Pete Rose, and the mesmerizing Powel Crosley, Jr. sculpture by Korean artist Naim June Paik, which pays homage to the father of modern telecommunications.

Also in Eden Park is the respected **Krohn Conservatory** (513–421–4086), one of the nation's largest public greenhouses. Wander through a tropical rain forest, duck while a spectacular 20-foot waterfall cascades overhead, or dry out in the desert greenhouses filled with prickly cacti and delicate multicolored orchids. All of Cincy gathers here for seasonal events, which include festive holiday floral shows.

Dinner: Hungry yet? You can't leave the city without eating at its most famous restaurant. **Maisonette** (114 East Sixth Street; 513–721–2260) has racked up five stars year after year and accumulated more Mobil stars than any other restaurant in the country. Reservations—well in advance—are a must. Maisonette is not only a critic's choice, but a people's favorite as well. It's known for its impeccable service and outstanding entrees such as grilled quail with champagne mustard or romantic rack of lamb for two. Unlike its Gallic counterparts, however, it's also known for its friendly staff and warm midwestern welcome. Expensive. (A tip for the budget-minded: The restaurant's bistro-style lunches are very reasonable, about $10 for a selection that ranges from classic cassoulet to seafood crepes.)

Evening entertainment in Cincinnati takes many forms. You might take in a play at the **Cincinnati Playhouse in the Park** (513–421–3888), one of the city's most intimate theaters (there's also a great view of the city from the parking lot). Baseball fans who see red will want to head for **Riverfront**

Stadium, one of the nation's most scenic ballparks and home of the world-famous **Cincinnati Reds,** the oldest team in the country (call 513–421–7337 for ticket information). Other options include the **Cincinnati Ballet** (513–621–1919), **Cincinnati Opera** (513–241–2742), even boot-scootin' at **Coyote's** (606–341–5150) in nearby Fort Mitchell, Kentucky, which has the largest dance floor in the Midwest.

Day 3

Morning

Breakfast: The meandering Ohio River plays a large part in Cincinnati's history and is one of the city's most scenic spots. Pay it proper homage with brunch on one of the few remaining riverboats, the ***Mike Fink*** (Greenup Street; Covington, KY; 606–261–4212). Docked across the river in Covington, Kentucky, under the Queen City's famed Roebling Bridge (it was designed by the same architect and served as the prototype for the better-known Brooklyn Bridge), it's a floating restaurant popular for birthday or anniversary celebrations. The brunch spread includes egg specialties, meats, seafood, baked goods, and more.

Tired of being docked? Take to the river with a ride on one of the **BB Riverboats** (800–261–8586), the city's oldest and largest riverboat company. From the modern Funliner to the steamboat-era *Becky Thatcher* and the authentic sternwheeler *Mark Twain,* BB offers more than thirty different cruises. They're docked at Covington Landing across from the Riverfront Stadium.

Afterward, abandon your sea legs for a walk on terra firma at the **Riverfront Park.** Bicentennial Commons at Sawyer Point is one of the city's newest and most beloved parks. Built in honor of the city's bicentennial, it skirts the river and boasts an impressive roster of recreational facilities and scenic overlooks. When you enter, look up and see the Cincinnati Gateway Sculpture, a whimsical three-dimensional work that pays homage to the city's history. (Interestingly enough, the sculpture was also quite controversial. Many residents were offended by the bronze winged pigs—a reference to the city's onetime nickname "Porkopolis," because of its pork industry—but others loved them. Today the sculpture stands as a playful reminder to residents not to take themselves too seriously.)

While at the park, why not take a turn at the 21,000-square-foot roller-skating pavilion, a favorite of the city's in-line enthusiasts? Maybe you'd rather join in a game of sand volleyball or just wander the 4-mile riverwalk, where you can trace the city's time line from prehistory and enjoy the great views of the graceful Kentucky antebellum mansions across the way.

The city's history is also the focus at the **Cincinnati Historical Society**, housed not far away in the Museum Center at Cincinnati Union Terminal

(1301 Western Avenue; 513–287–7011). Some cities choose to honor their past by tearing it down piece by piece in the name of progress. This is not so in preservation-minded Cincinnati, which, when faced with an unused Art Deco train station the size of fourteen football fields, decided to turn it into not one, but three, fantastic museums.

Union Terminal was built in 1933 and once hosted up to 215 trains and 34,000 people daily. It closed in 1972, victim of America's love affair with the automobile. Now restored to its original grandeur, it stands as one of the country's most spectacular remaining examples of streamlined Art Deco architecture, with a magnificent soaring rotunda filled with murals and other distinctive details. Inside the bright, soaring space—it covers some 500,000 square feet—are three popular attractions, including the Cincinnati Historical Society, the Cincinnati Museum of Natural History, and the Robert D. Lindner Family Omnimax Theater.

For an overview of the city's long and lively history, check out the historical society first. Here you can trace the city's development from frontier river town to modern metropolis. Costumed interpreters escort you on a journey through time, from a frontier cabin to a 1940s-era gas station. Along the way, you can visit a settler's cabin, board an old-fashioned flatboat (a plaque nearby calls its the "moving van of the frontier"), and climb on an original 1923 trolley used in the city until 1951.

Afternoon

If geology is your thing or you brought the kids, the **Cincinnati Museum of Natural History** (513–287–7000 or 800–733–2077) captivates visitors of all ages. The emphasis here is on the natural and geological history of the Ohio Valley, including the Ice Age (where you can walk through a mock glacier), an exhibit on area caverns, and one exploring the dinosaurs that once walked the same soil. The popular Omnimax theater takes movies to new heights. Your local multiplex will pale in comparison to this 5-story, 72-foot domed screen. Special technology enables you to experience every scene and motion with gut-wrenching clarity. Past films have explored *Destiny in Space* and the natural wonders of *Yellowstone* and have even gone *To the Max* with the Rolling Stones.

Fuel up for the ride home with a taste of the city's famous chili. Sold all over Cincinnati (the city has more chili parlors per capita than anywhere else in the world), it's a favorite in the diner at the Museum Center. Have it your way or try the city favorite—served over a plate of spaghetti with diced onions, red beans, and cheddar cheese. For those who'd rather cool down than heat up, the train station's original **Rookwood Ice Cream Parlor** sells sweet treats in an atmosphere or glowing walls and floors of authentic area-made Rookwood tile.

Afterward, stop and shop at the three great stores in the Museum Center complex. The **Collector's Shop of the Cincinnati Museum of Natural History,** the **Children's Shop,** and the **Heritage Shop** of the Cincinnati Historical Society sell gifts and goods that make great souvenirs of your weekend visit to the Queen City.

There's More

Animals. The Cincinnati Zoo (3400 Vine Street; 513–281–4700) has been called "America's sexiest zoo" by *Newsweek* magazine. Among the world leaders in the breeding of endangered animals, it's a family favorite, with exhibits that range from rare tiny spiders to huge Komodo dragons, the world's largest and most dangerous reptile. Other highlights include Bagus and Rapunzel, the only breeding pair of Sumatran rhinos left in the world, and an ambitious cat house with rare, white Bengal tigers.

Antiques. Waynesville, about 20 miles north, is considered Southern Ohio's antiques capital and is a charming and picturesque side trip. Call (800) 433–1072 for information.

History. The Cincinnati home of Harriet Beecher Stowe, author of the famous *Uncle Tom's Cabin,* has been restored and now serves as a museum, gift shop, and cultural center. It's at 2950 Gilbert Avenue; (513) 632–5120.

Scream Machines. If the kids are in tow, Kings Island (6300 Kings Island Drive, Mason; 513–398–5600) is just 24 miles north of downtown Cincy. One of the largest theme parks in the country, it features a replica of Paris's Eiffel Tower, seven areas with stage shows, thrill rides, a 15-acre Waterworks park, and more.

Ship Shape. Cincinnati is one of the many colorful ports visited by the *Mississippi Queen,* the *Delta Queen,* and the new *American Queen,* all part of the steamboat trips offered by the Delta Queen Steamship Company (800–543–1949). These overnight paddlewheel steamboats are the last to ply our nation's rivers and offer three- to sixteen-night cruises that explore "Mark Twain's America" and more.

Sun and Fun. The Beach (2950 Waterpark Drive, Mason; 800–886–7946) is the state's largest water park, with thirty slippery slides and watery attractions spread out over more than 35 acres. It's conveniently located across from Kings Island.

Washington Slept Here. Listed on the National Register of Historic Places, the Golden Lamb (27 South Broadway, Lebanon; 513–932–5065) is Ohio's oldest operating inn. Daniel Webster, Charles Dickens, Mark Twain, and ten U.S. presidents have slept here. The inn is also known for its hearty dinners and its impressive collection of Shaker and Victorian antiques on display throughout the inn. The charming town of Lebanon is a destination in itself, a great day trip with antiques shops, boutiques, and restaurants.

Special Events

January. Travel, Sports, and Boat Show
February. Auto Expo
March. Home and Garden Show
April. Reds Opening Day
May. Delta Queen Homecoming
    Taste of Cincinnati
June. KidsFest
July. Riverfront Stadium Festival
September. Oktoberfest Zinzinnati
October. Light Up Cincinnati
November. Festival of Lights

Other Recommended Restaurants and Lodgings:

Restaurants

Barcelona's (Fourth and Race Streets; 513–333–0003) is the place for tapas and other Spanish specialties. There are also nightly entertainment, a full bar, and late-night hours. Moderate.

The **Diner on Sycamore** (1203 Sycamore; 513–721–1212) is a casual eatery set in an authentic 1950s diner, with a varied menu that includes seafood, meat, and fish entrees. Moderate.

Main Street Brewery (1203 Main Street; 513–665–4677). The city's first brew pub has a full–service restaurant and lively nightly entertainment. Moderate.

La Normandie (118 East Sixth Street; 513–721–2761) has been a downtown tradition for more than sixty years. It's located next to the Maisonette downtown and is famous for its dry-aged steaks and fish. Expensive.

Lodgings

The **Cincinnatian Hotel** (601 Vine Street; 513–381–3000) is located in the heart of downtown and is the area's only four-star hotel. It draws raves as one of the city's most luxurious and intimate hostelries, with personalized service, a concierge, twenty-four-hour room service, and elegant guest rooms. Rates: $160–$245 per night.

Garfield House Suite Hotel (2 Garfield Place; 513–421–3355) is downtown's only all-suite hotel, with the city's largest suites and complimentary breakfast daily. Rates: $150–$325 per night.

Hyatt Regency Cincinnati (151 West Fifth Street; 513–579–1234) has recently renovated guest rooms connected by Skywalk to the Convention Center, restaurants, and more. Rates: $139–$229 per night.

The **Westin Hotel** (Fountain Square; 513–621–7700) is one of the city's most centrally located hotels and within walking distance of all the city's top attractions. It has 450 deluxe rooms and suites, two restaurants, and a fitness center. Rates: $135–$175 per night.

For More Information

Greater Cincinnati Convention & Visitors Bureau, 300 West Sixth Street, Cincinnati, OH 45202; (513) 621–2142.

Ontario Escapes

Windsor

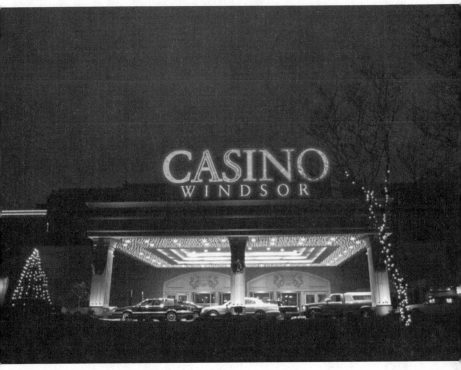

The new Casino Windsor attracts optimists from all over North America.

Betting on Windsor

_____ 2 NIGHTS _____

Casinos • Restaurants • Shopping • Wildlife

Wander downtown Windsor's streets and you'll swear you're in another country. And you are—despite this city's proximity to Detroit (it's just a tunnel or bridge ride away), Windsor, Ontario, is very much a Canadian city. There's a certain European flair on the streets and in the cafes that you won't find across the border.

Detroiters have long enjoyed this city's rich and varied restaurant offerings—everything from Chinese to gourmet French. More recently, however, the city has become known as the gambling capital of Canada—the country's equivalent (albeit markedly tamer) of Las Vegas or Atlantic City. Casino publicity claims it has become the country's top commercial attraction. Since opening in 1994 it has attracted thousands of visitors from across the United States and Canada.

The strength of the American dollar doesn't hurt, either, making a weekend in Windsor a great deal as well as great fun. If you're looking for a quick trip that still gives you that delicious sense of being away from home, this is it. Windsor has plenty of family-friendly activities, bu leave the kids at home if you're looking to gamble.

Day 1

Afternoon

There's no need to leave early. From Detroit, Windsor is a fast tunnel or bridge ride away. Of the two, the four-lane bridge is more scenic, offering great views of the Detroit River and the Motown skyline from its 152-foot center. It opened to traffic in 1929 and ranks as the world's longest international suspension bridge, stretching 1.75 miles between Canada and the Unites States. The recently renovated tunnel, however, is more convenient, whisking you right into the heart of downtown Windsor. Skip it if you're claustrophobic, however. It reaches a maximum depth of 75 feet beneath the surface of the Detroit River. Back-ups can be frustrating during peak travel such as rush hours.

Dinner: Windsor is known for its fine restaurants, many of which are housed in renovated historic structures. Friday night is generally less crowded at the tiny **Cook's Shop/The Pasta Shop** (683 Ouellette; 519-256-5233), located in a former brownstone. Reservations aren't required, but they're usually a good idea. Specialties include the succulent rack of lamb and the pastas—all made on the premises. Moderate.

If you're interested in a few laughs, check out **Yuk Yuk's** (430 Ouellette; 519-256-5233), Windsor's home of stand-up comedy. The lively club has hosted cut-ups such as Jerry Seinfeld, Jim Carrey, and Emo Phillips.

Lodging: If you're looking for convenience and plan on courting Lady Luck into the wee hours, you can't do better than the **Compri Hotel**, (333 Riverside Drive West; 519-977-9777 or 800-267-9777), located next to the casino. This modern chain hotel (it's called Doubletree in the United States) has 207 rooms (ask for one with a skyline view) and offers both a great location and reasonable prices as well as a "Stay, Play and Win" package that includes a cooked-to-order breakfast, twenty-four-hour tea and coffee, dinner at your choice of four first-class city restaurants (including taxes), $10 in casino tokens, free parking, a bottle of wine, and more—all for just $150 Canadian per night. There's also a tempting "Romance by the River" package at the same rate. The hotel's 5,000-square-foot Compri Club and its large health club offer stunning views of downtown Detroit across the way.

Day 2

Morning

Breakfast: Grab a quick bite in your hotel (a made-to-order breakfast from room service is included in your room rate) before setting out on foot to explore Windsor's downtown. Detroit's skyscrapers cast a long shadow over downtown Windsor, but that's the only reminder you'll have of your home across the way. Ouellette Avenue, the main drag, offers a bevy of sophisticated European-style boutiques and welcoming coffeehouses and bistros where your dollar is worth about 35 percent more (to get the best exchange, use your plastic).

From your hotel, wander along Ouellette. Skip the ordinary T–shirt and souvenir shops, but don't miss the deals at **Shanfield–Meyer** (119 Ouellette; 519–253–6098), which has attracted Americans and Canadians alike for more than fifty years with great deals on fine porcelain, sparkling crystal (including an entire room devoted to Waterford), and other goodies. Also on Ouellette is a **Columbia Sportswear Outlet** (527 Ouellette; 519–252–5203), which offers deals on signature ski jackets and outerwear. If you're looking for something to read while you're away, check out **South Shore Books** (164 Pitt Street West; 519–253–9102), which stocks a choice selection of American and Canadian titles as well as gambling how-to's such as *The Complete Idiot's Guide to Gambling Like a Pro.*

If you're curious about Windsor's history, stop at the stone **Francois Baby House** (254 Pitt Street West), located in an 1812 structure that sits in the shadow of the nearby casino and Hilton Hotel. Its exhibitions trace the individuals, cultures, and events that contributed to the city's development.

Round the corner of Pelissier Street and you'll find more tempting shops, including those housed in the vintage 1908 buildings known as Park Place (405 Pelissier). Other favorites include **Resourceful Child Books** (1675 Ottawa Street; 519–977–7464), with a great selection of books in English and French, and **Delicate Touch Lingerie** (3877 Dougall Street; 519–972–9675), with lacy underthings and weekend wear for yourself or a friend. **Native Wonders** (131 Park Street; 519–977–0663) is the city's only Native American–owned gift shop and gallery and specializes in aboriginal art and collectibles.

Lunch: **Plunkett's Bistro-Bar** (28 Chatham Street East; 519–252–3111) is marketed as "a little bit of Toronto in downtown Windsor" and is an attractive urban eatery with a wide range of entrees, including soups, salads, and more creative fare. In summer, chic patrons prefer to sit outside on the patio that faces the street and provides the perfect vantage point for people-watching. Moderate.

After lunch, head down to the waterfront to **Dieppe Park,** where you can relax on one of the many benches and watch the huge freighters sporting colorful flags of many nations pass by (surprisingly, the Detroit River is the world's busiest international waterway).

Afternoon

After wandering around downtown, all roads lead to the **Devonshire Mall.** Here the **Art Gallery of Windsor** (3100 Howard Avenue; 519–969–3732) holds court among other, more predictable shops and boutiques. Ironically, the art gallery was once located where the casino is now (the casino rents space until the permanent location is built sometime in 1997). In a surprising mix of art and commerce, the museum decided to rent space for the interim in Devonshire Mall. To get there, just take Howard Street out of downtown and you can't miss it. At the gallery you'll find more than twenty-five hundred pieces in the permanent collection, including an important gallery of Canadian art and a lively children's gallery that offers a view of art past and present. The museum also boats more than thirty traveling exhibitions annually. Don't miss the gift shop, known as the **Uncommon Market,** which sells a wide range of Canadian crafts and design as well as the usual museum-shop books, note cards, and jewelry.

Most of the rest of the mall is predictable, with a lot of the same stores you'll find at home, although some merchandise is different and you'll still enjoy the great exchange rate. One standout, however, is **Marks & Spencer** (519–966–1940), an outpost of the famous "Marks & Sparks" department store in London, England. Here you'll find all their signature clothing, as well as British foodstuffs such as distinctive teas, chewy toffees, frozen crumpets, steak and kidney pies, even a few frozen bangers (sausages). It's a fun place to pick up a few souvenirs or treats to enjoy once you're back home.

Afterward, head for Erie Street, home to one of the largest concentrations of Italians outside Italy. Located between Ouellette and Howard avenues and also known as "Via Italia," it boasts more than sixty interesting specialty stores, small family restaurants, cafes, and tempting ethnic bakeries. Be sure to stop for a frothy cappuccino or tangy gelato to tide you over until dinner.

Dinner: Erie Street is also the home of one of the city's best-known restaurants. **Spago** (690 Erie Street; 519–252–2233) is listed as one of the best restaurants in Canada in the well-known *Where to Eat in Canada* (Oberon Press). It's known for its veal, seafood, and homemade pastas; be sure to make reservations, however, as its fills up quickly on weekends. There are also simpler dishes such as tangy pizza and Italian-style sandwiches. The kitchen grows its own herbs, which are used extensively in the tasty cuisine. Moderate.

Afterward, there's still time for a night on the town. Casino Windsor and the new Northern Belle are open twenty-four hours a day, seven days a week.

Leave the tux and the glitter at home, however. The dress code here is casual, and you'll be more comfortable in a pair of pants and a sweater.

Casino Windsor (800–991–7777) opened in 1994 and has three floors (approximately 50,000 square feet) of gaming, including roulette, blackjack, baccarat, big six, pai gow, and Caribbean stud poker. If all this means nothing to you, you'd better stick with the slot machines. There are more than seventeen hundred one-armed bandits that are happy to eat your hard-earned money (but be sure to exchange your coins for tokens, however, since quarters aren't accepted). The temporary locations accomodates four thousand optimistic gamblers. The new permanent casino, when it opens in early 1998, is expected to have almost twice as much gambling space.

The **Northern Belle** (800–991–7777) is the newer of the two casinos. Docked just east of the tunnel, it's an authentic Mississippi paddlewheel riverboat with the flavor of the spicy South. It has 23,000 square feet of gaming, including eight hundred seafaring slots. Like the interim casino, it's open twenty-four hours per day.

If your idea of music is more symphonic than slots, the **Windsor Symphony** (519–252–6579) offers an extensive series of concerts at downtown's Cleary Auditorium throughout the year.

Day 3

Morning

Breakfast: Skip the hotel's free meal and opt for a meal in the city's well-known **Chinatown,** located not far from the University of Windsor. Here you'll find **Wah Court Restaurant** (1689 University Avenue West; 519–256–4755) whose dim sum brunch has been attracting locals and in-the-know visitors for years. Foodies claim it's the best dim sum they've had outside of San Francisco. Inexpensive.

If you're looking for something a little more traditional, the brunch spread at the **Park Terrace Restaurant** in the Windsor Hilton is also a good bet and features meat, cheeses, and breakfast fare as well as a wide selection of Ontario wines.

Afterward, venture out for a Sunday drive to the wineries in nearby Essex County (see "There's More") or head for home. Before leaving, however, check out the newly renovated **Duty Free Shoppes** for a souvenir or two of your "time abroad." Here you'll find bargains on everything from Parisian perfumes to Spanish porcelains.

There's More

Birds. "Let there be one place on earth where no money changes hands," wrote naturalist Jack Miner. To achieve that goal, he established Jack Miner Bird Sanctuary (Kingsville; 519–733–4034) in 1904, primarily for aiding in the migration and conservation of Canada geese and ducks. Since 1909, almost one hundred thousand migratory geese and one hundred thousand wild ducks have been tagged here. Today the sanctuary includes a museum, a nature stadium, and a pond where birds can be hand-fed. Admission is free, in accordance with Miner's will. The best times to visit, however, are October, November, and in the spring. Birds are flushed out at 4:00 P.M. in daily "air shows."

Gardens. Colasanti's Tropical Gardens (P.O. Box 40, Ruthven, 519–326–3287) has the largest selection of cacti and tropical plants in Southwestern Ontario, as well as exotic birds and gardens, domestic and miniature animals, wicker and crafts, even amusement rides for the kids. After wandering through the fifteen greenhouses filled to the brim with flora and fauna, head for the on-site restaurant and cafe, which serves everything from refreshing apple cider and homemade soups to chicken dinners and a famous Sunday brunch. Check with customs, however, if you plan on bringing botanical goods across the border.

Parks. Point Pelee is Canada's most southerly mainland point, a slender tip of land that juts out into lake Erie. It's accessible by ferry from March through December and is internationally known for its spring and fall concentration of migrating birds and for its fall migration of monarch butterflies. The trip takes about seventy-five minutes each way. Point Pelee National Park (519–322–2365) is a great place to hike, bike, swim, or canoe, or just wander the island's Heritage Centre (519–724–2291), which has exhibits on the area's rare flora and fauna as well as its natural and human history and area shipwrecks. If you'd like to check out some of those wrecks for yourself, the Pelee Passage Dive Centre (519–326–3483) offers adventures for novices as well as expert divers.

Reptiles. Did you know that snakes have legs? After a visit to Windsor's Reptile World (853 Division Road; 519–966–1762), you will. This new attraction is the only reptile exhibit in Essex County and one of the largest in Canada. It offers a fascinating glimpse into the world of reptiles and amphibians. You'll even be close enough to count the teeth on a huge crocodile!

Wineries. If you're looking to venture out beyond the city limits, surrounding Essex County has a number of excellent estate wineries. Colio Estate Wines (1 Colio Drive, Harrow; 800–265–1322) is known for its award-winning Vidal Icewines as well as for Pinot Gris and Rieslings Traminers. It offers daily tours of the wine-making process and free samples at its Harrow location. D'Angelo Estate Winery (5141 Fifth Concession, Anderdon Township; 519–736–7959) grows more than seven varieties of vinifera and three types of

French hybrids and offers year-round tours by appointment. The Pelee Island Winery (Kingsville; 519–733–6551) dates back to 1865 and is the country's southernmost winery as well as one of its largest estate vineyards. Year-round tours are offered three times daily.

Special Events

May. Pelee Festival of Birds, Point Pelee National Park
June. Strawberry Festival, La Salle
　　　Carousel of Nations, Windsor
　　　Art in the Park, Windsor
July. International Freedom Festival, Windsor and Detroit
August. Harrow Peach Festival
　　　Tecumseh Corn Festival
September. Via Italia Bicycle Races, Windsor
　　　Ruthven Apple Festival
October. Oktoberfest, Windsor
November–December. Poinsettia Festival, Windsor

Other Recommended Restaurants and Lodgings

Restaurants

Casa Bianca (345 Victoria Avenue; 519–253–5218) is housed not far from the casino in a white nineteenth-century Victorian home complete with gingerbread. It serves homemade pastas and other Italian favorites in a relaxed and elegant setting. For a special treat, ask to have one of chef Aldo Cundari's specialties prepared at your table. Moderate.

La Cuisine (417 Pelissier Street; 519–253–6432) is a tiny upstairs cafe with wonderful French food, including classics such as onion soup, quiches, and fancier fare at dinner. Inexpensive to moderate.

The Mini Restaurant (475 University West; 519–254–2221) is one of the few authentic Vietnamese restaurants in Windsor and attracts diners from all over the region. Inexpensive.

Shin-Shin (978 University West; 519–252–1449) is the kind of local restaurant that the natives keep to themselves. It's known for its Szechwan and Peking specialties.

Tunnel Bar BQ (59 Park Street East; 519–258–3663) has been an area favorite since 1941. It's located across from the tunnel (of course) and is known for its tangy ribs and chicken as well as for its flaky homemade pastries. Inexpensive.

Lodgings

Quality Suites by Journeys End (250 Dougall Avenue, 800–228–5151) is the only all-suite hotel in downtown Windsor. Located just a block from the casino, it offers attractive 450-square-foot two-room suites with king-size bed, a large bathroom, and a separate sitting area. There are no water views, but this is the place to stay if you brought kids. Rates: $90–$150 Canadian per night.

The 22-story **Windsor Hilton** (277 Riverside Drive West; 800–445–8667) is more expensive than the other downtown hotels, but it offers some of the best vistas of the Detroit skyline (the hotel is angled so that each of the 303 rooms has a view). A tip: Be sure to ask for accommodations on one of the renovated floors. They're worth the little bit extra. The Park Terrace and River Runner Bar & Grill offer full-service cuisine on site. Rates: $140–$220 Canadian per night.

Ye Olde Walkerville Bed & Breakfast (1104 Monmouth Road; 519–254–1507) is located in a vintage 1903 home in the city's historic Walk-erville district (so named for the huge Canadian Club plant that dominates the area). Guest rooms are furnished in antiques and reproductions; common rooms include a comfy loft with TV, VCR, and stereo as well as a baby grand piano and a fully stocked bar. Rates: $59–$129 Canadian per night.

For More Information

Convention & Visitors Bureau of Windsor, Essex County, and Pelee Island, City Centre, Suite 103, 333 Riverside West, Windsor, Ontario, Canada N9A 5K4; (519) 255–6530 or (800) 265–3633.

Toronto

Casa Loma is one of Toronto's most unusual sights.

Broadway North

———————————— 2 NIGHTS ————————————

Sports • Museums • Nightlife • Shopping • Restaurants • Theater

Not long ago, Toronto was considered one of North America's dullest cities. Its Sunday closing laws were a national joke, and it was regularly compared with its chic French-speaking neighbor, Montreal, and found wanting. So the city's transformation into the country's largest and most exciting metropolis is more than a little surprising. Today once-tame Toronto is the Manhattan of Canada—

center of the country's fashion, publishing, and art worlds. It's also called "Hollywood North" because of the volume of film and television production done here. In North America, only Hollywood and New York serve as locations for more film and commercial work than Toronto. Feature films shot in Toronto include *Sea of Love, Three Men and a Baby,* and *Moonstruck,* made by Toronto resident Norman Jewison.

This once-stodgy enclave of Scottish bankers and British expatriates has become a booming metropolitan area with a population of 3.5 million, including burgeoning Chinese, Taiwanese, Thai, Sikh, Portuguese, and Caribbean Islander communities. It's also a big draw for visiting Americans, who find its *joie de vivre* exciting and the strength of the United States dollar an added bonus.

Day 1

Afternoon

Toronto is a four-hour drive from Detroit via Queen's Highway 401. You'll probably want to take off Friday to get in a full three-day stay. Plan on getting out of town as early as possible to make it to Toronto in time for lunch. You might even want to stay through Monday for a full-fledged minivacation. If you do, be sure not to leave visiting the museums until the last day as most of them are closed Monday.

If you'd like to leave the driving to someone else and enjoy the ride along the way, you can ride the rails to Toronto. **VIA Rail Canada** offers service from Windsor, Ontario, across from downtown Detroit for about $80 Canadian round-trip in economy class. For an added $100 you can treat yourself to the special service and fine dining offered in VIA 1 first class, which includes a three-course meal, larger seats, cocktails, and more. For reservations and ticket information, call (800) 561–9181.

There's plenty of time for serious sight-seeing on Saturday and Sunday. Save your first day for chilling out, Canadian style. Wander around the neighborhood near your hotel, cool your road-weary heals over a glass of wine (try one of the great local Ontario vintages) or a cappuccino at a charming bistro, or explore one of Toronto's ethnic enclaves such China Town, the Greek-inspired Danforth, or Little Italy.

Little Italy is the center of the city's Italian neighborhood and home of its largest ethnic group. It's a bit more of a melting pot now (Canadians prefer to call it a mosaic), but it still has genuine trattorias and outdoor cafes as well as small gatherings of old Italian men smoking cigars or drinking dark red wine and playing bocce ball. It's also the place for perfectly prepared pastas and other kinds of heart-warming comfort food, Italian style. Three restaurants in the area worth a try include **Café 82 Diplomatico** (594 College Street; 416–534–4637), **Trattoria Giancarlo** (41 Clinton; 416–533–9619), and **Sotto Voce** (595 College Street, 416–962–0011). Depending on what time you arrive in town, they're good choices for lunch or dinner.

If you'd like to take in a little nightlife, Toronto offers plenty of choices. As in any city, the club and bar scene can be famously fickle, and clubs come and go like fashion trends. The **Warehouse District** at Richmond, Adelaide, and John streets is always a sure thing, with clubs such as Syn, Atlas, Whiskey and Fluid Lounge Saigon, consistently packing in the crowds. One of the newest hot spots is the **Joker** (318 Richmond Street West; 416–598–1313), a $1.5 million, four-floor extravaganza complete with a palace and court jester. This 20,000-square-foot showpiece houses up to one thousand hipsters each night as well as six bars, an Internet to surf, pool tables, and dance floors.

Lodging: Toronto has thousands of nice hotel rooms. For about the same price as a regular room in the other hotels, however, you can enjoy a spacious suite at **Cambridge Suites** (15 Richmond Street East; 416–368–1990). All of the 230 well-decorated suites have a living and dining room, a separate bedroom, an oversize bathroom, a minibar with microwave, and extra-nice amenities. Rates: $130–$190 per night, including breakfast.

Day 2

Morning

Breakfast: Cambridge Suites has a better-than-usual continental breakfast consisting of yogurts, cereals, fruits, fresh breads, bagels, juices, and coffee. If you're still hungry, however, head for the **St. Lawrence Market** near the harbor, a mecca for area foodies and galloping gourmets. Housed in a vintage brick building are hundreds of butchers, bakers, and sausage makers, each with fragrant food stalls filled with taste treats of all varieties. Even if you're not hungry, the market is a sight to see.

Once you've had your fill, you may want to get your bearings with a guided tour of the city. Scores of companies offer standard sight-seeing tours, all of which provide a good introduction to the city's many attractions. For something really unusual, however, sign on for a tour by bike, rickshaw, or underground. **Neighbourhood**

Bicycle Tours (416–463–9233) offers city cycling adventures; **Rickshaw Walas, Inc.** (416–703–4469) lets you ogle the city's hot spots via authentic rickshaw; **Toronto Underground City Tours** (905–886–9111) takes you deep into the subterranean world beneath the city. If you're curious about the city's historical inhabitants, sign on for a tour of haunted Toronto with **Ghostwalk** (416–501–0615).

Whatever your interest or mode of transportation, you'll want to explore Yonge Street during your weekend stay. Yonge is listed in the *Guinness Book of World Records* as the longest street in the world. It begins at the city's lakeshore and runs an incredible 1,178 miles to Fonda, North Dakota, before it ends. In Toronto, the famous strip is both fun and flashy, with a mix of sleaze and sophistication found nowhere else.

Afternoon

Lunch: **Marche Movenpick** (42 Yonge Street; 416–366–8986) is a European market transported to Toronto's busiest street. Inside this cavernous restaurant are more than ten food stations where diners are free to wander and take their pick from hundreds of food and drink choices. Sushi, seafood (try the bouillabaisse or the pasta with smoked salmon), pizza, pastries, ice cream, bakery goods, and gourmet items to take back to your hotel make this a must-stop when strolling Yonge. Inexpensive to moderate depending on how much you eat.

Yonge Street is also home to **Eaton Centre** (Yonge and Dundas streets; 519–343–2111), the city's largest shopping center. With 350 stores, including the flagship **Eaton's,** it's a favorite of Americans and Europeans looking to take advantage of the exchange rate. Another popular place is the **CN Tower** (301 Front Street West; 416–601–4741), reportedly the world's tallest free-standing structure. On a clear day you can see Blue Mountain and the Toronto Islands. Whatever the weather, you can enjoy futuristic pinball and laser tag games, explore virtual reality at the new Ecodek, or dine in the world's highest revolving restaurant. Craving an adrenaline rush? Take in the outdoor observation deck, where you'll walk on air—or at least on a new glass floor that's 1,122-foot above street level.

Plan on an early dinner so you can catch a show at one of the city's famous theaters. In 1962 Toronto had only two professional theaters; today it boasts more than 140 and is the third-largest theater center in the English-speaking world (it ranks behind only New York and London). Big splashy musicals such as *Sunset Boulevard* and *Phantom of the Opera*—the latter running since 1989—have earned the city the nickname "Broadway North." Repertory companies include the **Royal Alexandra Theatre** (260 King Street West; 800–461–3333), the longest-running theater in downtown Toronto, and the **Canadian Stage Company** (416–368–3110), which presents contemporary Canadian productions as well as classics at a number of area venues. Other sure crowd pleasers include the long-running retro hit, *Forever Plaid* at the **New Yorker Theatre** (651 Yonge Street; 416–872–1111) and the hilarious satire, *Forbidden Hollywood* at the **Atlantis Complex** at Ontario Place (955 Lakeshore Boulevard; 416–260–8000).

If you're looking for something really different, sign on for a tour of the **Elgin and Winter Garden Theatre Centre** (189 Yonge Street; 416–363–5353), the last operating doubledecker theater in the world. A Canadian National Historic Site, it includes the opulent Elgin Theatre and the Winter Garden, the world's only fully restored roof-garden theater.

Not a theater fan? Toronto is also a fanatical sports town. The National Hockey League's Toronto Maple Leafs play in historic Maple Leaf Gardens. In hockey, only the rival Montreal Canadiens have won more Stanley Cups. The Toronto Blue Jays, part of major-league baseball's American League, prove that the boys of summer are not just an American phenomenon. The team won the Eastern Division title in 1985, 1989, 1992, and 1993 as well as the World Series in 1992 and 1993. Since moving into their hew home, the SkyDome, the Blue Jays have drawn more than three million fans and have sold out practically every game.

Dinner: The Centro Grill (2472 Yonge Street; 416–483–2211) is an intimate, four-star eatery with a facade of etched glass, granite, and marble and a welcoming interior featuring huge blowups of owner Franco Prevedello's hometown of Asolo, Italy. Massive columns, a bright blue ceiling, and salmon-colored walls are a backdrop for the creative cuisine, which features specialties such as rack of lamb with tomato, garlic, Spanish capers, eggplant, and salsa. All baking is done on the premises. Moderate to expensive.

Day 3

Morning

Breakfast: Enjoy continental breakfast at Cambridge Suites, then head out to market. The American dollar is at such a premium in Canada that it would be a shame not to take advantage of the exchange rate. One ever-tempting place to do so on the weekend is the **Sunday Market** (416–410–1310), when more than eighty antiques vendors take St. Lawrence Market and hawk their wares in an arena reminiscent of Bermondsey Market in London. Another one hundred fifty or so dealers can be found at the city's **Harborfront Antique Market** (390 Queen's Quay West; 416–260–2626), located just south of SkyDome. Canada's largest antiques market, it's open daily year-round but has more exhibitors (and therefore more goodies) on the weekend. You'll find lots of British imports, many dating back centuries.

Torontoans are a fashionable lot. Many of the shops have a decidedly European flair and carry designers' and brand names unavailable at home. If you're looking to import a few fashions to your home in the United States, head for **Hazelton Lanes,** a chic enclave in the picturesque high-rent district known as Yorkville. Here you'll find tiny storefronts jammed with the latest in everything from cigars to clothing, handmade papers to homemade pastas. A few of the more famous outposts include Polo/Ralph Lauren, Laura Ashley, and the Provence-inspired Pierre Deux, but there are also many local boutiques and shops unique to Toronto.

Afternoon

Lunch: Yorkville has many wonderful restaurants and bistros. One of the best, however, is **Studio Cafe** in the elegant Four Seasons Hotel (21 Avenue Road; 416–928–7330). AAA voted Truffles, the hotel's fancier restaurant, the best restaurant in Canada, but the Studio Cafe offers lighter, more informal and equally accomplished dining in a modern, avant-garde atmosphere. The fish and pasta dishes are excellent. Moderate to expensive.

It's not surprising that this fashionable district is home to two of the city's best museums. The **Royal Ontario Museum** (100 Queen's Park at Avenue Road; 416–586–8000) is one of the city's—and the country's—premier, with a new wing dedicated to European decorative arts and a fascinating working paleontology lab. Don't miss the popular galleries dedicated to Ancient Egypt or dinosaurs or the rare Bat Cave and Chinese Tomb. Not far away is the **George Gardiner Museum of Ceramic Art** (111 Queen's Park; 416–593–9300). The Gardiner is North America's only specialized ceramics museum. It houses a beautiful collection of Italian majolica, English Delftware, Meissen figurines, and other priceless pieces.

If you're museum-hopping, one you won't want to miss is the **Art Gallery of Ontario** (17 Dundas Street West; 416–979–6648). One of the largest and finest art museums in North America, its fifty galleries contain an encyclopedic collection, from pre-Columbian to contemporary Canadian. Don't miss the smooth and sinuous Henry Moore Sculpture Center, which houses the largest collection in the world of

Canadian life. Entry is included with the $7.50 per person admission fee to the art gallery.

If you're into shoes, put your best foot forward and head to the **Bata Shoe Museum** (327 Bloor Street West; 416–979–0078). You may have thought that Imelda Marcos had the most shoes under one roof, but that dubious distinction belongs to this well–heeled new museum. It even looks like a giant shoe box, and is filled with 4,500 years of shoe history, all collected by Sonja Bata, whose husband has shoe manufacturing plants around the world. Displays range from papyrus sandals worn during biblical days to rocker Elton John's nosebleed-inducing platforms.

Before jumping back on Queen's Highway 401 and heading home, plan a stop at **Ontario Science Centre** (770 Don Mills Road, North York; 416–429–4100) just outside the central city in North York. A hit with scientists and nature lovers alike, it gives you the chance to walk through a steaming tropical rain forest, make a fool of yourself in a shadow tunnel, and enjoy a bird's-eye view in the city's first Omnimax theater. Open year-round.

There's More

Amusements. Paramount Canada's Wonderland (9580 Jane Street, Vaughan; 905–832–7000) is a huge, 300-acre theme park with more than 140 attractions, including Splashworks Water Park, Kid's Kingdom play area, Canada's largest wave pool, *Star Trek* and Hanna-Barbera characters and more. Open weekends in May and fall; daily from late May through Labor Day.

Animals. The Metro Toronto Zoo (361A Old Finch Avenue, Scarborough; 416–392–5900) is one of the world's best zoos, with five thousand animals in seven tropical pavilions. A must if you have kids.

Art. The Group of Seven is a well-known group of Canadian painters. Their work is featured at the McMichael Canadian Art Collection (10365 Islington Avenue, Kleinburg; 905–893–1121). Also featured are Inuit, First Nations, and contemporary Canadian works. There are also an on-site restaurant and gift shop.

Castles. Casa Loma (1 Austin Terrace, Toronto; 416–923–1171) was built for financier Henry Pellatt. It features unusual architecture, elegant furnishings, secret passageways, and an 800-foot tunnel connecting the mansion to its luxurious riding stables. The adjacent gardens are a lush oasis of dancing fountains, sculpture, and floral displays.

Cruises. A number of companies offer boat and yacht tours of the Toronto harbor. The *Empress of Canada* (260 Queen's Quay West; 416–260–5547) is the city's newest, with large panoramic win-

Cruises. A number of companies offer boat and yacht tours of the Toronto harbor. The *Empress of Canada* (260 Queen's Quay West; 416–260–5547) is the city's newest, with large panoramic windows and a contemporary decor. At the other extreme is the Great Lakes Schooner Company (249 Queen's Quay West, 416–260–6355), with the 96-foot, three-masted schooner *Challenge* that sails daily on one- and two-hour sailing tours. If you've something more southern in mind, check out the *Jubilee Queen* (207 Queen's Quay West; 416–203–7245), a 120-foot river showboat with sweeping staircases, Tiffany lamps, spacious dance floors, and on-board dining.

Entertainment. Ontario Place (955 Lake Shore Boulevard West, Toronto; 416–314–9811), the province's well-known park dedicated to entertainment, celebrated its twenty-fifth anniversary in 1996. Since opening it's been known for its Cinesphere IMAX films, rides (including the new Rush River Raft Ride), attractions, and restaurants. The park is open from mid-May through Labor Day; admission is free most days.

Golf. There are seven respected courses in the Toronto area, including Glen Abbey in Oakville (905–844–1800) designed by Jack Nicklaus; Lionhead Golf & Country Club (905–455–8400), with two championship courses; and St. Andrews Valley (905–727–7888), the country's highest-rated public golf course.

History. Fort York (100 Garrison Road, Toronto; 416–392–6907) is an early-nineteenth-century fort that re-creates the drama of the War of 1812 and the history of early Toronto. Open year-round, it includes tours, displays, and military reenactments.

Hockey. This is Canada, after all. The national game is celebrated at the Hockey Hall of Fame (BCE Place, 30 Yonge Street, Toronto; 416–360–7735), which traces the sport's evolution through displays, movies, trophies, and interactive exhibits.

Indoor Excitement. Fun City (114 Clayson Road, North York; 416–749–5000) is the world's largest indoor amusement facility, with a go-kart track, miniature golf, seven batting cages, basketball, bumper cars, and more than two hundred video games.

Skiing. Blue Mountain (RR #3, Collingwood, ON L9Y 3Z2; 705–445–0231) is the area's best-known ski area and Ontario's largest four-season resort. It features the highest ski vertical, with thirty trails and sixteen lifts.

Snowmobiling. Want to really chill out? Sign on for one of the tours offered by Canadian Snowmobile Adventures (800–465–7378). The company takes the adventurous on guided snowmobile treks along 20,000 miles of groomed trails and through thick Canadian forests.

Theater. What began in 1961 as a weekend event in postcard-pretty Niagara on the Lake is now an annual summerlong event. The Shaw Festival (P.O. Box 774, Niagara on the Lake, ON; 800–267–4759) sics as well as modern drama and comedy against the bucolic backdrop of Stratford, Ontario. Both venues are a ninety-minute drive from downtown Toronto.

Water Wonderland. Wild Water Kingdom (7855 Finch Avenue West, Brampton; 905–369–9453) is Canada's largest water theme park, featuring a half-acre wave pool, tube and river rides, kids' watery playground, batting cages, and miniature golf. Open summer only.

Wineries. The Wine Council of Ontario (110 Hanover Drive, St. Catherine's; 905–684–8070) operates a number of vineyards within a two-hour drive of Toronto. Acres of vineyards produce some of the finest grapes in the world, with many wineries opening their doors and cellars for tasting and tours. Contact the council for more information.

Special Events

January. International Boat Show
February. Canadian International Auto Show
March. Canadian Music Festival
April. National Home Show
May. Toronto International Pow Wow
     Lilac Festival
June. Symphony of Fire Fireworks Festival
     Downtown Jazz Festival
     Taste of Toronto
July. Canada Day Celebration
     Caribana Fest
August. Canadian National Exhibition
     Canadian International Air Show
September. Toronto International Film Festival
October. International Festival of Authors
     Canadian Ski Show
     Autumn Artsfest
November. Royal Agricultural Winter Fair

Other Recommended Restaurants and Lodgings

Restaurants

Chiaro's (37 King Street East; 416–863–9700) is located in the opulent King Edward Hotel. Specialties including Dover sole, New York steaks, rack of lamb, and other French-inspired cuisine served in a plush gray dining room. Expensive.

Joso's (202 Davenport Road; 416–925–1903) is the place to be if you're a member of the international artistic community. Owner Joso Spralja is an artist, musician, and restaurateur and has filled his two-story restaurant with sensual paintings and large, intriguing wall hangings. Food is unusual and healthy, with a number of Italian and seafood specialties. Moderate to expensive.

North 44 Degrees (2537 Yonge Street; 416–487–4897) refers to the city's latitude and to this trendy modern eatery. Specialties inside the metallic-looking dining room include rack of lamb, angel hair pasta, and a mixed appetizer platter. You'll also find a popular wine bar on the upper level and entertainment on weekends. Expensive.

Truffles (21 Avenue Road; 416–964–0411) is best known for its wonderful wine list, which features rare European and North American vintages. Murals, paintings, and ceramics by local artists decorate the dining room, which serves cuisine based on the gastronomic offerings of Provence, France. Specialties include Quebec duck and a rack of lamb with mustard seed sauce. Pastries are made on the premises. Expensive.

Downtown Lodgings

Clarion Essex Park Hotel (300 Jarvis Street; 416–977–4823) has 102 recently renovated guest rooms and suites in an intimate, European-style hotel within walking distance of Eaton Centre. The on-site Bistro Restaurant offers three meals daily. Rates: $85 Canadian per night and up.

The **Delta Chelsea Inn** (33 Gerrard Street West; 800–243–5732) is centrally located near the theater district and downtown shops and restaurants. It's especially popular with families, with an innovative Delta Dolphin swim program for kids and a drop-off Children's Creative Center. An added plus: Kids age five or younger eat free; kids ages six through eleven eat at half off. Rates: $125 Canadian per night and up, although package deals are often available.

King Edward Hotel (37 King Street East; 416–863–9700) is one of the Leading Hotels of the World and an elegant European-style inn.

Built in 1903, it was remodeled in the early 1980s and boasts a vaulted ceiling, marble pillars, and palm trees in its lobby. The 310 guest rooms are well furnished, with sumptuous marble bathrooms. Rates: $125 Canadian per night and up for weekends.

Novotel Toronto Centre (45 The Esplanade; 416–367–8900) is close to the Harbourfront, theaters and the St. Lawrence Market. Facilities include health club, whirlpool, restaurants, and more. Rates: $115–$165 Canadian per night.

Radisson Plaza Hotel Admiral (249 Queen's Quay West; 416–203–3333) is a well-run 157-room hotel near the Harbourfront and St. Lawrence Market. Its Commodore's Dining Room is rated four diamonds by CAA/AAA. Rates: $115–$175 Canadian per night.

The stately **Royal York Hotel** (100 Front Street West; 416–368–2511) is a huge landmark hotel across from Union Station. It has 1,365 rooms as well as a health club and ten on-site restaurants. Rates: $129 Canadian per night and up.

Yorkville Lodgings

Four Seasons Toronto (21 Avenue Road; 416–960–5200) is in the heart of the fashionable Yorkville district and is Toronto's only five-diamond hotel. Rates: $230–$305 Canadian per night.

Hotel Inter-Continental Toronto (220 Bloor Street West; 416–960–5200) has 209 elegant guest rooms and eleven suites. Art Deco and Edwardian touches are found throughout the public spaces and the guest rooms. Deluxe facilities include twenty-four-hour room service, free shoe shine, a skylight lap pool, and more. Rates: $185–$1,150 Canadian per night.

Bed and Breakfasts

If you'd like to experience the warmth of a bed-and-breakfast inn, the city offers many options. **B&B Homes of Toronto** (44 Yonge Street; 416–363–6362) represents twenty homes in many of the city's best neighborhoods. The competing **Bed & Breakfast Guest Houses Association** (416–368–1420) represents a large selection of distinctive Victorian homes in downtown Toronto.

For More Information

Metropolitan Toronto Convention & Visitors Association, Queen's Quay Terminal at Harbourfront Centre, P.O. Box 126, 207 Queen's Quay West, Toronto, ON M5J 1A7; (416) 203–2600.

Indiana Escapes

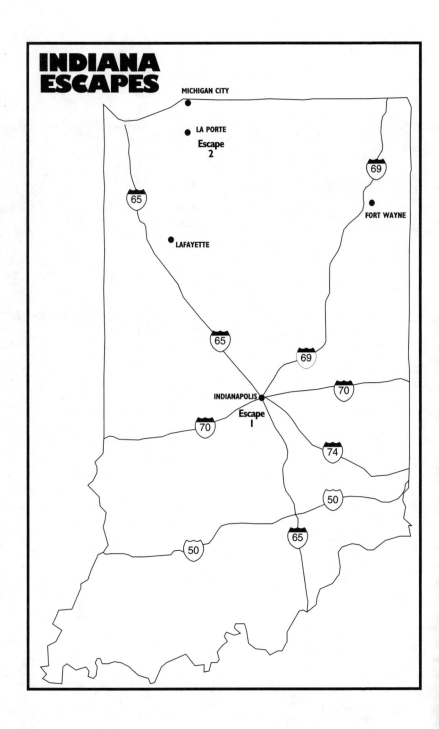

INDIANA ESCAPES

MICHIGAN CITY

LA PORTE

Escape
2

69

FORT WAYNE

65

LAFAYETTE

65

69

INDIANAPOLIS

70

Escape
1

70

74

50

50

65

Indianapolis

The Indianapolis skyline rises like a beacon above the surrounding plains.

Hoosier Hospitality

———————————— 2 NIGHTS ————————————

Museums • Sight-seeing • Speedway • Theater • Amateur and
Professional Sports

For many Detroiters, Indianapolis seems like just another notch on the mid-western rust belt. Dismissing the nation's twelfth largest city so easily, however, would be a mistake. Today's Indianapolis has built a reputation for its sporting facilities, world-class attractions, performing and visual arts, and legendary Hoosier hospitality. There's more than enough to fill a weekend.

Residents are quick to point out that Indianapolis, not Detroit, was the first automobile capital. In the early 1900s, more than sixty car makes were produced here, including Duesenbergs, Marmons, and Stutzes. Detroit's assembly line production soon replaced Indy's custom-made vehicles, however, and by the mid-1930s only three auto manufacturers were left. Today Indianapolis manufacturers produce automotive parts rather than finished cars. The city's most famous connection to cars is the annual **Indianapolis 500** automobile race, which draws about four hundred thousand spectators each year.

And while Detroit is still working on its renaissance, one is in full bloom in Indianapolis. A sure sign is the Circle Centre Mall, which opened in fall 1995 and is linked by skywalks to downtown hotels. Anchored by tony Nordstrom's and the Parisian's, the mall has about one hundred stores, as well as nightclubs and movies. It's a source of pride for local downtown boosters and popular with both residents and visitors. Indianapolis is also a mecca for sports lovers of all varieties. Besides the Indy 500 for auto racing fans, there are professional football (Colts) and basketball (Pacers) teams. The new Victory Field is home of the Indians minor-league baseball club. As *TV Guide* put it, "Indianapolis never met a sport it didn't like."

Day 1

Morning

Indianapolis is 284 miles from Detroit, a drive of about five hours. To get there, take Interstate 75 south to Interstate 80 west and then continue to Interstate 69 south, which goes right into downtown Indianapolis.

The city is easy to get around. Architect Alexander Ralston, who worked with Washington, D.C., planner Pierre L'Enfant, laid out the city on a mile-square grid. At its center is **Monument Circle,** the starting place for four diagonal spoke streets. Monument Circle, in the heart of downtown, is home to a number of historic landmarks. The best-looking one is the 284-foot Soldiers and Sailors Monument, completed in 1902 as a Civil War tribute (a new Civil War museum is also planned for the site). For a bird's-eye view of the city, take the elevator or stairs to the top of the 284-foot obelisk. In summer, you'll be able to see picnickers and people-watchers on the circle below; in winter, it's home to both carolers and Christmas lights.

The modern heart of the city, however, is **Circle Centre Mall** (49 West Maryland Street; 317–681–8000), a sparkling new mall that epitomizes the new Indianapolis. City leaders had the foresight to save 3 blocks of landmark stores and office facades, some dating to the 1800s. When the buildings were demolished, their fronts were stored and later incorporated into Circle Centre Mall, thereby preserving the original look of downtown. The $314 million shopping center, with Nordstrom's and Parisian's as its anchors, has revitalized the city's heart since it opened in 1995.

This is power shopping at its best. Besides the big department stores, the mall is also home to more than one hundred smaller boutiques, including the first-floor **Back Home Indiana** (317–630–4663), chock full of paintings, furniture, books, and other items by Indiana artisans. The most unusual spot is the fourth-floor virtual world, billed as the world's first digital theme park. Here you can don a headset and travel to Mars or compete against pilots in a space race known as "Red Planet." The mall is linked to the respected Artsgarden, six hotels, and the Indiana Convention Center and also houses restaurants and entertainment, including **Flashbaxx** (317–630–5483), a funky tribute to the 1970s disco scene. After a visit, you'll never think all malls are alike again.

Afternoon

Lunch: Indianapolis Monthly voted the **California Cafe 82 Bar & Grill** (Circle Centre; 317–488–8686) "Indy's Hippest Eatery." It has a California-cool interior and a menu that features lighter fare such as seasoned fish and an eclectic daily special. You'll feel as if you've been transported form the heartland to the West Coast. There are also a separate espresso bar and an in-house bakery. Moderate.

One of the highlights of a weekend here is a trip to the **Indianapolis Children's Museum** (3000 North Meridian Street; 317–924–5431). With more than five floors of hands-on adventure for explorers of all ages, it's a family favorite. It's even fun if you don't have kids. Plan on arriving early, as lines can be long for the most popular exhibitions and displays, including the turn-of-the-century hand-carved carousel. During your visit, you'll barter for goods in an eighteenth-century fur-trading post, sit behind the wheel of a roaring race car, and explore a limestone cave. The antique doll and model train collections are the largest in the country. Be sure to stop and let the kids spend the allowance in the "Kid Stuff" shop, which features goodies all priced $5.00 or less. If you have preschoolers, there's also an expansive playscape. Admission can be steep if you have a large family ($6.00 for adults; $3.00 for kids ages two to seventeen; under two free), but it's worth every penny.

Union Station. (39 West Jackson Place; 317–267–0701) is another of the city's restored masterpieces. Housed in a breathtaking 1888 railroad station, it was the first of its kind in the world and featured Rookwood columns, ornate plasterwork, and stained-glass windows. Today it houses specialty shops, restaurants, and nightspots.

Dinner: **Louisiana Street Restaurant and Bar** (123 West Louisiana Street; 317–631–2221) in Union Station has been called the city's best-kept secret by the *Indianapolis Star*. It specializes in spicy Creole cuisine, with an excellent blackened swordfish. If you've brought the kids and would rather skip the station's abundant fast food, try **Norman's Union Station** (317–269–2545) for tasty and affordable soups, sandwiches, and family-friendly entrees such as burgers and pasta as well as a great Sunday brunch.

Lodging: If you've decided to splurge, the place to do so is the **Canterbury** (123 South Illinois Street; 317–634–3000). This British-style hotel features ninety-nine rooms with four-poster beds, Chippendale reproductions, and marble baths. Public rooms, including the parlor, with its carved wooden fireplace—are spacious and sophisticated. Rates: $150 per night and up. The hotel's restaurant is known for its Dover sole, rack of lamb, veal dishes, and its to-die-for dessert souffles. Expensive.

If you've brought the family, the **Crowne Plaza Union Station** (123 West Louisiana Street; 317–631–2221) has affordable weekend packages and the rare chance to sleep in one of twenty-six Pullman train car rooms. Opt for one of the 276 regular rooms if you're claustrophobic, however. All rooms are centrally located adjoining Union Station and are adjacent to Circle Centre Mall. Rates: $130–$175 per night.

Day 2

Morning

Breakfast: **Le Peep** (301 North Illinois Street; 317–237–3447) has been voted one of the city's best breakfast spots since 1988. Specialties include frittatas, French toast, overstuffed omelettes, and four types of casserole-like "pampered eggs." Inexpensive.

No trip to Indianapolis would be complete without a visit to the **Indianapolis Motor Speedway Hall of Fame and Museum** (4709 West Sixteenth Street; 317–484–6747), located just west of downtown. This is mecca to motoring fans: You can take a $2.00 bus ride around the famous 2.5-mile track or ooh and aah at the adjacent museum, which features one of the world's largest and most varied collections of racing, classic, and antique cars as well as more than thirty Indy winners. There are also a half-hour film on the track's history, plus racing memorabilia, a great gift shop, and more.

If track and field is more your speed, check out the **Hall of Fame** in the RCA Dome (317–261–0483), which chronicles the greats such as Jim Thorpe, Babe Didrickson, Jesse Owens, and Bruce Jenner through records and achievements that date back to the late 1800s. And if you still haven't had enough of sports, head for the **National Art Museum of Sport** (850 West Michigan Street; 317–274–2339), which houses the nation's largest collection of art with sport themes, including works by Winslow Homer and George Bellows.

Afternoon

Lunch: The **Rathskeller** (401 East Michigan Street; 317–636–0396) is housed in the Athenaeum, which was designed by the grandfather of well-known native son Kurt Vonnegut, Jr. It's an Old World–style eatery that serves up dark German beer along with German specialties from brats to sauerbraten. There's also a full menu of American favorites. Moderate.

You may know the city best for its motor sports, but Indianapolis's "other" history takes center stage at the **Indiana State Museum** (202 North Alabama Street; 317–232–1637). A frequent stop for Smithsonian traveling exhibitions, this showplace in the original hall concentrates on the state's natural and cultural history. Popular displays include an ancient glacier, city streets from 1910, and—of course—a section on the world of modern sports. Admission is free.

Dinner: If you're into meat and potatoes, you won't do better than the **St. Elmo Steakhouse** (127 South Illinois Street, next to the Circle Centre Mall; 317–637–1811), a city landmark since 1902. It's been voted the best downtown restaurant for five straight years by readers of *Indianapolis Monthly*. Specialties include a hefty twenty-ounce New York–cut sirloin steak, a carnivore's dream, and a tangy shrimp cocktail. The restaurant's excellent wine cellar has been cited with an Award of Excellence from the *Wine Spectator,* every year since 1991. Expensive.

Indianapolis is credited with having some of the oldest and best jazz clubs in the country. After dinner, check out the **Chatterbox** (435 Massachusetts Avenue; 317–636–0584) or the **Jazz Cooker** (925 East Massachusetts Avenue; 317–253–2883) for a little late-night rhythm.

Day 3

Morning

Breakfast: Grab an eye-opener at your hotel, but save room for brunch at the **Garden on the Green Restaurant** (317–926–2628), part of the Indianapolis Museum of Art. For just $10.00 per person ($6.75 for kids) you'll choose from a buffet that includes a variety of enticing hot and cold breakfast dishes (including a wonderful cheese strata) and lunch items. Reservations are required.

After brunch, don't miss the **Indianapolis Museum of Art** (1200 West Thirty-eighth Street; 317–923–1331), one of the oldest in the country. Set on 152 lush acres, it includes four pavilions featuring African, medieval, and Renaissance art, plus eighteenth- through twentieth-century European painting and decorative arts in period settings. Other attractions include a beautiful botanical garden, shops, greenhouses, a concert hall, a theater, and more.

Western art in the middle of the heartland? At the **Eiteljorg Museum of American Indians and Western Art** (500 West Washington; 317–636–9378), seeing is believing. The adobe Eiteljorg is home to one of the nation's finest collections of American western and Native American art and artifacts. Highlights include works by Charlie Russell, Frederic Remington, and Georgia O'Keeffe as well as Native American objects. The museum was a gift to the city from a coal baron and is part of the **White River State Park.** There are also daily films and demonstrations and a large museum store. This is one museum kids love as much as adults do.

There's More

Antiques. The Historic Fountain Square neighborhood (110 East Prospect Street; 317–686–6010), not far from downtown, boasts 150 antique dealers in three malls. You can also dine at three vintage lunch counters, an old-time soda fountain, even a restaurant featuring classic southern cookin'.

Cultural Center. The Madame Walker Urban Life Center (617 Indiana Avenue; 317–236–2099) was named after the country's first black woman millionaire. Originally used as a Vaudeville stage, the 1927 Art Deco building fell into disrepair after World War II and received a $3 million facelift in 1988. It now serves as an arts and cultural center for Indianapolis's African-American community as well as the site of the popular weekly "Jazz on the Avenue" concerts.

Sports. Professional, semipro, amateur: Whatever your pleasure, Indy has something for you. The Pacers tip off at Market Square Arena (300 East Market Street) and the Colts kick off at the Hoosier Dome (100 South Capitol Avenue). For information on both, call (317) 239–5151. Baseball fans can check out the AAA affiliate Indianapolis Indians, a farm team of the Cincinnati Reds. For tickets, call (317) 269–3545.

Water. Old Indiana Family Fun-N-Water Park (7230 North 350 West, Thornton; 800–653–4639) in suburban Thornton is Central Indiana's largest water playground, with more than thirty rides, four stages, and a popular petting zoo.

Special Events

May. Indianapolis 500
June. Talbot Street Art Fair
       Midsummer Fest
July. Indiana Black Expo, Indiana State Fairgrounds
August. Indiana State Fair, Indiana State Fairgrounds
       Brickyard 400 Race
September. Penrod Arts Fair

Other Recommended Restaurants and Lodging

Restaurants

Acapulco Joe's (365 North Illinois Street; 317–637–5160) is a lively and inexpensive ethnic eatery. It was the city's first Mexican restaurant and is still considered one of its best. Moderate.

Bazbeaux Pizza (334 Massachusetts Avenue; 317–636–7662) is the place for pizza that's made with homemade doughs and sauces as well as fifty-two tasty toppings.

Essential Edibles (429 East Vermont Street; 317–266–8797) is an award-winning gourmet vegetarian restaurant located in the basement of a former Catholic girls' school near theaters and art galleries. It features specialties such as the Wander India sampler plate and the veggie burger as well as a popular carry-out market. There's live jazz on Friday and Saturday nights. Moderate.

The **Majestic** (47 South Pennsylvania Street; 317–636–5418) features fresh seafood such as stuffed Florida pompano and bluepoint oysters in a vintage 1895 building. Moderate to expensive.

Pesto (303 North Alabama Street; 317–269–0715) is a light-filled Italian bistro featuring casual dining and entrees such as veal scallopini rolled with spinach, proscuitto, and fontina cheese over polenta or farfalle pasta with shrimp, artichokes, and basil. It's also a great lunch spot. Moderate.

The **Porch** (in the Hyatt Regency Indianapolis; 1 South Capitol Avenue; 317–632–1234) offers dark woods and contemporary art in a setting inspired by midwestern architect Frank Lloyd Wright. Specialties include steaks and pastas as well as a scrumptious Sunday brunch. Moderate to expensive.

Lodging

Westin Indianapolis (50 South Capitol Avenue; 317–262–8100) has 573 rooms as well as a heated indoor pool, Jacuzzi, and health club. It's adjacent to the Hoosier Dome and Convention Center. Rates: $95–$140 per night.

For More Information

Indianapolis Convention & Visitors Bureau, 200 South Capitol Avenue, Indianapolis, IN 46225; (317) 639–4282.

La Porte County

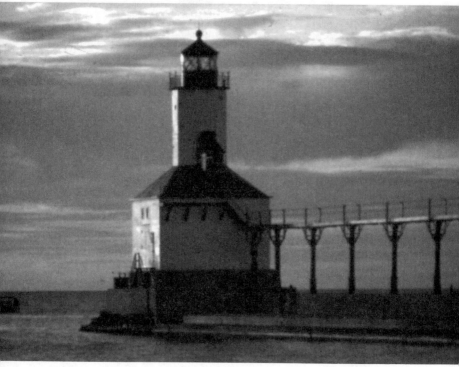

Washington Park's lighthouse offers great views of Lake Michigan.

Doin' the Dunes

──────────── 2 NIGHTS ────────────

Dunes • Antiques • Bicycling • Outlet Mall

───────────────────────────────────

Why would anyone from the Detroit area want to visit Indiana's dunes when we have our own share of scenic shifting sands back home in Michigan? There are many reasons. Surprisingly, beyond the superficial grime of the area's steel mills lies an unspoiled and untamed landscape that rivals the best in the Midwest. The 13,000 acres of Indiana Dunes National Lakeshore inspired midwestern poet Carl Sandburg to write that "the dunes are to the Midwest what the Grand Canyon is to Arizona and Yosemite to California... a signature of time and eternity."

Indiana's dune country is spread over three counties (Lake, La Porte, and Porter). A good base of operations is La Porte County's Michigan City, which has a range of bed-and-breakfast inns as well as one of the best outlet malls in the Midwest.

Day 1

Afternoon

La Porte County is a four-hour drive from Detroit along Interstate 94. Plan on arriving in time for a late dinner in the town of La Porte.

Dinner: **Roskoe's** (1004 Lakeside Street, La Porte; 219–325–3880) is a lively lakeside venue with a popular sports bar and a menu that ranges from meaty steaks and sandwiches to lighter fare such as seafood and salads. Moderate.

Lodging: **Creekwood Inn** (Highway 20/35 at Interstate 94, Michigan City; 219–872–8357) is a serene and secluded English country inn that's surprisingly close to I–94. A recently added conservatory overlooks 33 wooded acres of surrounding trails, creeks, and gardens. Rates for the twelve rooms range from $110 to $125 per night, including a continental breakfast of freshly prepared homemade pastries, cereals, and more. There's plenty to fill you up and fuel your adventures ahead.

Day 2

Morning

Breakfast: Creekwood Inn has a nice spread of fresh baked goodies, coffee, and juices to get you going.

Few people come to this part of Indiana without "doin' the dunes." The breathtaking **Indiana Dunes National Lakeshore** stretches along Lake Michigan's southern shore and covers 18 miles. Administered by the U.S. Park Service, it's a remarkable landscape of uncrowded beaches, bird-filled marshes, oak and maple forests, and towering dunes made up of ever-shifting sands. On really windy days you can even set a sand pail or tote bag on the beach and watch as a miniature dune forms around it.

King of the dunes is **Mt. Baldy**, a "live" 123-foot dune that continues to move each year. If climbing isn't your forte, you can walk through the area's relaxing woodlands full of wildflowers and songbirds, swim on sandy beaches, picnic under a canopy of trees, tour a historic homestead, or join in one of the special events such as

March's Maple Sugar Time festival or September's Duneland Harvest. For a map and more information, contact the park superintendent in writing at 1100 North Mineral Springs Road, Porter, IN 46304–1299, or by phone at (219) 926–7561.

Lunch: The lakeshore is the perfect picnic spot, and it would be a shame not to enjoy it. Pick up a meaty sandwich, salad, or one of twenty-five delicious desserts and something to wash it all down with at **5th Street Deli** (431 Washington Street, Michigan City; 219–872–5204). Sandwiches are named after celebrities. Inexpensive.

Afternoon

Save Saturday afternoon for exploring historic Michigan City. The town was settled in 1831, when Major Isaac C. Elston bought land near the mouth of nearby Trail Creek, where it converged with Lake Michigan. In 1833 he platted a town, which he named Michigan City. Because it was the northern terminus of the Michigan Road and had navigable waters, it grew quickly. By 1836 it had become a city, elected its first mayor, and attracted industries such as the Barker Car Company and the Zorn Brewery. By the 1920s, the area gained a reputation with Chicago's elite as a popular resort community.

The thirty-eight-room **Barker Mansion** (631 Washington Street; 219–873–1520) is known as "the house that freight cars built" and was once the residence of millionaire John H. Barker. Built in 1857, it's listed on the National Register of Historic Places and has daily tours year-round. Don't miss the beautiful gardens and the third-floor ballroom.

Not far away, on Eighth Street, is the **John G. Blank Center for the Arts** (312 East Eighth Street, 219–874–4900). An area showcase, it's known for its 1895 Tiffany windows as well as its more recent collection of prints and photos of the Indiana dunes. There's also a regular traveling exhibit, usually featuring the work of a local artist.

Save your big shopping day for Sunday, when you'll need lots of energy to navigate the 130 stores of the Lighthouse Place outlet mall. If you can't resist ducking in a few doors while you wander, some good stops include **Elegant Gypsy** (727 Franklin; 219–872–6001), with home furnishings and art, and **B & A Hobbies** (408 Franklin; 219–874–2382), where railroad buffs of all ages can indulge their romance with the rails.

Speaking of hobbies, antiques lovers will find collectibles of all vintages and values at the area's many antiques stores and malls, including **Coachman Antique Mall**, the area's largest, in nearby La Porte (500 Lincolnway; 219–326–5933), **Antique Junction Mall,** also in La Porte (711 Lincolnway; 219–324–0363), and **Stocking Bale Antiques** in Michigan City; (227 West Seventh Street, 219–873–9270).

Need some air? Head for Michigan City's **Washington Park**, where you'll find more than enough to keep you busy into the evening, including a fine museum dedicated to the state's oldest lighthouse (219–872–6133). Built in 1858, it's full of lore relating to shipwrecks, maritime history, and the "big lake." It's open from 1:00 to 4:00 P.M. Tuesday through Sunday only. Washington Park is also home to a fine small zoo, picnic areas, fishing spots, and more. The zoo, built in 1928 on the side of a sand dune, has an observation tower that was added by the Works Progress Administration in 1933. While it's not for the faint of heart, it offers an incredible view and rises high above the zoo with a vantage point from the top that stretches from the southern tip of Lake Michigan to the Chicago skyline.

Dinner: **Matey's Restaurant & Beer Garden** (110 Franklin Street; 219–872–9471) is a casual and friendly eatery located across from Washington Park. It has a natty nautical interior and a menu that features seafood and casual entrees. It's a great place in summer, with an outdoor patio, and also serves breakfast and lunch daily. Inexpensive to moderate.

Afterward, you may choose to walk off your meal with a tour of nearby **Long Beach and Lake Shore Drive,** which was developed as a resort area where Chicago residents could escape on weekends. The "cottages" that line the shore remain and include many architectural styles, including some by famous architects such as Frank Lloyd Wright.

If you have any energy left, consider catching a play at one of two excellent in-town theaters. The **Acting Company of Michigan City** (215 West Tenth Street; 219–872–4221) is the state's only all-original company, with family-friendly musicals, plays, and holiday performances offered in a seventy-five-seat venue year-round. The **Canterbury Theatre** (907 Franklin Street; 219–874–4269) is housed in a 125-year-old downtown landmark and stages six performances annually.

Day 3

Morning

Breakfast: Creekwood Inn or **Sweet Pea's Gourmet** (711 Wabash; 219–873–0637), located in "The Works" across from Lighthouse Place. It features hot-from-the-oven French pastries as well as croissants and gourmet coffees. Inexpensive.

Ready to shop 'til you drop? **Lighthouse Place** (219–879–6506) is one of the main reasons for heading to this part of the Hoosier State. Yes, we have outlet malls in Michigan, but this one has many stores that you can't find anywhere else. Two of the best are the Crate & Barrel, home to all the stylish housewares found in the popular catalog—at prices that are 30 to 70 percent less (I found wonderful place mats that retailed for $9.00 apiece originally for just 99 cents). Another standout if you have kids or like colorful clothing is Oilily, a Swedish company known for its crazy quilt patterns and bright layers. Other good stops include Burberry's of London, Carol Little, Ann Taylor, and Benneton.

All in all, Lighthouse Place has a whopping one hundred stores as well as restaurants, entertainment in good weather, and a charming old-fashioned trolley the kids love when your feet get tired. There's also an adjacent area known as "The Works" in a renovated Pullman Railroad Factory building, with small specialty shops and railroad memorabilia. If you need a sugar boost, Scoops in the mall offers sweet treats and is worth a visit just for the Pullman Railroad Car Factory memorabilia on the walls.

Afternoon

Lunch: The **Pullman Cafe and Club Car Lounge** (219–879–3393) in The Works across from Lighthouse Place is a good place for a quick lunch before you hit the road. You can rest your feet over a bowl of homemade soup and a healthy sandwich or try one of the daily lunch specials. Inexpensive.

There's More

Animals. Washington Park Zoo (219–873–1510) is open April through October and houses more than two hundred animal species. It's also one of the state's oldest and largest zoos.

Automobiles. Housed in a spectacular building near La Porte, the Door Prairie Museum (2405 Indiana Avenue, La Porte; 219–326–1337) displays more than one hundred years of the history of the "horseless carriage," including the world's first car, an 1886 Benz Motor Wagon. There are also Auburns, Deusenbergs, Fords, Rolls Royces, Tuckers, and more, as well as classic airplanes and antique toys. Open May 1 through November 30.

Gardens. Quail Ridge Farm (3382 East 1000 North, La Porte; 219–778–2194) is a must-visit for green thumbs and landscape lovers, with more than fifty thousand perennials and ten thousand herbs as well as themed plantings such as gardens inspired by Shakespeare, the Japanese, Native Americans, the prairie, the woodlands, and more. The farm was designated a "hidden treasure" by the state and also has a tempting gift shop.

Golf. Northern Indiana has five respected courses: South Bend's Blackhorn (219–232–4653), La Grange County Country Club

(219–463–2906), Lake James Golf Course (219–833–3967) in Angola, Swan Lake/US Golf Academy in Plymouth (800–582–7539), and Zoll-ner at Tri-State University in Angola (219–665–4269).

Military History. Vets and others who love vintage weapons and related memorabilia flock to the Great Lakes Museum of Military History (1710 East U.S. Highway 20, Michigan City; 219–872–2702) to see uniforms, flags, posters, and more.

Water Park. Splash Down Dunes (150 East U.S. Highway 20, Porter; 219–929–1181) is the first water park in the region, with the Midwest's largest wave pool and the tallest water slides in the state.

Yellow Brick Road. The Yellow Brick Road Gift Shop and Fantasy Museum (State Highway 49; 219–926–7048), in nearby Chesterton, is a small shop and museum dedicated to Dorothy and her furry friends. It houses memorabilia from the classic film *The Wizard of Oz* and has attracted both movie stars and munchkins since it opened in 1978.

Special Events

March. Maple Sugar Time Festival
May. Hoosier Coho Club Fishing Tournament
June. Columbia Yacht Race
July. Summer Festival
August. Lakefront Art Festival
  Boat Show
September. Duneland Harvest
  Oktoberfest
October. Pioneer Days
December. Santa Parade

Other Recommended Restaurants and Lodgings

Restaurants

Copper Penny Bar & Grill (10 Commerce Square, Michigan City; 219–878–1235) is a friendly neighborhood tavern with reasonable daily specials as well as seafood, steaks, and ribs. Inexpensive.

Le Franklin (521 North Franklin Street, Michigan City; 219–872–4500) is just two blocks east of the outlet mall and features bistro-style cooking in two dining rooms. Lunch and dinner daily. Moderate.

194

Lodgings

The **Brickstone Bed and Breakfast** (215 West Sixth Street, Michigan City; 219–878–1819) has four rooms named after the seasons in a former parson's home from 1880. Run by a friendly mother-daughter team, it's bright and airy and convenient to Lighthouse Place shopping. Rates: $78–$136 per night, including breakfast.

Holiday Inn (5820 South Franklin Street, Michigan City; 219–879–0311) is a great idea if you've brought the family, with a Holidome indoor recreation center and an indoor pool. Rates: $84–$145 per night.

Hutchinson Mansion Inn (220 West Tenth Street, Michigan City; 219–879–1700) is the kind of place that many people dream of living in. The elegant 1875 residence has stained-glass windows, high ceilings with elaborate decoration, and antique furnishings in its ten rooms. There are also luxury suites in the carriage house. Rates: $82–$135 per night.

For More Information

La Porte County Convention and Visitors Bureau, 1503 South Meer Road, Michigan City, IN 46360; (219) 326–8115 or (800) 634–2650.

Index

About the Author

Khristi Sigurdson Zimmeth is a freelance writing and contributing editor of *Michigan Living* magazine. She is also a former editor of *Travel & Leisure* magazine and *The Magazine of the Detroit Institute of Arts*. Khristi has traveled in and around Detroit extensively and currently lives in Michigan with her husband and two children.

Also of Interest from The Globe Pequot Press

Family Adventure Guide: Michigan $9.95
Hundreds of attractions and events ideally suited for family
adventure in Michian.

Off the Beaten Path: Michigan $10.95
Devoted to travelers with a taste for the unique. Covers those
places in Michigan that most tourists miss.

Great Family Vacations: Midwest & Rocky Mountains $14.95
Find family adventure in the states of Michigan, Ohio, Illinois,
Iowa, Kansas, etc.

Short Bike Rides in Michigan $10.95
Challenging treks and pleasant excursions for the enthusiastic
biker.

Other books in this series:

Quick Escapes From New York City	$14.95
Quick Escapes In and Around Toronto	$14.95
Quick Escapes In the Pacific Northwest	$14.95
Quick Escapes From Chicago	$12.95
Quick Escapes From San Francisco	$13.95
Quick Escapes From Washington D.C.	$13.95
Quick Escapes From Los Angeles	$14.95
Quick Escapes From Atlanta	$14.95
Quick Escapes From Dallas/Fort Worth	$13.95

Available from your bookstore or directly from the publisher. For a
free catalogue or to place an order, call toll-free 24 hours a day
(1-800-243-0495), or write to The Globe Pequot Press, P.O. Box
833, Old Saybrook, Connecticut 06475-0833.